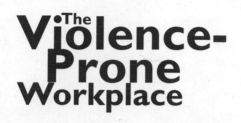

The Violence-Prone Workplace

The Violence-Prone Workplace:

A New Approach to Dealing with Hostile, Threatening, and Uncivil Behavior

Richard V. Denenberg

and **Mark Braverman**

ILR Press an imprint of

Cornell University Press   ITHACA AND LONDON

First published 1999 by Cornell University Press

Printed in the United States of America

Library of Congress Cataloging-in-Publication Data

Denenberg, R. V., 1942–
    The violence-prone workplace : a new approach to dealing with hostile, threatening, and uncivil behavior / Richard V. Denenberg and Mark Braverman.
        p.   cm.
    Includes bibliographical references and index.
    ISBN 0-8014-3396-7 (cloth)
    1. Violence in the workplace—United States—Prevention.
    I. Braverman, Mark.   II. Title.   III. Title: New approach to dealing with hostile, threatening, and uncivil behavior.
    HF5549.5.E43D46   1999
    658.4′73—dc21   99-40898

Contents

▼

PART III Alarms, False Alarms, Threats, and Panics

PART IV Benefiting from Experience: Strategies for Preventing Violence

PART V Documentary Resources

Preface

This book reflects in large part experience the authors have gained as principals of Workplace Solutions, a consortium of professionals in crisis management and conflict resolution. The mission of Workplace Solutions is to demonstrate the value of a multidisciplinary approach to the issue of workplace violence. In marrying the insights of crisis management and conflict resolution, the organization emphasizes collaborative problem solving and the involvement of all stakeholders in the planning process. The organization has fostered the creation of pilot programs in the public and private sectors and has helped to plan emergency interventions.

Workplace Solutions is funded by the William and Flora Hewlett Foundation, whose philosophy is that problems are best solved by consensual means:

> Recognizing that the origin of conflict can be traced to defects in methods of communication and participation in policymaking, the Foundation assists organizations that demonstrate means of improving the processes of decision making on issues of major public importance. The Foundation's interest is focused primarily on facilitating and convening organizations that explore new

ways of approaching contentious public policy issues through collaborative action that addresses the legitimate interests of all involved parties. [Annual Report for 1996]

Our objective in this book is to allow readers to benefit from the experience of others rather than having to learn the same lessons the hard way. To that end, the discussion is keyed to case studies—actual incidents in which there was violence, a threat of violence, or at least a perception that violence had been threatened. The incidents are analyzed and the findings integrated with practical strategies for transforming a crisis-prone organization into one that is crisis-prepared. A recurring theme is that the transformation is best accomplished with all stakeholders acting in concert to achieve the mutual goal of security and safety. To reach that goal, it is imperative for labor and management to operate in a joint problem-solving mode.

Although a number of books on workplace violence have been published in recent years, they generally adhere to the "cook-book model," relying on patent recipes for avoiding violence. But unduly simplistic formulas fail to ensure that the reader understands the phenomenon under scrutiny.

The case studies presented here, in contrast, impart a genuine understanding of violence on the job because they illustrate the mistakes that are commonly made in responding to perceived threats or dangers. Unlike lists of rules, these poignant, true stories remain vivid in the memory. The value of the cases is further enhanced by a framework emphasizing the Critical Decision Points. Every act or threat of workplace violence—from the stark horror of a mass killing to the disruption of a "false alarm"—engenders a series of critical decisions. Each of these decisions represents a point where an alternative action might have been taken. The Critical Decision Points section at the end of each case highlights those moments and demonstrates their effect on the outcome.

In addition, references to the cases are integrated into the six chapters of discussion that follow, helping to draw out the significance of each incident. The reader thus learns from actual experience—a reality-based approach that should appeal to workplace decision makers looking for practical strategies to enhance safety.

We have designed the book for workplace specialists of various kinds: human resources managers, employment lawyers, safety and security personnel, corporate medical directors, Employee Assistance Program staff, and labor relations neutrals, such as arbitrators, mediators, and fact-finders. Union officers, particularly those involved with Labor-Management Committees dedicated to health and safety issues, will also benefit.

The book is equally applicable to the unorganized workplace. In the absence of a collective voice, it behooves individual employees who feel endangered or fearful at work to make their concerns known to their employer. Reading this book will help the individual discuss the matter knowledgeably with the employer, providing useful ideas for improving workplace safety.

The book is divided into five parts:

Part I is an introduction to the phenomenon of workplace violence, based on empirical data, such as surveys by government agencies and professional organizations, as well as other evidence. We consider the prevalence of the problem, its possible causes, and its variety of forms. Readers are introduced to the classification system devised by the California Occupational Safety and Health Agency (Cal/OSHA), which is the most useful and widely recognized taxonomy of workplace violence. Using a standard classification system is essential for tracking trends and comparing data from various industries and regions.

Part II offers detailed narratives of five notorious incidents of mass murder in the workplace and a discussion of their policy implications. Although such disasters represent a small proportion of the total volume of violence on the job, the episodes discussed here are significant because, taken together, they cost more than 20 lives and have helped to draw attention to a disturbing phenomenon. They portray violence in its most extreme form. It is events such as these that have made many employees feel insecure and spurred the search for effective means of preventing violence.

Too often people hear snippets of news blaring from a radio or glimpse a lurid headline about a violent incident without taking the time to become fully acquainted with the facts. In the five chapters of Part II, we go behind the headlines and the generalities to examine in detail what happened and why. Overall, we conclude from our examination of the record that such incidents typically are not random, senseless, or unexpected, as popularly believed, but result from disputes that have been allowed to fester.

Part III presents accounts of equally significant incidents in which violence was considered likely or a threat was perceived. Only one of these resulted in actual violence. Included are instances of domestic violence overspill, racial and ethnic tension, corporate culture change, downsizing resentment, and other typical situations. Both public sector and private sector settings are featured. We evaluate the adequacy of each organization's response to the threat, indicating where mistakes were made because of poor information, bad judgment, absence of a clear policy, faulty coordination, or irrational fears. Absorbing these lessons can help avoid similar mistakes.

The cases are based on actual events, although names and some other details have been changed for the sake of privacy and brevity. Each case has been reconstructed from a variety of sources. We conducted extensive interviews with participants—among them managers, union officials, arbitrators, attorneys, and journalists. We also examined news accounts and original documents: decisions of arbitrators and public personnel boards, court filings and special reports—often commissioned as a postmortem to a horrifying event. In some cases, we or our colleagues have been directly involved in a professional capacity. No confidential information has been disclosed, of course.

Part IV discusses techniques and model programs for preventing workplace violence, based on principles gleaned from the case studies in Parts II and III, as well as our personal experience. The reader learns how to construct a violence risk profile of an organization, how to form crisis response teams (also known as violence prevention and response teams), and how to undertake advance planning for extreme behavioral crisis. Emphasis is given to collaborative techniques that are designed to enlist the support of all stakeholders, including labor and management. Part IV also considers the usefulness of dispute resolution in relieving tensions that might otherwise flare into violence, and it deals with the special case of violence in schools.

Part V provides documentary resources, including sample violence prevention policies and federal government guidelines. We have eschewed a single model policy, believing that it is better to illustrate the wide variety of approaches that actually have been adopted. Workplaces differ markedly in their needs, and a single policy is unlikely to be suitable for every setting. The samples included in this collection can, however, serve as starting points for policy development and modification in the reader's own workplace. The policies are excerpted, rather than reprinted in full, in the interest of succinctness and in order to focus on the unique features of each document. The sample policies complement Chapter 19, "Designing a Violence Prevention Program," which compares and analyzes various types of employer policy.

Part V includes excerpts from the U.S. Occupational Safety and Health Administration's guidance for the health care industry. Violence is particularly prevalent in that industry, one of only two that have merited special attention from OSHA. The Equal Employment Opportunity Commission's guidance on workers with psychiatric disabilities is also included because violent episodes often have mental health dimensions.

In writing this book, we have benefited from the assistance of several institutions and numerous individuals. We are grateful to the Hewlett Foundation for its financial support and to B. Stephen Toben, program officer of the foundation, for having confidence in our vision: the synthesis of crisis management and conflict resolution.

Each of us is married to a partner who is also a collaborator in the professional sphere and a principal of Workplace Solutions. We are indebted to our wives, Tia Schneider Denenberg, arbitrator and mediator, and Susan R. Braverman, M.S.W., for sharing their own experiences in resolving crisis and conflict in the workplace. We are also grateful for their unfailing understanding while the book was in progress.

We were fortunate to have the research assistance of Lisa Ternullo, who displayed admirable skill and tenacity on our behalf. Gordon Law, librarian of the Cornell University School of Industrial and Labor Relations, generously made available to us the rich resources of his institution, and Donna Schulman, who directs the library's New York City branch, extended hospitality as well. ILR School Dean David Lipsky provided a home for Workplace Solutions during its startup phase.

We gained much from discussions with colleagues in a variety of disciplines who are knowledgeable in workplace issues. They read portions of the draft, gave us interesting leads, alerted us to fascinating cases, and in general facilitated our quest for understanding. Among those colleagues are David Alexander, Terry Amsler, Jordan Barab, Robert and Bonnie Castrey, Robert Conti, Craig Cornish, E. C. Curtis, M.D., Gerry Fellman, Claudia Goldin, Marcia L. Greenbaum, Jim Haley, David Hinds, Eileen and Richard Hoffman, Wayne Horvitz, Jennifer Kaplan, Cheryl King, Lewis Maltby, Jean McKee, Yoshimi Muto, Jonathan Rosen, Ken Swan, Robert Taylor, and Lisa Teems.

Portions of the book have been adapted from articles we wrote for the *Dispute Resolution Journal* (issues of March 1996 and November 1998). The material is used with the permission of the American Arbitration Association, publisher of the journal.

RED HOOK, NEW YORK   R.V.D.

NEWTON, MASSACHUSETTS   M.B.

PART I

VIOLENCE AS A WORKPLACE ISSUE

CHAPTER 1

Introduction: An Everyday Event

The front page carries the story: a desperate employee, enraged at having been fired or passed over for a promotion, returns to the workplace to exact his revenge. He heads for the vice president's office, confronting him with a revolver. He rakes the halls with a deadly spray of automatic weapons fire, eliminating those who slighted and humiliated him, spoiling his career prospects. He saves a bullet for himself, leaving behind him grieving families and a workplace traumatized, terrified, and forever changed.

Eruptions of murder and mayhem, as well as lesser expressions of anger and hostility, are everyday events in America's plants and offices, taking a cumulative toll in heightened insecurity and lowered productivity. The issue of violence has been propelled to the forefront of the workplace agenda by events like the 1991 massacre at a Royal Oak, Michigan, postal facility in which four employees died at the hands of Thomas McIlvane, a discharged worker (Chapter 3). The Michigan shooting was part of the infamous series of multiple slayings by U.S. Postal Service employees that took the lives of more than 35 persons in ten years. But there is little reason to believe that post offices alone are at risk.

In an insurance industry survey, one out of four workers reported being harassed, threatened or physically attacked on the job in the previous

12 months.[1] Moreover, more than half of 500 human resource managers surveyed by the American Management Association reported incidents or threats of violence in their companies in the previous four years. Thirty percent of the managers reported multiple occurrences.[2]

The National Institute of Occupational Safety and Health (NIOSH) calculated that 6,965 work-related homicides occurred from 1980 to 1988.[3] By 1990, the U.S. Centers for Disease Control reports, homicide had "surpassed machine-related incidents as the second leading cause of work-related deaths."[4] NIOSH and the Bureau of Labor Statistics data show that homicide accounts for 17 percent of all deaths in the workplace.

A 1993 survey conducted by the Society for Human Resource Management (SHRM) found that one-third of workplaces sampled had seen a violent incident in the previous five years. Three quarters of the incidents involved fistfights and fully 17 percent involved a shooting.[5] Three years later the same organization discovered evidence that the menace had grown. A nationwide survey of human resource managers found that "the number of violent incidents at work continues to rise." Nearly half the 1,000 managers in the follow-up survey reported one or more incidents in their workplaces since the beginning of 1994.[6]

Regional surveys also reveal deep concern among managers. One in five of the southern California human resource directors surveyed by Thomas Staffing Services, a personnel agency based in suburban Orange County, reported having an experience with workplace violence in the previous three years. Half of the directors worried that a violent incident might occur at their companies in the future. Concern was most pronounced among managers at companies with more than 250 employees and in the medical, high technology, and aerospace industries. Sixty percent of the executives said that they had taken "specific security precautions to prevent . . . employee-generated violence."[7]

Human resources managers, like those responding to the surveys, are commonly victims,[8] and women are particularly likely to be targeted.[9] The danger to women is borne out by worker compensation data generated at state level. For example, in Oregon, "women suffer a disproportionate percentage of the violent incidents," according the state Department of Consumer and Business Services. Although females make up only about a third of compensation claimants, they represent 57 percent of the claims involving violence. In the fields of health care services and education, more than two thirds of the Oregon workers bringing claims of violence were women.[10] In Texas, according to its Worker Compensation Commission, homicide "was the leading manner of death in the workplace for females, accounting for almost half of their occupational injury total" in one study period (1990–91).[11]

Professionals are by no means immune to threats of violence. The American Bar Association conducted an informal survey in 1997 of 253 attorneys who specialized in family law. Sixty percent of the respondents reported being threatened by the opposing counsel's client, and fully 17 percent had been threatened by their own client. A law school dean commented ruefully: "People think attorneys are safe targets because no one likes them."[12] Violence has been so indelibly associated with working life that it figures in fictional portrayals. Cindy Sherman made her debut as a movie director with a 1997 film titled *Office Killer*. Its antiheroine is Dorine, described by a reviewer as "a mousy drudge who, after being downsized, accidentally kills one snotty yuppie and then decides to go for the whole office."[13]

Owing in part to the relatively free access to guns, the United States is often thought of as a particularly violent country, yet the Geneva-based International Labor Organization concluded in 1998 that workplace violence was a planet-wide phenomenon. Violent incidents "occurring at workplaces around the globe suggest that this issue is truly one that transcends the boundaries of a particular country, work setting or occupational group," according to an ILO report.[14] The organization urged that "the full range of causes that generate violence should be analyzed and a variety of intervention strategies adopted. The response to workplace violence is too frequently limited, episodic and ill-defined."[15]

Attacking the Command Structure

Violent incidents often appear to be random acts of slaughter but upon close examination reveal a calculated attempt to decapitate the command structure of the workplace. Such assaults might be labeled "organicides"—efforts to destroy the organizational hierarchy that has been responsible, in the assailant's eyes, for his or her troubles. Here are several examples:

- Los Angeles, California, 1995—Willie Woods, a police department maintenance employee who had received a poor performance evaluation, hunts down and shoots to death four officials of his agency. Each is a carefully selected target: a department supervisor.[16]
- Wixom, Michigan, 1996—Gerald Atkins, a camouflage-clad gunman who is described as a "militia wannabe," storms a Ford auto plant and kills its manager with a semiautomatic rifle. Atkins was on "a quest to destroy some vague conspiracy he said he felt existed between management and the White House."[17]

- Milwaukee, Wisconsin, 1997—Anthony Deculit, a postal clerk in the Central Processing and Distribution Center, shoots a supervisor in the face as he hands her an inventory ticket. The supervisor had reprimanded him for sleeping on the job. Deculit also kills an employee with whom he had feuded and wounds a third worker.[18]
- Santa Ana, California, 1997—Arturo Reyes Torres, a highway worker who has been discharged for theft, returns to a California Transportation Department yard and kills his former supervisor, along with three other employees, with automatic weapons fire.[19]
- Hartford, Connecticut, 1998—Matthew Beck, an accountant who had been denied out-of-classification pay, uses a 9-mm pistol to murder the president of the state's lottery corporation, a quasi-public authority. He also kills three of the corporation's senior managers: the chief financial officer, the vice president of operations, and the information systems manager.[20]
- Apex, Nevada, 1998—Frank Lemos, an experienced heavy equipment operator at a chemical plant, crushes to death the plant production superintendent with the bucket of a 100-ton front-end loader and destroys several buildings. The supervisor had worked with Lemos for more than three decades but a few years earlier had opposed his worker compensation claim.[21]

The Wixom incident, in particular, illustrates the urge to attack the command structure. The assailant did not know the manager. Identifying him

> by his white shirt and two-way radio, Atkins chased [him] from the plant, wounded him in a parking lot, then stalked him back into the facility where he cornered him in a room, shooting and shouting "wimp" to [the manager's] pleas for mercy. Atkins was selective in his targets. None of the rank and file workers were injured. He chatted with some and warned others to flee before surrendering to police after a three-hour siege.[22]

The desire to retaliate against workplace authority is evidently a powerful motive: four of the six perpetrators were willing to give their lives for the sake of revenge. Deculit and Beck were suicides. Torres and Lemos committed "suicide by cop," forcing law enforcement officers to become their executioners (see discussion of the Torres and Beck cases in Chapters 4 and 5).[23]

Often the shooter takes advantage of an intimate knowledge of the workplace. In 1989, Joseph Wesbecker, a former union officer at the Standard Gravure Printing Company in Louisville, Kentucky, entered a company lunchroom armed with an AK-47 assault rifle, two 9-mm pistols and

1,000 rounds of ammunition. He opened fire on his former work mates, killing eight and wounding twelve. Wesbecker maximized the number of his victims by launching his attack at a time when he knew the lunch room would be filled with workers waiting for a shift change. In the Nevada incident, similarly, Lemos made perverse use of a workplace skill—his recognized ability deftly to maneuver a machine that is nearly three stories high. Ironically, he had won an award for his safe handling of that equipment.

Gun-wielding multiple killers like McIlvane, Beck, and Wesbecker are the classic—and dreaded—manifestation of workplace rage. But fatal violence is still relatively rare, accounting for less than 4 percent of all documented incidents. Nevertheless, fatalities are merely the tip of the workplace violence iceberg. In many workplaces resentment routinely displaces cooperation and communication. Hostility surfaces as threats, intimidation, harassment, stalking, and verbal degradation. Advanced information technology has brought with it anonymous "cyberstalking," an electronic form of harassment. Some employees are chronically in conflict with supervisors and fellow workers, or bent on retaliating for discipline or perceived slights. Domestic abuse, as well as simmering ethnic, linguistic, and cultural rivalries, may disrupt the workplace. And workers sometimes become embroiled with nonemployees, such as customers.

Much of the aggression is nonphysical. "The new profile of violence at work," according to an ILO representative, "gives equal emphasis to physical and psychological behavior, and . . . full recognition to the significance of minor acts of violence."[24] A study based on survey evidence concluded that "verbal and passive forms of aggression were rated as more frequent . . . than physical and active forms of aggression."[25] Nonphysical attack can do significant damage. Emotional abuse is recognized by the ILO and other bodies as "psychological violence." The two main forms are "bullying" and "mobbing." Bullying consists of "vindictive, cruel, malicious or humiliating attempts to undermine an individual or groups of employees." Mobbing is a concerted effort by a group of employees to isolate a coworker through ostracism and denigration.[26] Bullying has also been described, from a union perspective, in the following terms:

> Persistent, offensive, abusive, intimidating, malicious or insulting behavior, abuse of power or unfair penal sanctions which make the recipients feel upset, threatened, humiliated, or vulnerable, which undermines their self confidence and which may cause them to suffer stress.[27]

Abusive behavior, according to social psychologist Loraleigh Keashly of Wayne State University, includes "yelling or screaming, use of derogatory names, the 'silent treatment,' withholding of necessary information, aggressive eye contact, negative rumors, explosive outbursts of anger, and ridiculing someone in front of others." Designed to secure compliance, psychological violence can be extremely damaging, as Keashly points out, "in terms of the target's sense of him/herself as a competent worker and person."[28] It adds to workplace stress, thus contributing to the potential for physical violence. And it depresses productivity: "rudeness actually can affect the company's bottom line," the *Washington Post* has observed.[29]

Varieties of Workplace Violence

California's influential state safety agency, known as Cal/OSHA, has formulated a threefold classification of violent incidents in the workplace:[30]

Type I, which accounts for most lethal violence, results from crimes committed by strangers and intruders, such as robbery and burglary. Those occupations that are peculiarly vulnerable to criminality—such as taxi driving or clerking at all-night markets—suffer the most Type I violence.

Type II is violence perpetrated by nonemployees—customers, clients, patients, or students—with whom workers deal from day to day. When an unruly airline passenger assaults a flight attendant aboard a plane, it is an example of Type II violence. As part of their duties, many employees routinely come in contact with nonemployees who for one reason or another may become violent or assaultive. An informal regional survey of union representatives in southern states found that grocery store clerks commonly scuffled with customers, teachers were often attacked by their students, and librarians were harassed by patrons who happened to be gang members or displaced mental patients. Many of these episodes involved weapons or excessive physical force.[31] A vivid example of the perils of retailing occurred in 1995, as a major northeast retail chain was declaring bankruptcy. When the chain abruptly stopped giving refunds for defective merchandise, outraged customers flung VCRs and other appliances at store clerks, inflicting minor injuries.

Health care workers are commonly assaulted by their patients or by the relatives of patients, many of whom are distraught about the fate of their loved ones or upset at a perceived lack of adequate treatment. According to the U.S. Bureau of Justice Statistics, nurses are victims of assault (nonfatal) at a rate of 24.9 per thousand, much higher than the average of 14.8 per thousand for all occupations.[32] As might be expected, the demented or schizophrenic pose an especially high risk. A study of injuries in a psychiatric hospital in the state of Washington, published in the *Journal of Industrial Medicine*, found that 60 percent of worker compensation claims resulted from patient assaults.[33] In 1998, a nurse in Buffalo, New York, was bludgeoned to death by a psychiatric outpatient while visiting her at home.[34]

But violence occurs in all kinds of health care settings, including surgical and pediatric units. There has even been a notorious episode of hostage taking in a maternity ward.[35] Assisting long-term care patients with bathing and dressing also has its hazards: proximity heightens vulnerability. Emergency rooms are another cause for concern; patients have often been rushed there from scenes of crime or drug overdose while still bearing a gun or knife. Overall, write two authorities on nursing, "increased violence in the general population as a means of solving problems, increased use of mind altering drugs and alcohol abuse, and the increased availability of weapons may all contribute to the problem of violence in the health-care setting."[36]

The reported incidents probably underestimate the actual amount of violence, since many health care workers fear that an altercation with a patient will lead to discipline—regardless of fault. In a 1996 arbitration case, for example, a New York State facility moved to discharge a nurse for allegedly punching a patient who was being moved to a "quiet room." The arbitrator, however, found no convincing evidence of a punch. Rather, the record demonstrated that the nurse was struggling desperately to free himself from the grasp of the patient, who was about to bite the back of his neck.

Public sector employees, especially those who deliver social services in this era of fiscal restraint, are also vulnerable to outbursts of anger. According to a union that represents such employees: "More depressed, unstable, and desperate people are waiting in longer lines to talk to fewer workers who have less time to dispense dwindling services and reduced benefits. The result is frustrated clients—clients who may already be unemployed, depressed, homeless and possibly mentally ill. Some, understandably, become violent."[37] One of the most harrowing examples of these dangers occurred in 1992. Four employees of a county social service department in upstate Watkins Glen, New York, were shot to death by a "deadbeat dad" who had been pursued for child support by the department (Chapter 6).[38] Unemployed persons may take out their frustrations on job agencies. In 1993, Alan Winterbourne, an out-of-work computer engineer, burst into the state Employment Development Department office in Oxnard, California, killing five staff members and wounding four others with a gun.[39] The Watkins Glen shooter committed suicide, and Winterbourne was killed by police at another employment office.

Type II also includes the domestic sphere—violence or a threat against a spouse or partner that affects the workplace, as when an ex-husband stalks his wife at her office. Increasingly, family discord, domestic violence, alcohol and drug abuse, and other social ills intrude into work life. An abusive domestic environment has been a particular liability to female workers. In a typical example, a service representative for a telephone company was discharged because her boyfriend repeatedly threatened to attack her at work, terrifying her co-workers and disrupting the office (Chapter 9). In the Wixom plant shooting, the manager's killer (a non-employee) professed at the trial to be suffering from "delusional eroto-mania," a nonreciprocated attraction to a female production worker who had spurned him. The defense counsel asserted that the accused held plant management responsible for coming between them, but the jury evidently concluded that her rejection of him was a only secondary motive for the attack; the main motive was "anti-social rage against authority."[40]

According to the U.S. Department of Labor, "Seventy-four percent of employed battered women are harassed by their abusive partners at work, causing 54 percent to miss at least three full days of work a month and 20 percent to lose their jobs."[41] These figures do not take into account battering that is unreported to employers owing to the absence of guaranteed protection and counseling. Only a few corporations have adopted protective policies. Delegates to the 1995 convention of the AFL-CIO called upon unions to deal with "instances where members' personal safety and job security are threatened as a result of being subject to domestic violence."[42] In the main, however, the extent of domestic overspill and the toll on health, productivity, and morale has yet to be fully recognized.

Type III is internecine violence: an employee attacking co-workers, as in the printing plant incident, or supervisors, as in the "organicides" detailed above. Frequently, the perpetrator has been discharged or suspended and is bent on revenge against the supervisor who imposed the discipline and the co-workers whom the perpetrator, fancifully or not, holds responsible for his plight—perhaps because he considers them informants against him. In 1994, an employee of the Extron Electronics Company in Santa Fe Springs, California, was dismissed for "unsatisfactory performance," only to return a few weeks later and shoot to death three former co-workers.[43] Two years earlier, an employee of the General Dynamics Corp., who was fired for habitual tardiness and absences, killed a labor negotiator at the company's plant in San Diego and severely wounded his former supervisor.[44]

Personnel closely connected with the disciplinary, grievance, and arbitration processes are often targeted when claims are not upheld. Among those killed at Royal Oak was the main employer witness in the arbitration hearing at which McIlvane contested his discharge. In a similar incident, James Brown, a representative for the postal service at arbitration hearings, was killed in Las Vegas, Nevada, in 1996 by Charles Jennings, a discharged employee whose grievance had been rejected by an arbitrator.[45] Such incidents demonstrate that merely separating a person from employment does not necessarily lessen the threat to the workplace; it often increases the danger. Although arbitration may be "final and binding" in a legal sense, when there is a propensity for violence the award may be only the beginning.

Complaint hearings and meetings between supervisors and subordinates have sometimes been occasions for violence. At a Colorado Department of Transportation hearing in 1998, an accountant, Robert Scott Helfer, drew a semiautomatic handgun and shot to death an Equal Employment Opportunity (EEO) officer. He also wounded the department's regional director. The hearing was about a harassment complaint by a female co-worker whom he had allegedly threatened over a canceled order for office furniture. Helfer, a department official said, was "just making a person's life miserable."[46] He was killed by a state police captain, whose headquarters were in an adjacent building.

That same year, two supervisors and the president of a union local representing federal workers died during a seemingly routine labor-management meeting at a U.S. Agriculture Department inspection facility station near Los Angeles International Airport. David Rothman, who headed Local 28 of the National Association of Agricultural Employees, apparently shot his colleagues and then turned the weapon on himself. Thirteen bullets were fired from a .380-caliber semiautomatic handgun about ten minutes after the start of the meeting, which was convened to discuss employee schedules. As in the Colorado incident, the circumstances underlying the California shooting potentially involved an EEO issue.[47]

A Type III incident also may involve elements of domestic dysfunction, as when there is a real or imagined relationship between co-workers. In 1993, Mark Richard Hilbun, a suspended letter carrier, opened fire in the postal facility in Dana Point, California, targeting co-workers and the supervisor who was trying to discharge him for stalking a female employee. Hilbun, whose T-shirt was emblazoned with the word "Psycho," had become convinced that the world was coming to an end and that God had ordered him to take the woman by kayak to Baja California, where they would re-create the human race. His obsession cost the lives of two persons and left seven others severely wounded.[48]

Type I incidents are by far the most common, but the Type II and

Type III varieties share a significant trait: they are acts committed by persons with whom a worker interacts routinely. Unlike the crimes perpetrated by intruders, Type II and Type III violence both arise from continuing relationships that are intrinsic to the business of the organization.

A special form of Type III violence is sabotage. The very technology that creates job stress also affords a weapon for striking back at the employer by exploiting its vulnerabilities. In two notable instances, during 1997–98, a financial services company in New York and an engineering firm in New Jersey suffered losses as great as $10 million when their computer systems were sabotaged. The police arrested discharged employees, whose motive for techno-sabotage was believed to be revenge. One of the suspects had been the subject of numerous complaints from colleagues and was considered "rude and abrasive" by supervisors.[49] The other, who was said to have planted a "logic bomb" timed to detonate three weeks after he had been discharged, "had simmering personal problems with his co-workers."[50]

Although many companies worry primarily about penetration by insidious hackers from outside, a 1998 survey conducted by the Computer Security Institute, a San Francisco–based association of information security professionals, found that computer attacks by their own employees were actually a more serious threat. Of the respondents who acknowledged unauthorized use, 70 percent reported from one to five incidents originating inside the organization, and it was these insider breaches—ranging from sabotage to reading another person's E-mail—that accounted for the most serious damage.[51] The organizations that could place a dollar value on the damage reported an aggregate annual total of nearly $137 million in losses. Disaffected employees, it seems, have been silently taking revenge against their employer by exploiting vulnerabilities they discovered on the job.

Damage akin to a natural disaster was caused in October 1997, when San Francisco suffered a major blackout that was traced to a single power substation. The switches there had been deliberately set incorrectly, and an employee with a key was considered the most likely culprit.[52] It is obvious that the nation's technical infrastructure is vulnerable to employees who give vent to hostility by adopting Luddite tactics. The knowledge that employers' own equipment can be turned against them increases the sense of embattlement and mistrust.

Whose Problem Is It?

There is little dispute that violence affecting workers is a serious and broad-based problem. However, the nature of the problem and the best way to address it are matters of intense controversy. Sadly, the workplace violence issue has become yet another battleground in the struggle between unions and employers. As workplace violence has achieved visibility, it has generated an entire industry of consultants. Rather than advocate a balanced approach, many of these consultants focus on Type III violence exclusively, trading on the distorted stereotype of a homicidal, paranoid worker who must be stopped before he wreaks terrible vengeance. The consultants advise employers how to protect themselves against retribution by angry workers and how to shield themselves from lawsuits by employees exposed to violence. Yielding to the pressure for quick fixes and easy targets of blame, training videos and manuals typically promise to show managers how to predict which workers will become violent.

This approach understandably disturbs union representatives, who argue that employers are using the workplace violence issue to rid themselves of troublesome, activist employees and to avoid responsibility for real safety problems. As unions correctly point out, only a small percentage of workplace violence takes place between workers. Yet to the unions it always seems to be the "violent employee" who becomes the center of the discussion. Their members mainly report injury and murder by people from outside of the workplace or by clients and patients—not by their fellow workers. As usual, it is the victims who are being blamed for the crimes, the unions argue, and the consultants are complicit in this injustice.

Typically employers do not attempt to discover what concerns workers have about violence and which experiences may have disturbed or alarmed them. Employers also commonly neglect to create a stakeholder alliance that draws unions and other critical constituents into the assessment and planning stages. Without such stakeholder participation and "buy-in," efforts to ensure protection are unlikely to succeed.

An employer that remains focused exclusively on worker-on-worker violence risks alienating and demoralizing the workforce. Employees who feel at risk of becoming victims of violence–from any source–will be reluctant to bring the hazard to the attention of the employer if they believe that they are viewed by the management as potential perpetrators. Such workers will feel mistrusted and readily believe that the employer cares little about what really concerns them. By failing to define the potential threat accurately, the employer misses an opportunity to forge a coalition around a concept with universal appeal: a safe working environment.

Perhaps the ultimate quick fix is the hasty resort to termination. The goal of "safe termination," a ubiquitous buzzword, is to induce an employee who may be consumed with a sense of injustice to depart quickly without taking physical reprisal. Guidelines for safe termination prepared by a New England consulting organization urge clients, "Be brief. . . . Remember—the less said the better." The guidelines suggest that terminations should take place early in the week so that the discharged workers "can immediately commence their job searches and focus on positive activities" rather than brooding during the weekend. The guidelines also advise against holding the termination meeting "in your own office, where you may be 'trapped' into a longer meeting than you anticipated."[53]

But a precipitate discharge can exacerbate rather than alleviate risk. A full explanation of the reason for a disciplinary action is less likely to produce a volatile response than giving an employee short shrift. Instead of trying to hold the employee at arm's length while abruptly showing him or her the door, the employer ought to explore the source of the troublesome behavior. The employer might gather useful information about the nature of the stresses that a worker experiences. It makes little sense for an organization to live in fear of its own employees yet remain incurious about their thinking. A more constructive approach is to view each incident as an opportunity for intelligence gathering and a chance to identify organizational weaknesses.

Labor-Management Polarization

Polarization around the issue of workplace violence is the classic lose-lose standoff. All are put at risk when deadlock and paralysis stand in the way of addressing possible dangers or when jockeying for power within an adversarial relationship takes precedence over ensuring the health, safety, and general well-being of the workforce. Forging effective health and safety alliances between labor and management is not always easy. Despite the establishment of OSHA and the proliferation of Labor-Management Safety Committees, the issue is often marred by mutual recrimination and partisan struggle. However, the obvious benefits to both sides of the table when the risk of violence is reduced affords a powerful incentive for breaking the deadlock.

Moreover, unlike subjects such as pay scales, job security, and work rules—the staples of the labor-management relationship—threats, intimidation, or dangerous behavior require more than a formal process of negotiation. They demand teamwork, consensus, and trust. The conventional pattern of labor-management interaction—management promulgates a policy unilaterally and the union grieves—creates vulnerability rather than security, because the common interest in safety tends to be ignored when each party attempts to score points at the other's expense. All stakeholders in an organization must be able to agree on the nature of the danger and on a mutually acceptable response. Throughout the risk assessment process, they need to speak to each other candidly and rely on each other's good faith. Since a poor relationship between the parties increases the risk of harm, a nonadversarial approach is essential to keeping the workplace free from violence and fear.

The challenge is to preserve the health and well-being of workers amid relentless spasms of change. Increasing economic pressure on families and more controlled health care delivery contribute to an escalating rate of individual breakdown at work. Forced to assume more and more responsibility as their ranks are thinned by downsizing, supervisors and managers may ignore all but the most immediate production-related crises. Effective communication, sensitivity to individual concerns, and awareness of deteriorating morale are easily lost in a pressurized environment.

Unions often find themselves caught between the increasing strain on their members on the one hand and the employer's decreasing ability to handle human needs on the other. Acrimonious grievances and demands for union support of members result. In some workplaces, where labor-management collaboration and confidence in the Employee Assistance Program (EAP) are both low, unions regularly deal with incidents of violence, respond to marital crises, arrange for drug and alcohol abuse treatment, and manage threats of suicide. They often assume these responsibilities without the benefit of proper training, follow-up mechanisms, and coordination with the employer. Never have unions had more reason to work with the employer in defusing conflict and decreasing the frequency of threatening and violent incidents.

As the case studies in this book illustrate, a poor labor-relations climate promotes unfavorable outcomes to crises. When supervisors and employees are in a hyper-adversarial relationship, the parties are prevented from seeking real solutions. In an environment of tension, cries for help are seldom heard, and responses come late, grudgingly, or not at all.

Workplace violence is a systemic phenomenon. It is encouraged by "macro" social factors such as poverty, racism, crime, mental illness, substance abuse, and family dysfunction. It is also fostered by workplace-induced stress, resulting from changes in the employment relationship: downsizing, reorganization, increasing workforce diversity, growing workloads, and erosion of job security. The decay of group cohesion and communication channels is a significant contributory factor.

Confronting violence means, at bottom, accepting that even "normal" persons are subject to breakdown—and its sometimes violent consequences—when stress becomes unbearable. A good prevention program seeks to relieve the sources of stress. Rather than hunt for a few supposed "bad apples" in the barrel, we ought to examine the barrel itself, recognizing that violence is ultimately the product of social or organizational change and other factors that leave the working environment potentially volatile. The next chapter explores the multitude of components that contribute to this phenomenon.

CHAPTER 2

Origins of Workplace Violence

 widely published innovator in the emerging field of crisis management offers this powerful description of the current state of our world:

> We live in a crisis-prone and crisis-laden world. A world in which crises are omnipresent and proliferating. Every aspect of society faces damaging disruptions, upheaval and restructuring, which are the hallmarks of crises.[1]

The modern workplace is no exception. It is vulnerable to extreme behavioral crisis, often culminating in menacing threats or outbursts of savage violence. Violence, or the threat of violence, creates a climate of fear and hostility, disrupting the workplace. A crisis of that kind may be engendered by forces within the workplace or by the global phenomenon of rapid change in social institutions, such as the family.

T. C. Pauchant and I. I. Mitroff, two students of corporate crises, offer a compelling model in which they contrast the "crisis-prone" with the "crisis-prepared" organization.[2] The latter also might be called "crisis-resistant." Given the proliferation of human and environmental crises in modern society, they argue, corporations that deny the possibility of crises and do nothing to prevent them or to prepare for them are more likely to experience severe disruption and harm.

The differences between "crisis-prone" and "crisis-prepared" organizations may be summarized as follows:

The crisis-prone organization:

- Reacts to crises, rather than reading the warning signs that might allow problems to be prevented or mitigated.
- Pays lip service to human issues but pays real attention only to bottom line figures and business interests.
- Holds fast to denial, summarily expelling or punishing employees perceived as deviant, rather than confronting their behavior and its causes.
- "Delegates" responsibility for programs and policies involving employee welfare to lower echelons while top leadership remains remote, especially during times of change and stress.
- Directs communication in a crisis outward (e.g., toward the public, stockholders, and the media) rather than inward, toward employees.
- Remains mired in adversarial standoff, thwarting genuine internal communication and problem solving.

The crisis-prepared organization:

- Maintains effective systems for collecting, reporting, and analyzing signs of distress at an early stage.
- Cultivates a sense of mutual interest among stakeholders, including unions, in responding effectively to incipient strains.
- Develops and fully disseminates in advance a policy for dealing with potential and actual crises.
- Encourages a climate in which employees feel free to communicate their distress to management and management feels a responsibility to respond.
- Engages in effective problem-solving rather than confrontation.
- Does not deny problems or seek to avoid dealing with them by expelling or suppressing "deviants."

Crisis-prepared organizations recognize the early symptoms and signals of individual distress and breakdown, and have systems in place to respond. Signs of trouble precede every threat or act of violence. For example, a large number of grievances may indicate poor morale or labor-management conflict, or they may involve a single employee, who has submitted a claim for stress or complained of harassment. A crisis-prone organization will allow these early signs of conflict to go undetected. If managers respond at all to danger signals, they will typically invoke standard disciplinary, labor-relations, or occupational health procedures. Only when the crisis has erupted will direct action be taken.

If an individual who has reached the breaking point works in an organization that does not recognize the warning signs and has no mechanisms in place to reverse the spiral of stress, the potential for violence is created. Violence expresses an overwhelming sense of desperation and isolation, and a growing conviction that *nothing I can do will help or change my situation.* Effective violence prevention depends on the ability of the social or institutional setting to mediate or moderate the effect of stressors on the particular individual at risk. In some cases, the workplace itself may be the source of the stress, so the role of the setting becomes even more significant.

Crisis-prone organizations stress their workers and are ineffective in recognizing the signs of stress-related breakdown. Although many of the sources of job-related stress have been well known for decades, a number of new, severe work stressors are making an appearance. Together, they increase the likelihood of individual breakdown and organizational dysfunction.

Competitive Pressures

Relentless global market forces demand constant changes in methods of production and workplace organization. Employees find themselves having to perform in new ways and more efficiently. Owing to the introduction of new technology, workers who may have spent decades in blue-collar jobs, wearing tool belts, may suddenly find themselves staring at computer screens, having been transformed willy-nilly into white-collar technicians. Although technology may make for efficiency, it often requires difficult adjustments in terms of work habits and self-image—often without adequate training, support, and guidance.

Team production methods introduce novel demands. Mandatory overtime, fatiguing production goals, and erratic scheduling may intensify the pressure. Shift schedules can disrupt circadian rhythms and family responsibilities, while monotonous tasks and "lean and mean" styles of work organization may also take a toll.[3] Abrasive co-workers or autocratic supervisors create additional stresses, particularly when mergers have led to a clash of corporate cultures or uncertainty about the goals and priorities of the amalgamated organization.

Ubiquitous threats of mergers, takeovers, and midlife "career crash" feed anxieties. In an era of mass layoffs and "re-engineering" in both public and private organizations, workers haunted by fear of unemployment struggle to remain in jobs that yield only stagnant or even declining real wages and scant security. Once regarded as long-term assets, whose loyalty was cultivated, employees have become liabilities, to be shed whenever possible or turned into "contingent" workers. A North American auto union leader lamented,

> Contrary to so much that is being written about workplace change, our jobs and our workplaces in the closing years of this century are actually getting worse. What we see in broader social terms—efforts to undermine our social wage, cut actual wages, reduce our standard of living, erode universal rights and entitlements, and weaken progressive organizations—is reflected in our workplaces by insecure employment, contingent pay, flexible workers, intensified work, and efforts to weaken and compromise unions.[4]

His assessment is supported by a prominent political theorist, who has observed that

> an unprecedented sense of personal economic insecurity . . . has suddenly become the central phenomenon of life in America, not only for the notoriously endangered species of corporate middle managers, prime targets of today's fashionable "downsizing" and "re-engineering," but for virtually all working Americans except tenured civil servants—whose security is resented.[5]

The consequences of such insecurity may resemble the effects of psychological trauma: irritable and hostile behavior, anger, mistrust, mood swings, depression, and withdrawal from social and family supports. At the same time, shrinkage of child care, health care, and mental health services means that many come to the workplace already stressed and perhaps suffering from untreated mental or substance abuse disorders. Changes in the structure of health care delivery—largely related to the advent of "managed care"—have also weakened the safety net for individuals and families. Preventive and therapeutic care for mental health and chemical dependency conditions has been restricted under managed care, increasing the frequency and severity of behavioral symptoms that affect productivity.

Loss of Personal Autonomy

To some extent, a surrender of personal autonomy is intrinsic to the industrial discipline upon which Western prosperity rests. In the nineteenth century, Frederick Winslow Taylor preached a gospel of "scientific management" that subjected each worker to the tyranny of the stopwatch in the name of efficiency. The reduction of manufacturing processes to measured, mechanistic tasks was sharply criticized, however, for depriving the worker of autonomy—the ability to use skills, exercise judgment and control the rhythm of work. Planning was separated from doing, turning the worker into a mindless robot. The humanistic critique of Taylorism, his biographer observed, held that scientific management "pitted workers as individuals against one another, made them claw at each other." Opponents of scientific management contended that it was fundamentally degrading:

> In reducing work to instructions and rules, it took away your knowledge and skill. In standing over you with a stopwatch, peering at you, measuring you, rating you, it treated you like a side of beef. You weren't supposed to think. Whatever workmanly pride you might once have possessed must be sacrificed on the altar of efficiency, your role only to execute the will of other men paid to think for you. You were a drone, fit only for taking orders.
>
> Scientific management, then, worked people with scant regard not only for the limitations of their bodies but for the capacities of their minds. . . . In the great Taylorist equation that spat out the Good News of high wages, high profits, and low prices, the quality of those eight or ten hours on the job itself had been banished from the calculation.[6]

As the basis of the economy shifts from smokestacks to cyberspace, from manual work to knowledge-based work, the efficiency principle has been translated to the white-collar realm, leading to what has been called the "Taylorization of management."[7] But human nature seems as resistant as ever to a machinelike style of work that compresses a maximum amount of effort into a minimum amount of time. An international survey of business executives, conducted in 1996 by Benchmark Research, a division of the Reuters news organization, revealed that "half of all managers complain of 'information overload,' which increases already high levels of stress and can lead to ill health." The survey—titled "Dying for Information?"—suggested that managers who felt overwhelmed by the flood of job-related data were suffering from a new disorder: Information Fatigue Syndrome. The symptoms, according to Reuters, include "paralysis of analytical capacity, increased anxiety and self-doubt, and a tendency to blame others." The psychologist David Lewis of the International Stress Management Association, who designed the study, asserts that "when compelled to choose among a series of options, in the face of vast amounts of potentially important information and against the clock, we move into a state of excessive stress."[8]

In his book, *Data Smog: Surviving the Information Glut*, the cultural critic David Shenk argues that the inability to cope with the onslaught of information is due to the primitive hard-wiring in the human brain. Because we have the same limited equipment as our hunter-gather ancestors, he maintains, we suffer from advanced stages of "Info-biological Inadequacy Syndrome," a condition he likens to Attention Deficit Disorder.[9]

Information fatigue is also intensified by the inability, under modern technological conditions, to get away from the office; many business travelers receive dozens of E-mail messages a week when they are on the road. In the office there are interminable meetings to cope with the deluge of information. Managers apparently must meet more often because organizational downsizing requires frequent face-to-face contact among the thinned ranks of the survivors.[10] A study by the executive search firm Ray & Berndtson discovered rising levels of "meeting stress" linked to the increasing amount of time being wasted in unproductive discussions.

Technology, in the form of fax machines and modems, seemingly has liberated many employees from the need to come to the office at all. More than a million employees are considered "telecommuters" because they work from home and communicate with supervisors without having to make an appearance. But even these workers find themselves subject to stress associated with a feeling of inability to escape work pressures. Many telecommuters told reporters for the Public Broadcasting System "that they are blurring the lines between work and home-life to the point where they are actually never 'away' from work."[11] The loss of a sense of control can be directly related to hostile or violent behavior.

Surveillance

Technology has hastened the erosion of autonomy by making possible various forms of surveillance on the job that can measure individual productivity in sophisticated ways—a giant computerized stopwatch, so to speak. In addition, employees are commonly subjected to biochemical analysis: random, scheduled, and "for cause" drug testing. Such testing has helped to erase the traditionally firm distinction between on-duty and off-duty conduct, since one's free-time behavior can lead to workplace discipline.[12] Employees' phone calls may be monitored, their computer keystrokes counted, and their movements tracked by hidden cameras, so that "unsuspecting workers feel betrayed, then paranoid," as a newspaper's exposé discovered.[13] A survey by the American Management Association in

1997 found that two thirds of mid-size and large companies take advantage of new technology to keep watch on their employees.[14] The range of surveillance was surprisingly broad, as an analysis of the survey by a civil liberties group pointed out:

> The survey . . . found that 35 percent of companies spy on their employees by taping telephone calls or voicemail, intercepting computer files and electronic mail, and videotaping employees at their job. The most common method of surveillance, practiced by up to 37 percent of companies, involves monitoring the telephone numbers and duration of calls made by employees.[15]

An illustration of how surveillance may unfairly intrude into worker privacy is provided by a decision of an Administrative Law Judge for the National Labor Relations Board. He found that an employer in Syracuse, New York, had installed a video camera in an employee break room for the purpose of overhearing workers' conversations about forming a union. This action interfered with their legal right to engage in collective activity, the judge held, in a case that led to the reinstatement of a discharged worker.[16] The ability to monitor employee communications, particularly E-mail, has played an increasingly large role in the appearance of threat of violence cases in the workplace.

The rise of the Internet offers another opportunity for surveillance. Many employees regrettably spend their employer's time on "recreational surfing" through entertaining but nonproductive web sites, including sports and pornography home pages. In response, a growing number of companies have adopted Internet use policies and introduced software that filters and monitors use of the Internet; some employers begin by blocking sexually explicit sites and monitoring the rest.[17] Although the employer's interest in preventing abuse is clearly legitimate, the result nevertheless is a decrease in personal autonomy.

Future technical advances promise even closer monitoring of electronic channels of communication. Computer programs known collectively as "censorware" will exhaustively screen all E-mail, according to a newspaper report, for "anything the program considers obnoxious, racist, religious, sexual or threatening." The scanning tool can spot off-color language and jokes about "Ebonics" as well as ethical lapses. In trial runs, about 15 percent of communications proved to be offensive. Although the goals of the surveillance—such as deterring racial and sexual harassment—may be laudable, such relentless scrutiny of expression inevitably creates an oppressive atmosphere.[18] As Jonathan Rauch has cogently argued, "there is no way to prevent workplace offense that does not also quickly lead to broad repression of speech."[19] Professor Eugene Volokh of the University of California at Los Angeles has urged that only "targeted vilification," not overheard comments, be considered harassment.[20]

Like experimental laboratory animals, employees may be required to undergo a form of compulsory physiological research known as performance monitoring. One version is a computerized "critical tracking test" with the proprietary name of Factor 1000: "Before starting work, the employees take a simple test, similar to a video game, that measures hand-eye coordination; they try to keep a swinging pointer centered on a computer screen."[21] The test measures psychomotor skills, hand-eye coordination, and mental acuity or alertness. The results are compared to a baseline score, representing the employee's personal average on previous tests. Another system, designed to detect diminished capacity to perform, probes the employee's ability to reproduce number sequences, comprehend written material, recognize patterns, and utilize short-term memory.[22]

Cumulative Physical and Mental Reactions

Medical researchers have begun to examine the possible adverse effects of stress on health, both physical and mental. The neuroscientist Bruce S. McEwen has coined the term "allostatic load" to refer to the long-term, cumulative effects of stress on the body.[23] Although the precise mechanism is not yet known, studies of laboratory animals suggest that stress reduces levels of acetylcholine, a chemical that promotes healthy brain functions, and thus in humans "might cause memory and other mental problems through a similar biochemical effect."[24]

A major source of one's lifetime stress load is the workplace. Those who experience job strain exhibit more stress-related illness than do other workers.[25] There is evidence that high psychological demand combined with low "decision latitude" (the ability to act autonomously and exercise discretion)—creates a special health danger. Even the physiology of low-autonomy workers is affected. Empirical studies by Dr. Peter Schnall, a physician at the New York Hospital–Cornell Medical Center, found that their blood pressure is permanently elevated[26] and that they are at greater risk for structural changes in the heart.[27]

In a 1997 study of blue- and white-collar workers, Dr. Redmond Williams of Duke University found that lack of control, combined with heavy demands and repetitive work, produced an increase in depression, anxiety, and hostility. Women were particularly vulnerable: "The women who were in the highest 25 percent of our sample with respect to their job strain score were depressed to a level that would be considered clinical," according to Dr. Williams, which meant that the condition was serious enough to warrant medical attention. Male workers, according to the Duke study, were more likely to react to job stress by becoming hostile.[28]

Although stress is a difficult condition to measure accurately, it may soon become practical to gauge its physiological effect by chemical means. Dr. Robert Chatterton of Northwestern University Medical School has discovered that the level of the enzyme amylase increases in response to stress. Since the chemical appears in saliva, it may be become possible to devise a simple chemical test for stress, akin to the tests used today to detect illegal drugs.[29]

In Japan, work stress has won legal recognition as a cause of death and a factor in suicide. "Karoshi," or death from overwork, has resulted in monetary awards to survivors, and the police identified "work-related problems" as a key factor in the increase in suicides among 50–59 years olds in 1995. In one case, the court held the employer fully liable for the suicide of an employee beset with work-related worries and ordered compensation to be paid to his family.[30]

The Fatigue Factor

Under conditions of global competition where time zones no longer matter, many employees have also suffered a diminution of autonomy by losing control over a basic physiological function: the sleep cycle. Although alcohol and other drugs have been prominently targeted as threats to work performance, research in human physiology is calling attention to what may well be a more imminent hazard: pervasive fatigue. Overly long shifts or erratically scheduled duty periods, researchers caution, can disrupt the body's "circadian" rhythm—the natural fluctuations in alertness that occur throughout the day. The result of disregarding the body's internal clock could be significant impairment and susceptibility to catastrophic error. These are a few examples:

- Scheduling pilots for long international flights without regard to time zone changes and biorhythm has been implicated in loss of attentiveness, somnolence, and even brief episodes in which all members of a cockpit crew were napping simultaneously.[31]
- A surprise government inspection discovered the entire night shift at Pennsylvania's Peach Bottom nuclear generating facility asleep. A re-

port on the incident noted that management had failed to recognize that the employees were affected by the nocturnal tedium of watching dials.[32]

- A study by the National Transportation Safety Board of 181 accidents in which truck drivers were killed concluded that fatigue was the single most prevalent causative factor (present in 57 cases, compared to 39 for drugs and 22 for alcohol).[33]

Experts on sleep disorders have pointed to a growing threat of "high-consequence errors" due to lapses of attention brought on by disruptive scheduling and the unremitting tempo of modern work. A group of the scientists who pioneered the study of "chronobiology"—the effect of time of day on the body's performance—issued a warning:

> The relentless push to operate transportation and other systems around the clock has meant catastrophe at times when people are least prepared to cope with it. . . . The safety problem is further exacerbated by regulations that permit prolonged and dangerous work schedules for personal reasons (for example, to earn extended free time) and by competitive forces that pit safety against economic gain or expediency.[34]

Job fatigue also may magnify the danger to the workplace of alcohol, illegal drugs, prescription drugs and over-the-counter substances, regardless of where they are used. In experimental settings, even moderate sleep deprivation has been shown to increase the risk of alcohol-related accidents. As a result of sleeplessness, the journal *Neuropsychopharmacology* reported, potential behavioral impairment related to prior ethanol consumption could exist, although "the evidence of that ethanol consumption would not be present. . . . [M]easurement of the level of ethanol in the system alone may cause underestimation of the degree of alcohol-related impairment."[35] In short, employees might be functionally impaired by pre-duty drinking although their blood alcohol concentration was negligible by the time they reported for work.

These findings add to a body of evidence, amassed in the last decade, which suggests that a postmetabolism "hangover effect" endures long after drinking has ceased. A Stanford University study found that pilot performance skills—such as the ability to keep on course—was significantly affected as much as fourteen hours after heavy drinking. In a similar study, experienced U.S. Navy pilots performed worse, by a variety of measures, during "hangover flights." At the moment, the FAA requires only eight hours to elapse between drinking and flying—the so-called bottle to throttle period—but such rules may need reevaluation in light of newer evidence.

Work-induced fatigue and its corollary—job stress—could exacerbate "road rage" and contribute to the abuse of psychotropic drugs. In the long-haul trucking industry, many drivers depend upon performance-enhancing chemicals for the stamina needed to achieve expected productivity levels. At truck stops amphetamines are traded as "go-fast" and "coast to coast"—names which graphically describe their function. The stimulants are aids in fulfilling often punishing driving schedules; such schedules have become common, in apparent indifference to how they are met. Of the drug-involved truckers identified in the NTSB accident study, 15 percent had used stimulants: an illegal amphetamine or over-the-counter substance. The stimulant users were more numerous than the users of any other single drug. (A smaller group—cocaine users—also might have been fighting off driving fatigue.)

Attempting to compensate for fatigue and stress could be a significant cause of chemical dependency. In Canada, transportation workers were asked in 1990 to pinpoint those aspects of their work that most inclined them to depend on alcohol or other drugs. Among the occupationally generated risk factors frequently cited were boredom and repetition, long hours, and job fatigue. The survey concluded: "Pressure and stress are seen as the major workplace contributors to the use of medications, alcohol or drugs among people in the various transportation jobs." The employees who mentioned pressure and stress most often (82 percent of respondents) were air traffic controllers—a finding with ominous implications for public safety.[36]

Self-medication is plainly a popular means of keeping pace with a demanding job, and such deeply entrenched patterns seem resistant to exhortations against the use of chemicals. Reshaping the work itself is another option. Students of circadian rhythm have proposed modification of standard work routines in the interest of safety, even if it requires departing from disciplinary tradition. Crew members who fall asleep aboard airline flights, for example, typically are discharged. Yet airlines have begun to heed the advice of sleep specialist David F. Dinges of the University of Pennsylvania Medical School, who recommends "individual crew member napping . . . at previously established periods in the flight." Since there is no substitute for real sleep, Dinges reasons, authorizing periods of rest rather than deterring them through punishment improves crew performance. This idea has been taken up by the Burlington Northern–Santa Fe Railroad, which allows sleep-deprived employees to cope with physiological needs by napping for 30 to 40 minutes.[37] By eliminating some factors that predispose employees to chemical coping, moreover, fatigue-reduction measures could become an effective strategy for preventing abuse.

Changing Workforce Demographics

Growing ethnic, linguistic, cultural and gender diversity is likely to breed intergroup tension. One factor is the accelerating pace of immigration. The percentage of the foreign-born in the U.S. population has doubled since 1970 and now stands at the highest rate in almost 60 years (8.7 percent). In heavily impacted regions, the proportion is much higher: nearly 25 percent of Californians, for example, were born outside the United States. Owing to immigration and differential birth rates, the U.S. Census projects, the ethnic composition of the population is likely to undergo a profound transformation in coming years. The proportion of Hispanics and Asians will probably swell, while blacks maintain their current share of the population. But non-Hispanic whites—the current majority group—are expected to shrink to half the population at most.[38] And a new ethnic category is emerging: the children of mixed parentage, who regard themselves as "multiracial." The number of children born annually to interracial couples quadrupled between 1970 and 1990, reaching 2 million in the latter year. A federal task force has recommended against recognizing "multiracial" as a separate census category, on the ground that it would "add to racial tensions and further fragmentation of our population," but it is clear that many persons of mixed heritage do regard themselves as a group apart, potentially adding many new pieces to the mosaic of American life.[39] Some, like the golfer Tiger Woods, who invented the telescopic term "Cablinasian" to describe his Caucasian-black-Indian-Asian lineage, may create their own unique mixed-heritage identities.

Illustrating the proliferation of identities, Wayne County, Michigan, which embraces Detroit, officially recognizes 105 distinct ethnic or national groups. Heightened diversification is likely to be particularly noticeable in the working-age population. This profound transformation is radically altering the demographics of the workplace and increasing the risk of pervasive intergroup tension on the shop floor.

Even a modest-sized company may have dozens of nationalities, mainly recent immigrants, on its payroll. Regrettably, there is reason to fear that diversity may result in divisiveness. Whereas dispute resolution theory has focused largely on conflict between a majority group and a minority group, recent survey research has found that "many minorities agreed with negative stereotypes of other minority groups even though they shared the sting of discrimination by the majority."[40]

In the absence of strong integrating forces, such as vibrant unionism and effective, leadership-driven programs to promote positive attitudes toward diversity, the workforce could become ethnically or culturally balkanized. The possibilities for dangerous misunderstanding are endless, particularly when there are linguistic differences. To prevent strife among linguistic groups, some employers have felt compelled to promulgate "English-only" policies, which prohibit employees from using other languages on the job.

The Spun Steak Company, a meat processing company in the San Francisco area, adopted such a policy because, according to its court filings, employees who were fluent in both Spanish and English used "their multilingual facility to abuse and harass their fellow employees." The U.S. Equal Employment Opportunities Commission considered English-only policies "presumptively invalid," on the ground that they constituted discrimination on the basis of national origin—a violation of Title VII of the Civil Rights Act of 1964. Nevertheless, Spun Steak's rationale impressed the U.S. Court of Appeals for the Ninth Circuit, which covers western states where a third of the nation's foreign-language speakers dwell. Despite the federal government's contention that the policy deprived some persons of the use of "the language in which they communicate most effectively," the circuit court upheld the employer, and the U.S. Supreme Court declined to disturb the circuit's ruling.[41]

An incident that took the lives of two persons and wounded four others in a plastics factory in 1997 stemmed from a misinterpreted foreign language conversation. Daniel S. Marsden, an inspector in the factory, overheard co-workers speaking in Spanish and believed—erroneously—that they were ridiculing him on the basis of his presumed sexual orientation. Before turning his 9-mm semiautomatic gun on workers in the office and warehouse, Marsden screamed, "I am not homosexual—you people are going to pay!"[42]

Here are some other examples of how ethnicity may incite hostility:

- A fire department in a large city has been dominated for generations by a white ethnic group. Affirmative Action has introduced minorities, particularly Hispanic, who have become the targets of unrelenting and vicious harassment and discrimination. The result is depression among the minority firefighters, frequent arguments, and fistfights.
- A lone Colombian man working with whites and African Americans in a manufacturing facility is the object of harassment because of his national origin. He is seen as a "drug dealer" and suspected of being vio-

lent. He becomes increasingly depressed and angry. One day there is a dispute about when his break is supposed to be over. When his supervisor tells him to get back to work, he makes a comment that is routine in Colombia but is perceived as threatening by the supervisor, who is an "Anglo." The worker is brought up on disciplinary charges for threatening violence.

- In a nursing home, line health care workers, who are largely from an inner-city, African American background, are supervised by white middle-class nurses. Frequent physical confrontations, which are normal for "the street" but unacceptable among staff members, are inconsistently controlled by supervisors, who are intimidated by the unfamiliar, confrontational style of their staff. For their part, line staff feel that supervisors do not treat them with respect.

The prevention of ethnically based hostility among workers and between workers and supervisors is one of today's most pressing policy issues. As part of violence prevention planning, employment specialists ought to develop a catalog of best practices and most effective dispute resolution techniques for dealing with diversity-linked conflict.

PART II

THE ANATOMY OF TRAGEDY: STUDIES IN MULTIPLE MURDER

CHAPTER 3

Royal Oak, Michigan:
A Post Office Massacre

On a gray November afternoon in 1991, the telephone answering machine of Thomas McIlvane, a discharged letter carrier, recorded a call, informing him that his arbitration case had been lost. After more than a year of proceedings, his termination by the United States Postal Service had been upheld.[1] A few days later, armed with a loaded semiautomatic rifle, McIlvane entered the main post office in Royal Oak, Michigan, where he had worked for more than eight years. Easily gaining entry through the rear loading dock (fellow workers later remembered having greeted him as he entered that morning), he headed for the management offices on the second floor. He found the four managers who had been involved in the discipline that had led to his firing, and he killed them. Then he took his own life.

The massacre at Royal Oak no doubt can be traced to a complex of causal factors. But it is worth asking: Did the system for resolving disputes play a part in this tragedy? Could it be responsible for the parties' failure to head off a looming disaster?

As an illustration of the dynamics of a workplace disaster, the Royal Oak incident deserves close examination. It could be argued that the grievant should never have been hired in the first place. Before joining the postal service, which accords hiring preference to veterans, McIlvane had been a

U.S. Marine. Owing perhaps to the obscurity of discharge records, postal authorities seem to have been unaware that his military career was marred by insubordination, use of profane and aggressive language toward superiors, destruction of equipment, and acts of overt violence, including an attempt to run over a fellow Marine with a vehicle. He had been disciplined repeatedly; the penalties included a three-month incarceration.

Management apparently misread the pertinent documentation: Defense Department Form 214. The form contains a blank to be filled in after "Character of Service." To qualify for a preference, the characterization must be either "Honorable" or "General (Under Honorable Conditions)." Although these characterizations seem semantically indistinguishable, there are crucial differences between them. An honorable discharge means that the service person has generally met the standards for "acceptable conduct and performance of duty." In contrast, a general discharge "under honorable conditions" signifies that "a member's service has been honest and faithful, but significant negative aspects of conduct or performance of duty outweigh positive aspects of the member's military record."[2] Therefore, according to a student of military practice, "under honorable conditions" has always indicated "an individual who had considerable difficulty adjusting to military life."[3] In short, the flawed nature of McIlvane's service should have been apparent from the type of discharge he had received. In addition, any periods of incarceration in military prison should have been ascertainable by checking dates entered in the "Time Lost" line of DD 214.

Beginning in early 1988, a few years after he had been hired by the postal service, McIlvane was often in conflict with authority. He became insubordinate. The incidents included:

- An alleged assault on a customer, which launched an investigation by the Postal Inspection Service, the agency's security force.
- Safety violations involving his vehicle, which led to a 14-day suspension.
- Throwing a pencil at a supervisor during an argument.
- Subjecting a female supervisor to a volley of epithets and threats.

There is an indication in his record that he had a fitness-for-duty examination that included a psychiatric component, but it is not clear why the examination was ordered. On August 8, 1990, a Removal Notice—in effect, a discharge—was issued. The triggering incident was an episode of "profane threats and insubordination" involving three supervisors. He filed a grievance against the notice.

During the next 15 months, while the discharge case was pending, more than 20 threats were documented. For example, the grievant phoned his former manager, saying, "You are the one who got me fired. . . . I'm going to be watching you, and I'm going to get you." At an unemployment compensation hearing several days later, McIlvane said to a supervisor, "You might win today, but I'm going to get you." At another point, McIlvane crumpled a form and threw it in the face of an office worker. He then told a manager, "I'm going to come up there and kill you."

At the arbitration hearing, the grievant denied making the remarks attributed to him in the notice and argued that he had been singled out unfairly for discipline. The arbitrator found, however, that the grievant had made "threatening and obscene statements" to supervisors. The opinion noted: "They were not uttered in a casual or joking manner and did not constitute mere 'shop talk.' Rather his statements were both insubordinate and intimidating ." The arbitrator continued: "By his own actions, the grievant has rendered himself unfit for continued employment. Efforts to rehabilitate him through progressive discipline and counseling failed prior to his discharge, and just cause existed under [the collective bargaining agreement] for his removal as an employee of the Postal Service."[4] Although confined mainly to behavior prior to termination, the opinion closed with the observation that the grievant's "conduct following the discharge certainly will not allow this arbitrator to return him to employment." That was evidently a reference to McIlvane's postdismissal remarks about what he would do if he lost the arbitration.

Perpetuating Stereotypes

The massacre at Royal Oak helped to perpetuate two enduring popular stereotypes about workers and managers at the postal service. The first is that of authoritarian management, presiding over an abusive, relentlessly demanding workplace. The second, interlinked stereotype is that of the "disgruntled" postal worker—angry, stressed to the breaking point, and ready to react with murderous violence if pushed too far. Sullen workers, the theory holds, are likely to erupt without warning in retaliatory violence against oppressive supervisors.

Neither of these images is more than a caricature. On-edge personalities are not unique to post offices, and the portrait of the mail-sorting center as a golgotha of management dysfunction and worker oppression is highly overdrawn as well. Since 1985, at least 35 postal workers have been killed by their colleagues. The most destructive outburst was a 1986 killing spree in Edmond, Oklahoma. Fourteen persons died in addition to the shooter, Patrick Henry Sherrill, a part-time letter carrier who had faced the possibility of discharge. Like several other perpetrators of such massacres, Sherrill became a suicide. Despite such spectacular incidents, however, the postal service, with a workforce totaling nearly 800,000, has a murder rate of only 0.6 per 100,000, which is less than the national average. When all causes of death are taken into account, a postal worker is 2.5 times less likely than the average worker to die on the job.

The service has been so eager to dispel the image of a violence-ridden institution that it has distributed lists of violent incidents occurring among other occupational groups, including famously peaceful categories, such as Amish farm workers.[5] Nevertheless, the postal service does not deny that its management style sometimes seems authoritarian. When he assumed the office of postmaster general in 1998, William J. Henderson pledged to "focus more on . . . employee relations" and to "take the negativism out of the environment."[6]

Some incidents are associated with periods of peak demand, a stress phenomenon by no means unique to the postal service. The service handles about 600 million pieces of mail annually, and during the annual holiday season the pressure to sustain the flow may be particularly intense. Milwaukee's 1997 postal shooting (see Chapter 1) took place at the city's central processing and distribution center, where 1,500 persons, including seasonal helpers, were coping with the holiday avalanche of mail. The perpetrator, Anthony Deculit, was a new father who had been formally warned for sleeping on the job—an indication that the fatigue factor (see Chapter 2) may have played a role in the incident. His repeated requests for a transfer to the day shift had been denied. Attempting to persuade him to put down his semiautomatic handgun, a co-worker at the downtown facility pleaded with him: "Tony, Christmas is right around the corner. In five days we'll be off."[7]

The incident occurred in the midst of a period of hectic, repetitious work with "a busy crunch time of mail sorting approaching."[8] A maintenance mechanic at the facility opined that drudgery was a factor:

With the sheer boredom of slogging through the mail day after day, along with the added strain of the last-minute Christmas rush, "it's just a matter of time before somebody goes off the deep end," [the mechanic] said. "Sure, it's repetition, a lot of repetition. It gets tedious. You start doing eight hours, 12 hours a day. . . . It's not a physically demanding job from the point of muscle, but it becomes physical on your mind."[9]

A former official of the American Postal Workers Union claimed that supervisors had picked on Deculit. She said: "It was just difficult for him to adjust, and management made it more difficult. There have been many problems with management, and management pushes people, they harass people and intimidate them."[10] His co-workers may have appeared to be part of the problem. One of the victims was a nonmanager with whom he had feuded. Taken as a whole, the circumstances suggest that two persons died because an employee was overwhelmed and exhausted by seasonal work pressure, aggravated by domestic demands—a new baby—unrelated to the postal service.

A Stage for Emotional Problems

In other incidents, it is clear that the postal service was simply the stage on which an employee acted out emotional problems that had originated elsewhere. The primacy of personal mental health issues clearly is evident in the 1996 Las Vegas incident, which took the life of Supervisor James Brown. Charles Jennings, 41, had been discharged by the postal service and had filed an appeal that was taken to arbitration. Brown represented the service at the arbitration hearing. A few days after learning that his discharge had been upheld, Jennings went to the facility with a gun, evidently hoping to kill the plant manager and several officials whom he blamed for his fate. He encountered Brown first and shot him during a struggle over the gun. It is unlikely that Brown was a primary target, since he was described by colleagues as "the most non-confrontational guy in the world."[11]

Jennings was convicted of first-degree murder. The trial revealed a long history of involvement with cocaine and suicide attempts. "A lot of pain came down," he testified, when the arbitration decision went against him. To cope with the pain, Jennings went on a substance abuse binge of several days. The plan to take revenge against his postal supervisors was formulated while Jennings, accompanied by a prostitute, was drinking heavily and using "crack." According to the defense attorney, the discharge had set in motion a precipitous downward spiral; Jennings changed from "a recovering addict to a new-and-improved addict."[12]

Another discharged postal worker, David Lee Jackson, seized a Denver mail facility on Christmas Eve in 1997, taking seven persons hostage. Jackson had been fired a year and a half earlier for threatening a supervisor and was trying to gain reinstatement through arbitration. A co-worker said that "Jackson had threatened to return to work someday to settle the score with the supervisor he had threatened before being fired."[13] The incident ended without injury.

Neither the Denver nor the Las Vegas case seems attributable to pressures inherent in the job of moving mail. Both cases appear to demonstrate, however, that discharge can trigger an extreme behavioral crisis. The perception of injustice creates a thirst for revenge, a pattern certainly not restricted to postal workers.

Fashioning a Response

Postal service unions typically blame the working environment—unbearable conditions and management practices—and such claims are often supported by psychologists. Management, on the other hand, prefers to blame individual personality factors. An academic study of the postal service has reached for a middle ground, finding the source of violence in the interaction between environment and personality: "authoritarian managers occasionally confront individuals with violent dispositions."[14] Attempting to isolate a single "cause" of violence may, however, encourage dubious one-dimensional strategies, such as developing an emollient management style or weeding out "potentially violent" employees.

Trying to identify a cause of violence makes less practical sense than examining the capacity of the organization to respond to the signs of stress or potential danger, whatever their origin. To ensure responsiveness, a broad, system-level analysis of the organization is required. Under such an analysis, the most salient feature of the Royal Oak massacre is that the perpetrator was able to carry out his threats without any effort by management or union to address the potential for violence or to work jointly to prevent it, even though they had a mutual interest in prevention.

What accounts for the inaction? One reason seems to have been the poor relationship between management and labor at Royal Oak. A breakdown in communication engendered overreliance on the formal grievance system. Even trivial disputes might end up in arbitration.[15]

Union. Some in the bargaining unit were disposed to view McIlvane's anger as an understandable, albeit extreme, response to heavy-handed supervisors. They seized the opportunity to confront management. Even those union representatives who were disturbed by the threats believed that it was their legal and moral duty to be the grievant's advocates; they were paralyzed by mistrust of management and a mistaken belief that they were obligated to keep information about his propensities confidential.

Management. Managers, too, were encumbered by adherence to a narrowly conceived role. They believed that invoking the conventional disciplinary procedure was a sufficient response to McIlvane's misconduct. Postal inspectors were reluctant to become involved because they believed that they were too often asked to respond to so-called behavioral emergencies that should have been handled by the labor-management relations staff. Already stretched to the limit in carrying out their security responsibilities, inspectors believed that the employment specialists once more were "crying wolf."

Arbitrator. The arbitrator alluded to the grievant's potential for violence, mentioning the postdischarge threats in the decision upholding the termination. But neutrals, too, are circumscribed by their professional role, even though they may well be potential targets. Maintaining impartiality requires a certain distance from the contending parties. The formal issue is whether the grievant should continue to be employed, but in the background may lurk even more crucial questions. Is the grievant a menace to himself and others, regardless of his employment status? Do threats require that steps be taken to warn or protect possible targets? These questions typically are not submitted to the arbitrator and go unanswered. Sadly, that is what appears to have happened in McIlvane's case.

Although the participants may act conscientiously within the framework of an arbitration proceeding, each is isolated in a narrowly defined role. The adversarial nature of the process, from the imposition of discipline to the arbitration hearing, obscures the mutual interest in workplace safety and thwarts practical consideration of menacing behavior.

Could Royal Oak have been avoided? It is impossible to know with certainty, but there can be no doubt that a few years later the same threats would have been handled quite differently. As a result of a joint labor-management accord in the Royal Oak postal district and many others, carefully designed violence prevention plans were put in place. They were typically administered by a team of management and bargaining unit members who had been trained in the handling of threats or suspected threats of violence. The plans were designed to be effective at any level of threat, from mild to acute. When a threat of violence is alleged or reported under such a system, the response is radically different from that which occurred in 1991.

If an employee speaks or behaves in a threatening manner in the workplace, he or she is confronted by the team, which investigates the alleged threat and, if warranted, requests that the employee meet with a threat assessment specialist. The specialist is a mental health professional who conducts a clinical interview and gathers collateral information from supervisors, co-workers, and family members. Until all the facts are gathered, the employee is placed on administrative leave with pay, effectively deferring any possible discipline. The results of the assessment are shared with the team and the employee.

This approach integrates the processes of discipline and psychological assessment into a single, comprehensive effort to make a well-informed judgment about the risk posed by the employee. The entire procedure is transparent, and neither party withholds information for tactical advantage, as happens in adversarial proceedings. It is likely that such a comprehensive investigation of McIlvane's threats would have uncovered his military record and other evidence that he was potentially out of control. Whereas the postal service ineffectively disciplined McIlvane over an eight-year period, contributing to the escalation of his dangerous behavior, the team intervention would have come at an early stage.

Why are we as a culture so taken with this issue of postal violence? Might not the image of the mailman-turned-monster be a reflection of what we feel at some level about the effect of work on our collective psyche? In *Modern Times* Charlie Chaplin created an unforgettable cinematic image of the assembly line worker who defies the production system that has robbed him of his autonomy. Perhaps fascination with employees who "go postal" is an expression of a belief, at some level, that the demands of work today—from the tool room to the board room—compromise personal dignity. Occasional outbursts of violence are the price paid for loss of self-determination. When we indulge in gallows humor about the postal service, we are probably voicing deep anxieties about our vulnerability to the demands of work.

CHAPTER 4

Santa Ana, California:
A Highway Worker's Revenge

It was December 1997, the season for Christmas festivities, but employees of the state department of transportation yard in Santa Ana, California, were attending funerals instead of parties. Flags were flying at half mast in the yard, which is not far from Disneyland, and a stone monument, topped by a white hard hat and a clutch of flowers, bore the names of the four men who were being buried. They were a supervisor and three workers who had fallen a few days earlier in a hailstorm of bullets from a semiautomatic weapon—an episode dubbed the "maintenance yard bloodbath."[1]

The perpetrator of the slaughter was Arturo R. Torres, who had worked for the department, known as Caltrans, for almost 15 years. He had been discharged a few months earlier on grounds of dishonesty, along with his brother, James, who was an eight-year employee. Despite its awful outcome, the incident originated in a mundane dispute. The subject was the disposal of scrap material by road crews.

The previous February, Supervisor Hal Bierlein had called his crew together at the end of the workday and read them the employer's guidelines for disposal of surplus property: salvaged material and scrap, such as aluminum rails. The guidelines reemphasized that salvaged materials were state property, which had to be sold for the state's benefit or, if valueless, taken to an authorized dump site. "Under no circumstances," the guidelines read, "shall a maintenance employee assume possession of such salable or unsalable materials." Each crew member, including the brothers, received a written copy of the guidelines in addition to hearing them read aloud.

The following week the crew took several lengths of galvanized iron rail from stock to replace the aluminum rail on a bridge. Bierlein and another supervisor were at the job site, equipped with a video camera. They watched the Torres brothers leave the site separately in state trucks and followed them. The brothers were videotaped entering and leaving the premises of a commercial salvage company.

Later that day, the brothers told the supervisor that they had disposed of scrap by taking it to a dealer instead of putting it in the state storage bins. They turned in $106.50 in cash along with a dealer receipt for that amount. The top of the receipt had been torn off, however. When the missing fragment was found, it contained the signature of a "Tony Fuentes" and a bogus driver's license number. The dealer supplied two other receipts, from late in 1996, signed by "Fuentes" and bearing the phony license number. They were for sales of aluminum— 451 pounds ($211.97) in one sale and 770 pounds ($369.60) in another.

During an investigation of the incident, the brothers claimed that they had been selling scrap for about three years but denied benefiting personally. Rather, they said, the proceeds went to a collective "kitty" that was used for employee barbecues and buying tools. They insisted that the supervisor had orchestrated the scheme, advised them to use a false name at the dealer, and even held the funds. They said they had been aware of the videotaping and believed that their actions were being misinterpreted. They believed they were being "set up."

The case was referred to an Administrative Law Judge, who held a hearing. After evaluating the evidence, the judge found that once the crew had been read the guidelines, the men were "on notice that even if past practice condoned selling salvaged materials to maintain crew 'kitties,' as of that date the practice was forbidden." The judge was unconvinced that "using a fictitious name to sign the receipts did not indicate a consciousness of wrongdoing. . . . (Although James Torres posed as 'Fuentes,' Arturo Torres was aware of the subterfuge.)" The judge added:

> Casting further doubt on [the brothers'] version is the concealment of the "Fuentes" name on the receipt which was provided to Bierlein. Signing a phony name, providing a phony driver's license number, and then concealing that information reflects a consciousness of wrongdoing.

. . . [After the brothers] sold the salvaged material, they realized that they had been observed doing so. They discussed the matter and decided to turn in the proceeds and the receipt, after removing the phony identification from the receipt. It is not believed that they would have turned in the money if they had not known that their sale had been discovered.[2]

The judge found that the "misappropriation of salvaged state property, and their using state vehicles in the sale" amounted to neglect of duty, willful disobedience, and dishonesty. He recommended that the two men be discharged, and the next month, October 1997, the State Personnel Board approved the decision.

In keeping with state policy, the discharged employees were instructed to stay away from their former work site, but nearly 1,000 persons were assigned to the Santa Ana yard, which remained open 24 hours a day. There was no identity check at the gate. Owing to the huge volume of traffic, the yard was effectively without access control—other than the wan hope that former employees would heed the warning to keep out.

Less than two months after the board ratified the discharge, Arturo Torres slipped back into the yard as scores of persons were entering and leaving. He carried a knockoff copy of an AK-47 (Kalashnikov) semiautomatic assault rifle, a shotgun, and a handgun. There was a popping sound as Torres began spraying a total of 144 bullets around the yard, holding the rifle alternately at his hip and his shoulder. According to the witnesses: "People were panicking . . . everybody was running for safety. It was pretty chaotic. . . . They hid behind desks, they hid on the floor. They tried to find safety in trailers that got sprayed with gunfire and they were on the floor trying to find exits to get away as quickly as possible."[3] The primary target was Supervisor Bierlein, but Torres also turned his weaponry on three co-workers, killing them and wounding a policeman before being killed himself by police officers in a grisly street shootout—another example of "suicide by cop."

The Santa Ana revenge attack illustrates that, far from being random, many workplace shootings are based on employment disputes that have escalated. In this instance, the dispute ostensibly involved pilferage. Pilferage traditionally warrants discharge, even though the value of the objects taken is insignificant, and arbitrators as well as administrative law judges often uphold terminations even when the material pilfered is trifling or considered scrap. Taking incidental items such a flashlight battery or a role of tape can lead to job loss. (The Torres brothers had sold more than $600 worth of scrap in the few months leading up to the discharge, a relatively significant amount.) Since it involves honesty, pilferage is also a charge for which prior good service is generally not considered a mitigating factor, as it is for many offenses. Reinstatement is considered inappropriate for an employee who has forfeited the employer's trust and confidence.

Nevertheless, Arturo Torres refused to accept the decision of the State Personnel Board and regarded himself as the victim of an injustice. A sense of injustice is a powerful motivating force, driving aggrieved employees to extreme behavior. The smoldering rage of the accused is clearly discernible in a remark he made to the judge during the hearing. Asked if he had acknowledged telling the supervisor that he had made a mistake in selling the scrap, Arturo replied, rather ominously, that "the mistake he made was trusting Bierlein." He clearly felt betrayed by the supervisor, who had become the chief witness against him.

Although Torres's retaliation was ruthless and wanton, some in the community sympathized with his sense of outrage. A columnist in a local newspaper, the *Orange County Register*, argued that he had been

> fired for doing something that had been a common practice for years. Scrap had long been sold for cash, and the money had been put in a kitty for work-group parties. I've seen no suggestion of anyone doing it for private gain.
>
> Caltrans supervisors not only condoned the practice, but also managed it. This misappropriation of public assets had tacit, if not explicit, approval by authority figures.
>
> Such practices not only financed parties (rationalized as morale boosters), but also made it easier for managers and supervisors to sustain budget projections based upon artificially high current expenditures. Thus, the practice became very self-serving for all, from top to bottom.[4]

Selling scrap, according to this theory, was a well-entrenched customary activity, something that employees may have come to regard as a past practice or "perk." It was foolhardy to expect that it could be extirpated at a stroke by departmental ukase. Indeed, there may have been a conflict between the formal "management culture"—in which a problem is presumed to be adequately addressed by writing a memo—and the informal "worker culture," which holds tenaciously to unwritten customs, especially those that confer benefits. The tragic reality may be that Torres's desperate resort to violence resulted from a clash of organizational cultures.

The judge accorded great weight to the fact that the supervisor had read aloud the memo reaffirming the policy of prohibiting private sale of scrap. But state officials' belief that a memo would command instant obedience may have been unrealistic. To begin with, the Torres brothers maintained that the reading had been too hurried to be comprehensible. The *Orange County Register* commented: "Many bureaucratic memos are never heeded, much less enforced. The huge quantity of them, plus selective enforcement, means that it becomes hard to discern which memos are for real."[5]

Thus, Arturo Torres may well have believed that the memo signified no real change and that prohibiting scrap-selling would amount to an arbitrary deprivation of a customary benefit. It follows that he would regard his discharge after 14 years of good service as treacherous—particularly if it were true that the scrap was being sold for the crew's collective purposes rather than for his private gain and that the supervisor was complicit.

The Santa Ana incident has been cited as additional evidence for a theory that public sector workplaces are particularly prone to violence because they are bureaucratic and impersonal and lack the objective feedback that private companies receive from their shareholders and profit-and-loss statements. Nevertheless, while some notable incidents have occurred in the public sector, they have been at least equaled in lethal magnitude by disasters such as Joseph Wesbecker's rampage through a privately owned printing plant (see Chapter 1). Stress pervades both private and public workplaces.

The shooting in Santa Ana also added to the controversy over gun control. Torres owned 17 guns legally. Friends said that he proudly showed off his collection, which included two AK-47–style assault rifles, three 12-gauge shotguns, five handguns, six rifles, and a revolver. The guns were kept in a metal safe in his den.

The assault rifle that caused mayhem in the maintenance yard was made in China and bought in 1988, shortly before a federal ban on the sale of such imported weapons took effect. It was one of the so-called image weapons, fierce-looking military-style rifles with big clips. The gun's remarkable bullet storage capacity—Torres carried five clips of 30 rounds—and rapid rate of fire enabled him to do much damage in a short time.

The imminence of the sales ban occasioned a frenzy of gun buying. According to California criminologist Ed Peterson, "People were lined up to buy them at any price. People who never would even think before about buying one of these guns panicked, figuring they'd better get one while they still could."[6] Torres, like the other gun lovers who had acquired such weapons before the restrictions went into effect, was allowed to keep the rifle—which was found in a pool of blood on the street where he had dueled to the death with the police.

CHAPTER 5

Hartford, Connecticut:
An Unlucky Day at the Lottery

Friday was dress-down day at the Connecticut Lottery Corp., in the leafy suburbs of Hartford, the state capital. Matthew Beck, a 35-year-old accountant, was at his desk by 8:00 A.M., wearing jeans and a leather jacket, which he kept zipped.[1] Under the jacket was a knife and 9-mm Glock semiautomatic handgun. Half an hour later, he plunged the knife into the chest of the lottery's vice president of operations and then strolled through the warren of cubicles to find the chief financial officer. She was in a meeting. According to a witness, Beck appeared in an open doorway: "He just aimed the gun right at her. He said, 'Bye-bye,' and he shot her three times." Terrified by the sound of gunfire, employees streamed from the building, diving into ditches or fleeing into nearby woods. Beck found the information systems manager and fatally wounded him too.

A former cross-country runner, Beck sprinted after the lottery president, Otho R. Brown, chasing him into a parking lot. Brown stumbled and fell to the ground. Just as police arrived, Beck fired at the executive, ignoring Brown's pleas to spare his life. When the officers approached, the killer put the gun to his own right temple and fired again, dying instantly.

The horrific slaughter, on March 6, 1998, marked the culmination of a troubled life for Beck. He was an able employee; some called him a "genius"—particularly in his mastery of computers, which were vital to the lottery. Yet Beck resented the way the company was managed and especially his bosses' failure to recognize his contribution properly.

Beck's emotional problems predated his employment. He earned a bachelor's degree from the Florida Institute of Technology but not before slashing his wrists—his first attempt at suicide. His adult life had been punctuated by hospitalizations for depression. After graduation, Beck worked as a security guard at a uranium plant and as a taxpayer assistance specialist for the Internal Revenue Service. He went to work for the lottery in 1989, when it was a state agency. In 1996 he accepted an invitation to join the reorganized lottery, which had recently become a quasipublic corporation and was designed to run as a business, earning profits for the taxpayers. Beck evidently believed that the new organizational structure would assure him greater opportunity for advancement. In his letter offering Beck a job, President Brown said, "Congratulations, I look forward to working with you in this new venture."

Beck came to be known as a steady employee who took his job seriously and never groused about having to work overtime. His co-workers recognized his computer skills, although they felt that he had difficulty explaining the technical concepts to them.

In January 1997, police were called to Beck's apartment because he was wielding a knife and threatening once again to kill himself. After that incident, he moved back to his family home with his father, the house in which he had grown up. He began to be treated by a psychiatrist, who prescribed an antidepressant and two sleeping medications. The depression was the most severe he had experienced, according to his father: "He was zombie-like and had a fixed stare. There was no inflection in his voice." Everything seemed hopeless to him. Despite his condition, Matt was allowed to keep his gun collection. He had a long-standing interest in firearms and held a gun permit. Posted at the Beck home was a forbidding sign: "Trespassers will be shot. Survivors will be shot again."

Valuing his computer skills, lottery management assigned Beck special work in data processing, yet they balked at his demand for two dollars an hour extra, which he claimed was the premium earned by others doing the same work. In August 1997, he filed a grievance through the Administrative and Residual Employees Union, his collective bargaining representative, claiming an entitlement to extra pay because he was working out of his normal classification. The lottery vice president denied the grievance, and it was appealed through the State Office of Labor Relations. The appeal succeeded: a hearing officer decided Beck was performing duties that properly belonged to a data processor. He was returned to his accountant duties, and he was declared eligible for back pay. On the day before the shooting, he telephoned his union to check on the determination of the amount of the back pay.

Beck desired a promotion from lottery accountant, in which title he earned about $45,000, to lottery financial analyst, the salary range for which topped out at $55,000. But lottery executives thwarted his desire, even though on paper he had the proper qualifications. Several newer hires had already been promoted to the analyst job. Co-workers believed that he had the necessary ability for the promotion. Unlike the pay claim, however, the denial of his promotion could not be challenged through the grievance procedure under the terms of the collective bargaining agreement.

In October 1997, Beck took a medical leave on the grounds that he was suffering from stress. The following month, while still on leave, he approached the *Hartford Courant*, the state's leading newspaper, to report abuses in the lottery system, which he believed compromised its integrity. According to Lyn Bixby, the reporter who spoke to Beck, he was "upset over the way he had been treated at work," and "his eyes were wild. He spoke with the precision of an accountant, enunciating his words sharply. His mouth grew so dry while we talked that frothy white spittle spots appeared at the corners of his mouth." Although he was on edge, he made no threats against anyone at the lottery and asked to remain an anonymous source.

Beck told the reporter that the lottery exaggerated the size of the jackpot in its advertising to attract bettors and that some retail lottery clerks went "fishing" for winning numbers by randomly punching numbers into their registers. As with many grudge-motivated tipsters, much of his information proved to be accurate, and the abuses were immediately acknowledged and corrected once the newspaper exposed them.

As his leave was ending, Beck wrote a series of letters to lottery officials, speaking of his despair at being relegated to what he considered a dead-end position. He returned on February 25, 1998, although he was entitled by statute and his collective bargaining agreement to take sick leave for a full six months. The only noticeable change was that his head had been shaved. Just ten days later came the lottery's bloody Friday.

The carnage of March 6 produced remarkably few changes at the lottery office beyond some physical alterations. When the surviving employees returned to work the following Tuesday, Beck's desk and chair had been removed—as if that might erase the memory of the shooting. The office layout was modified so that it no longer looked as it had on the fateful day. But the important issues raised by the events remained to be examined by policy makers.

That Beck was allowed by family and friends to live with a gun collection while being treated for acute depression and work stress is troubling. With the support of relatives of the victims, proposals were introduced into the state legislature to deny gun permits to persons suffering from acute mental illnesses and to create a new offense—"felony trespass"—that would allow a business to prohibit anyone from entering its premises while carrying a gun. But these measures stood little chance of passage. Although the governor somberly declared March 6 a "terrible day," his office announced that he "already feels the state has some of the strongest gun laws in the country."

What Went Wrong?

Beck's personality was impaired: he suffered from "Depressive Personality Disorder," which makes its victims "tend to brood and worry, dwelling persistently on their negative and unhappy thoughts."[2] Beck's tendency to brood was exacerbated by his inability to achieve recognition at work. The rejection of his request for promotion provoked a sense of powerlessness that was clearly intolerable for him.

The workplace failed to appreciate the danger in the combination of disaffection, access to guns, and a history of trying to use violence—the prior suicide attempts—to solve his problems. The two attempts were practice sessions, as it were, for the scene in the parking lot, where he finally turned the gun on himself after taking his revenge.

Analyzing the lottery disaster is complicated by the lack of any suicide note or clear expression by the employee about his feelings. Several points can be inferred, however, from the available evidence. To begin with, it is remarkable that Beck erupted in murderous rage after *winning* a grievance. In the more typical pattern, a grievant is moved to violence by losing a grievance. Beck may have viewed the grievance process as an ordeal and resented the employer for forcing him to go to such lengths to vindicate his entitlement to extra pay. Rather than leaving him euphoric, the win seems to have aggravated his hostility to the employer.

For Beck, being denied a promotion from the accountant classification was a major disappointment. No doubt he sensed the paradox in being good enough to be assigned extra duties that required special skills—but not good enough to become a financial analyst. Unlike pay, promotion was not a subject that could be appealed; management enjoyed complete discretion. Employers typically seek to add to collective bargaining agreements "management rights clauses" that confer broad discretion on executives and restrict the ability of employees to file grievances. It is worth recognizing, however, that such arrangements may exact a psychic toll in the form of resentment at the inability to have one's claims even considered. The sense of being ignored can be a powerful emotion. When they insulate themselves from employee complaints, employers may be eliminating an important safety valve and an indicator of unduly stressful working conditions. What is legally advantageous for the employer may be detrimental in other respects.

Were there warning signs? When he heard reports of shooting at lottery headquarters, the husband of one victim "remembered her worries about a worker who had filed a grievance. I was losing hope fast, and I thought that I knew who the gunman was. I was right." At union headquarters, similarly, the president had tuned into the radio broadcasts about the shootings; he remembers thinking, "I hope it's not Matt Beck." The thought crossed his mind because Beck was known to be angry about the denial of promotion and was the only member of the union who had an active grievance against the lottery.

Familiar with his personality, acquaintances of Beck were also concerned when they heard the initial reports. A friend from his days at the nuclear plant received a call from someone who had heard the news: "As soon as he said lottery, I said, 'I think I know.' I kind of got a little nervous, and I said, 'I think it might be Matt.' . . . If anything I thought Matt might have cracked. . . . I was shocked, but I wasn't surprised, let's put it that way."

On the other hand, there were signs that Beck was contemplating a future. He had just laid in a large supply of yogurt, a favorite food, according to his father, and had shown keen interest in the size of his back pay award. Beck took care to have his name withheld from the newspaper exposé to avoid jeopardizing his job. Concern about job tenure is difficult to reconcile with an intention of committing suicide.

Yet, in taking his own life, Beck followed a pattern common to perpetrators of workplace revenge murders. As a rule, the perpetrators are deeply depressed. They feel desperate, isolated, and rejected. Plagued by feelings of helplessness, they view violence as the final attempt to make a difference. Convinced that they are completely alone and unable to alter the way people treat them or perceive them, they seek revenge on their tormentors and release from their own pain. A logical inference is that ensuring better treatment for employees suffering from depression might go far toward ensuring workplace safety.

Keeping Beck away from guns might also have helped, but there was no basis for formal action in that regard, because there had been no clinical judgment that he was dangerous to himself or others or was unable to care for himself. No threats had been made.

Mental Health Care and Return-to-Work Issues

Inadequate mental health care may have played role in the lottery incident. Although Beck was receiving treatment for his underlying illness, it may not have been effective. According to a 1997 consensus statement by leading mental health experts, "There is overwhelming evidence that individuals with depression are being seriously undertreated," causing "long suffering, suicide, occupational impairment, and impairment in interpersonal and family relationships." Among the reasons given by the experts were therapists' "underestimating the severity" of the illness and the patient's "noncompliance with treatment."[3] Either of these factors could have contributed to the lottery incident, since Beck did not use all the illness leave time available to him, and he was cleared to return to work while still using powerful drugs regularly. In addition, there is the appearance of a family not organized well enough to take charge of a troubled member. If neither the family nor the employer plays an active role, an employee may be passively "treated," which means dispensing medicines and processing the patient through a series of crisis-oriented contacts, without any attempt to involve people in the patient's life.

The employer's policy was to allow an employee's own doctor to certify fitness to return. A more assertive approach, especially in cases of stress-related leave, would provide a greater margin of safety. An experienced management lawyer has commented: "Increasingly, employees are requesting and/or demanding time off due to stress, depression and the like. It is reasonable, if not necessary, to require, to the extent permitted by law, psychiatric clearance before such individuals return to work."[4]

There might be a standing rule that fitness to return should be ratified by an independent medical or psychological consultant upon "reentry" to the workplace. At a minimum, it is sensible for the employer to communicate with the therapist and the employee him- or herself . The employer should wish to know certain basic facts. How is the person doing? What was the contribution of the workplace to the stress? How may any such adverse effect be minimized or avoided after return? In Beck's case, reaching out to inquire about his condition might have also afforded him assurance that someone at work cared about his well-being. That, in turn, might have helped ease any sense of isolation.

In a study of more than 800 patients being treated for depression, a common symptom was functional work impairment, including—in 44 percent of the cases—interpersonal problems.[5] The need to improve the management of depression cases on the job is the goal of the D/ART Program, which stands for Depression Awareness, Recognition and Treatment. Established in 1989, it is a work site–targeted joint endeavor of the Washington Business Group on Health, an industry coalition, and the National Institute of Mental Health, a federal agency. D/ART estimates that 70 percent of the 17 million adults suffering from depression are in the workforce and that these workers account for half of all psychiatric disability claims. Absenteeism, diminished productivity, and depression-related suicide are among the possible consequences of the untreated disorder. D/ART urges employers to effect early recognition, encourage proper treatment, and provide whatever accommodation and work site supports may be necessary for complete recovery.[6]

The Role of Drugs

Suspicion also has fallen on the treatment drugs themselves. On occasion—the Wesbecker case discussed in the first chapter is one example—there have been allegations that a psychotropic drug used in therapy caused an outburst of violence. The drugs taken by Beck were powerful, to be sure. Lorazepam (a benzodiazepine) is a tranquilizer used in cases of acute psychotic agitation, and fluvoxamine (a serotonin uptake inhibitor) is an antidepressant and long-term treatment for obsessive-compulsive patients. Nevertheless, a major hospital-based study by the University of Chicago found that in the case of benzodiazepines "adverse reactions were rare"—only 0.05 percent of doses in the case of lorazepam. Moreover, "there were no reported cases of violent behavior" in the three years of the study.[7] On the other hand, noncompliance with a prescribed drug regimen or stopping the medication prematurely is a frequent feature of depression, often leading to relapse.

Whistleblower Syndrome

When he tipped the newspaper about lottery abuses, Beck was engaged in "whistleblowing"—exposing an employer's malfeasance in order to build public pressure for change. According to a study of committed whistleblowers (in a different industry) by the National Academy of Public Administration, they "exhibit a combination of some or all of the following beliefs":[8]

- Everyone must abide strictly by . . . regulations.
- Their allegations are correct.
- They must do the "right thing."
- The motivations of management and the government are suspect.

It is possible that the whistleblower's mind-set, and its attendant suspicion of the employer, interacted with the depressive aspects of Beck's personality to create a paranoiac view of his managers.

Clearly, not all aggrieved workers with a history of depression perpetrate workplace revenge murders. But we do know: (1) many employees suffer from depression; (2) a large number of these are inadequately treated or not treated at all for this malady; and (3) some sufferers blame their plight on their employer, eventually developing deeply held grudges. As their depression worsens, the risk of self-destructive and violent actions rises. The sad facts of this case point clearly to the need for closer attention to employees who may fit that pattern. There should be better treatment for employees with depression, improved methods for planning their return to work, and careful, caring attention to the employee with a depression-linked grudge. Attention to these lessons of the lottery tragedy will both help relieve suffering and reduce the likelihood of similarly grim outcomes in other workplaces.

CHAPTER 6

Watkins Glen, New York:
A Social Service Office under Siege

I t was autumn in upstate New York, and orange and red leaves covered the hills of the Finger Lakes region. In Watkins Glen, a bucolic town at the southern tip of Seneca Lake, the Schuyler County Building was open for business. On the second floor of a long narrow addition to the building, the staff of the Collection Unit, part of the Department of Social Services, was carrying out its mission of tracking down "deadbeat dads"— fathers who owe child support payments.

Avoiding the front entrance in favor of a side door, John Miller, a burly former county resident, climbed the stairs to the Collection Unit. He carried a 9-mm semiautomatic handgun. In barely a minute, Miller shot to death Unit Supervisor Florence Pike, 60, and three members of her staff: Investigator Phyllis Caslin, 54, and Account Clerks Nancy Wheeler, 48, and Denise Van Amberg, 28.

The slaughter, on October 15, 1992, was a devastating shock to the tightly knit community, where violent crime had been virtually unknown. Miller, who was employed by an Ohio trucking firm, had a specific reason for targeting the Collection Unit employees. A native of Schuyler County, he had left New York State more than 20 years earlier when his girlfriend became pregnant and named him as the child's father. While the Collection Unit and the courts pursued him for back payment, he persistently denied paternity. Several times he was arrested for nonpayment. A week before the killings, justice at last caught up with him. A court-ordered garnishment of his wages for the arrears resulted in the first deduction—$10—from his pay. Miller took time off from work and returned to Schuyler County.

On Wednesday, October 14, he visited his former girlfriend, then went to the Collection Unit. According to the unit's sole survivor, who was present that day and absent the next, he argued vehemently with Supervisor Pike but was not abusive. The clerical workers were suspicious, however, of a paper bag that he carried under his arm. One of them remarked, "Boy, that makes me nervous. He may have a gun in that bag."

On Thursday morning, Miller returned to the county building, which also houses the county legislature and the court. He found Ms. Pike sitting with a visitor in her small office. Ordering the visitor to leave, he shot the supervisor, walked to the office where the other unit employees were working and fired at those three women as well.

The police, whose headquarters were about 100 feet away, did not hear the shots but responded to urgent phone calls pouring from other offices. Officers first encountered Miller standing in the second floor hallway with his gun pointed to his head. Over the next several minutes, as officers tried to persuade him to drop his gun, they evacuated some county employees, although others stayed hidden under desks and in closets. Miller appeared calm. He said that he would not hurt anyone else, that he had "already hurt everyone" he was going to hurt. Confronted as he tried to leave by the stairs at one end of the hallway, he shot himself fatally in the head. On the back of a letter Miller had received from the department was a note, asserting that he "could not get satisfaction" and denying that he had fathered the child.

A Risk Denied

After the murders, surviving members of the Collection Unit acknowledged that they had been aware that violence could occur. Child welfare experts had pointed out that social services, family, and marital cases were are among the most volatile and dangerous. In fact, there had been instances of violence in neighboring counties that should have been taken as danger signals:

- A man applying for food stamps stabbed nearly to death an employee who told him he had not completed a form.

- The eleven enforcement officers of a county domestic relations office received personal threats and had their cars vandalized.
- An angry client attacked and beat an examiner at her desk in a county child-support enforcement office.
- A social service employee had been stalked and killed at home by a client seeking revenge against the department.

Typically, security increased at the site of each incident, but the counties failed to learn from each other's experiences. Schuyler County did not become alert enough to prevent John Miller from exacting his revenge.

The Collection Unit employees did sense danger the day before the killings. They were unnerved by Miller's angry demeanor and by the package he was carrying. They talked about him. It was learned later that one victim—the unit supervisor—had even mentioned her concern to her family. None of the employees, however, notified the police or their department head. Had they received violence prevention training, including practice in coordinated response with police, the staff would have been more likely to notify security forces when they felt fearful.

Since the Watkins Glen incident, the Civil Service Employees Association (CSEA), to which the victims belonged, has emphasized the importance of warning mechanisms. The union urges that client files be "red-flagged" when specific problems—such as a threat—surface. In this instance, the fact that Miller had journeyed from another state to remonstrate with the unit supervisor should have raised a flag, especially since there had been a significant change in his status: his wages had been garnished.

Warnings have also been emphasized in other states. In Oregon, for example, the American Federation of State, County and Municipal Employees (AFSCME) Local 1246, which represents workers at a secure youth residential facility, bargained for each employee's right to be warned of potential danger when reporting for a shift in a housing unit other than one's regular work location. The contract states that "the employee may contact the person responsible for the shift to inquire about any clients who may be dangerous."[1]

Warning Mechanisms

DSS offices throughout New York now use a variety of warning mechanisms in conjunction with coordinated response measures. One county, for instance, prohibits any person who makes a threat from visiting the office unless escorted by a sheriff's deputy. On some occasions, unfortunately, a deputy is not available for escort duty. Caseworkers become frustrated and may not seek protection the next time a threat is made, because they assume lack of availability.

For field caseworkers, warning systems have been especially important. In one county, a computer reporting system raises an alert if a warrant has been issued for anyone at an address that a caseworker is about to visit. If it seems prudent, a sheriff's deputy or at least a co-worker provides an escort. Caseworkers and sheriff's deputies receive training to ensure effective coordination, and over time the sheriff's department becomes expert at anticipating the needs of the caseworkers. Other counties, however, hesitate to use the warrant reporting system, owing to concerns about privacy and related legal issues.

In some states, social service field workers have negotiated contract language that guarantees them protection while carrying out their duties. In Ohio, AFSCME Local 3072 negotiated a buddy system. The agreement reads: "Social workers who are called out into a potentially hazardous situation should use law enforcement accompaniment. If law enforcement accompaniment is unavailable, the employee may take along a supervisor or another employee of the department."[2] In the same state, another AFSCME affiliate, Local 3098, bargained for the right to an escort in unsafe neighborhoods. The agreement explicitly incorporates a well-known safety exception to the principle that an employee is obligated to "work now, grieve later." It reads: "In any situation where an employee believes there is danger of immediate harm, the employee should take appropriate action first and then advise the supervisor of the action taken and reasons therefor."[3]

The importance of security for field employees was underscored by the brutal murder of a child-protection worker in Macomb County, Michigan, in 1998. Lisa Putnam, 28, was beaten to death while investigating a home from which two children had been removed on grounds of poor hygiene. The children's mother and aunt were arrested and charged with first-degree murder for the crime.[4] Police said that they attacked the social worker because she refused to reveal the name of the person who had lodged the complaint that led to the children's removal. As a result of the incident, the state added extra staff and equipped social workers with cellular telephones, although the union that represented the workers protested that the measures were "too little, too late."[5]

Community Response

The murder of the four women in Watkins Glen, an example of Type II workplace violence described in Chapter 1, galvanized the community. Shaken county employees were given the day off with pay and the opportunity to meet with counselors and clergy. State and local officials joined with the CSEA in planning security improvements for county offices.

Employees were asked about their concerns, and private sector expertise was tapped. The security department at Corning, Inc., a corporate neighbor, helped to develop a safety plan. A sheriff's deputy and a metal detector were stationed at the entrance to the county building. A receptionist was positioned behind bullet-proof glass at the DSS office, and a separate room was set aside for interviewing visitors.

Realizing the implications of the Watkins Glen incident, the CSEA conducted assessments of the 50 social service offices in the state. The findings were published in a 1993 "white paper," titled "A Matter of Life and Death." Acknowledging that the security needs of any particular site depends on the "age and location of buildings, multi-use sites, satellite offices, caseload history, population, proximity to urban centers and departmental organization," the union nevertheless found that "the most successful counties have considered common strategies and adopted similar approaches." The CSEA recommended:

- Clear and concise employee safety and building security strategies. Plans should be reviewed and updated at least annually and shared with employees.
- A security committee that meets on a scheduled basis, at least monthly. Membership on the committee should include employees designated by the union as well as supervisory personnel.
- Mandatory employee training. There should be initial training/ orientation for new employees, periodic refresher training for other workers, and specific training for each job title.
- An incident reporting system. The security committee should regularly review written incident reports for significant patterns and update the security plan accordingly.

At the statewide level, the CSEA called for the following:

- A study and public hearings on violence in the workplace, employee safety, and work site security.
- An interagency task force on security and safety training.
- A security standard, enforced by the State Labor Department, to protect employees.

Along with other unions, the CSEA proposed a statewide workplace violence standard and began discussions with the state's Hazard Abatement

Board. The state annual needs assessment reported that "staff and supervisors overwhelmingly wanted training on assessing and defusing potentially dangerous situations." As a result, the department allotted 85 training days. The state and unions sponsored a teleconference, "Safety: A Shared Responsibility," for employees. Joint union-management safety committees were given access to safety consultants.

Such collaborative efforts are crucial, because they give employees a sense that they have a voice in planning their own safety and a stake in making prevention measures effective. Evaluation of programs, updated site assessments and processing of data from incident logs benefit from the participation of those whose safety is at stake.

A Crisis Forgotten

Immediately after the October 1992 incident, Schuyler County and union representatives, along with police officials, strove energetically to prevent a recurrence of violence. They formed a committee that met regularly, and a similar working group was created at the state level to examine safety policy throughout New York. When security enhancements had been in place a few years, however, the sense of urgency began to fade. Despite the emphasis in the white paper on the need for continuous collaborative planning, the local-level joint committee became defunct. State officials also stopped working with unions and formed their own safety taskforce. But the taskforce members were unable to reach consensus or produce tangible achievements.

By 1997, the consensus in favor of vigorous prevention measures had so dissipated that the chairperson of the Schuyler County legislature proposed removing the metal detector from the building entrance. She preferred to place one detector at the entrance to the court and another at the entrance to the DSS office on the second floor, an arrangement that was generally considered inadequate to the potential threat. Although the chairperson insisted that she was merely responding to complaints from the public and employees, who supposedly resented the inconvenience and invasion of privacy, the CSEA and the sheriff objected to relaxing the security measures. The plan was shelved after being condemned at a public meeting that many county employees attended.

The Schuyler County experience demonstrates the difficulty of remaining vigilant, even when a workplace has sustained horrific casualties. Many county employees were deeply traumatized by the 1992 murders, yet even the memory of the four dead women failed to prevent the cooperative safety planning mechanism from becoming moribund within a few years.

Finally, then, this case stands as a paradox. The systems that were implemented by Schuyler County in the wake of the murders were exemplary. Officials took care to conduct an assessment and prepare a white paper. The components of the resulting plan are a model for violence prevention, integrating union-employer collaboration, training, reporting procedures and security measures. Yet vigilance began to give way to "practical" concerns as the memory of the tragedy ebbed. It may be that this story reveals the difference between merely responding to an incident, regardless of how comprehensive that response may be, and truly creating fundamental change. The moral of this case, perhaps, is that preventing violence in the workplace is not about putting out fires or simply tending to the needs of victims. Ultimately, true prevention results from the ability to undergo an enduring change of outlook on the basis of experience.

CHAPTER 7

Iowa City, Iowa:
The "Darkest Hour" of a Campus

I t was a was a gray, dreary afternoon on the tranquil campus of the University of Iowa in November 1991. The weather mirrored the mood of Gang Lu, a native of Beijing, China, who was a graduate student in physics. He walked into Van Allen Hall and entered Seminar Room 208. There he found Linhua Shan, another student from China, along with two professors of physics, Christoph Goertz and Robert Smith. Pulling out a registered .38-caliber handgun, Lu shot and killed all three men.

But he was not finished. He encountered Dwight Nicholson, chairperson of the Department of Physics and Astronomy, and T. Anne Cleary, the university's associate vice president of academic affairs. Lu left both of them dead. He then fired a bullet into Miya Rodolfo-Sioson, a student who was working in Cleary's office. Ms. Sioson survived but was bound to a wheelchair, totally and permanently paralyzed. Within 20 minutes of the start of the drama, Lu played out the denouement: he turned the gun on himself.

At first other professors in Van Allen Hall thought that the sounds were just high spirits left over from Halloween, which had been the day before. But in a few minutes the whole campus knew that what had taken place was no lark. Years later, the professor who discovered the bodies sprawled across the seminar room recalled it as "a terrible experience. It stays very vivid in my memory." It became, in the words of the *Daily Iowan* newspaper, the university's "darkest hour." Some spoke of a loss of innocence for this gentle Farm Belt community.[1]

Lu's swath of destruction seemed inexplicable at first, but the motivation soon became clear. Both he and Shan had received doctorates in physics. But Shan had won the department's prize for the best dissertation, which carried a stipend of $2,500, and had just been hired by the university. Lu believed that he, not Shan, should have won the prize. Lu was in dire financial straits, was having difficulty finding a job, and had been counting on the prize money to keep him from being forced to return to Beijing.

Lu had filed an appeal about the prize, but he felt that his claim was not being given fair consideration. The official who received his appeal was Associate Vice President Cleary, which is probably why she became one of his victims. Lu had targeted those whom he held responsible for his plight.

The shooting shook the hitherto cloistered academic community in Iowa City like an earthquake; the Ivory Tower had been invaded by the real world. But the event also set in motion a remarkable effort to respond to the human dimensions of the crisis by creating a "group healing process" and initiating long-term planning to ensure that there was no recurrence of violence.

The basis for the response was a little-known campus organization called the Administrative Liaison Group (ALG)—in effect a crisis response team, representing various departments of the university. It had been created without fanfare during the Vietnam War era and was prepared to cope with both natural and human crises—from periodic flooding of the Iowa River, which runs through the campus, to protest demonstrations. It had operated virtually unnoticed since the 1960s. But when Lu exacted his bloody revenge, the ALG broke cover and launched an energetic outreach operation.

A prime consideration was caring for those who might be suffering from stress and trauma as a reaction to the incident. A "Mental Health Resource Network," which contained the names of 40 mental health practitioners, was organized to provide personal counseling services, and numerous group "debriefings" were held on campus to help students and faculty cope with their reactions to the killings. Hundreds were counseled through individual or group sessions. As the university's ombudsperson was to later write, "People reached out to each other with compassion, they cared and they cried."[2]

Another challenge was dealing with the university's Chinese students and their families. The ALG worried about the possibility of backlash sentiment against the resident Chinese, and members of that community were ashamed, embarrassed, and concerned that they might be held responsible for Lu's murderous rampage. To counter these fears, the university president assured the Chinese community publicly that they were in no way responsible for the actions of a single distraught individual. The brothers of Vice President Cleary held a press conference to urge forgiveness and sent a message to the Lu family, declaring that they shared its sorrow.

There were also efforts to cut through red tape to achieve practical solutions on an urgent basis. One of those taking advantage of that service was the widow of Linhua Shan. Because her husband had been hired so recently, his employment paperwork had not been completed, preventing Mrs. Shan from collecting survivor benefits.

For the long term, the university decided to create an Emergency Preparedness Plan and to raise the profile of the ALG. The university's ombudsperson wrote:

> Today, in the nineties, it is to everyone's advantage to make the existence of the group, its leadership, and its role known. This would reassure the entire university community that we are prepared to face any crisis. It is a strength and a plus for the university to have an experienced, competent emergency response team in place, and its existence should be openly acknowledged and understood.[3]

The response team was to include the director of public safety, the university attorney, the director of personnel, the director of counseling services, and the dean of students. Each would be given a specific responsibility in a time of crisis.

It was also decided to familiarize everyone on campus with the details of the emergency response plan, in order to "give all members of the community a feeling of confidence that we are well prepared for whatever we may need to face." As part of the plan, an emergency coordinator was appointed for each building, an E-mail communication system was created, and provision was made for "immediate and sustained psychological support."

But the university went beyond mere structural change. It attempted to create a heightened awareness of "persons perceived as seriously troubled." Students, faculty, and staff members were urged to react quickly to signs of risk and to report potentially dangerous persons, so that a proper, professional evaluation could be undertaken. (In the year after the shooting, 11 reports were received.) A plan that used the university ombuds office as an anchor was put into effect:

Whether they are part of the team or not, ombudspersons can be helpful to their institutions throughout the academic year by being mindful of the special needs of clients who seem troubled or potentially dangerous. In order to assist our institutions in guarding against violence on the campus, we must give special attention to:

1. Identifying and assessing the needs of troubled individuals.
2. Helping to create a campus network to deal with troubled individuals.
3. Insuring that the rights of troubled individuals are protected.
4. Helping to maintain the confidentiality of troubled persons, particularly the nature of any illness they may have.
5. Maintaining close working relationships with colleagues who deal with the problems of faculty, students and staff on a daily basis, perhaps meeting regularly to discuss mutual concerns.
6. Monitoring the timeliness of grievance procedures.
7. Working closely with foreign student advisors to better understand and appreciate the special needs of international students and faculty.
8. Securing an adequate alarm system for the Ombudsperson's office.[4]

In January 1992, the university adopted an eight-page formal policy on violence. The statement urges that "the highest value be placed on the use of reason and that violence involving the university community be renounced as inimical to its goals." The policy also commits the university to taking action "when violence or harassment has the purpose or effect of unjustifiably creating an intimidating or hostile environment for work or learning." The following actions are among those prohibited.

- Physical assault or abuse.
- Sexual assault or abuse.
- Threats with weapon (display of a weapon accompanied by statements or actions which cause justifiable fear or apprehension).
- Verbal or other threats of physical or sexual assault.
- Damage or destruction of another's private property for the purpose of demeaning the owner or owners.[5]

There are annual commemorations of the event, and an action group, Iowans for the Prevention of Gun Violence, was created. Through these efforts, the memory of that day is kept alive and used to promote social and institutional change.

The Iowa episode involved an act of violence by a person not known for a violent temperament. But at another university the following year there occurred a similar shooting for which there had been many warning signs. The culprit was Valery Fabrikant, a member of the Department of Mechanical Engineering at Concordia University in Montreal, Canada. On August 24, 1992, he brought a handgun to campus and fatally shot four persons, essentially bystanders targeted at random.

The incident capped 13 years of shrill complaints and vituperation by Fabrikant, who was a hostile and disruptive force within the university. The origins of the episode have been summarized as follows by a Canadian lawyer:

> Fabrikant was hired by Concordia in 1979, literally off the street. As a Russian emigré with Italian papers, he dropped off his curriculum vitae and talked his way into an interview, during which he was hired on the first of a series of "soft-money" research appointments, first on staff and later on faculty. In one position after another with inferior status and no job security, he constantly wrangled with his colleagues, especially the clerical staff, and engaged in misconduct, including threatening and manipulating others, that should have been grounds for discharge.
>
> . . . Instead he went on to better appointments and higher salary. In 1985 he received a three-year appointment, which position was renewed in 1988 for two more years on soft money from a government source. At the time he engaged in an angry, irrational dispute with the purchasing department, which culminated in threats of litigation.[6]

By 1989, Fabrikant was complaining of mistreatment and exploitation. In his effort to obtain redress, he verbally abused and harassed the staff. He coupled his legitimate expressions of dissatisfaction with suggestions of violence. For example, he reportedly remarked, "I know how people get what they want; they shoot a lot of people." Many university employees feared that he carried a weapon. Indeed, at one point he applied for a permit to transport a handgun, but he needed the endorsement of his employer. For obvious reasons, the university withheld its assent.

The university did, however, accept his department's recommendation that he be offered a regular tenure-stream appointment on the basis of his research and teaching. After becoming a member of the faculty association, he filed two grievances, one seeking a promotion and the other seeking sabbatical leave.

Fabrikant also made allegations concerning the ethics of some colleagues. He provided extensive documentation, purporting to show conflicts of interest, bribery, professional misconduct, and illicit claims of authorship by two colleagues. In order to draw attention to his allegations, he carried out an intemperate and offensive campaign of E-mail messaging.

The university conducted investigations of these charges, but the investigators did their work poorly. One of two boards of inquiry appointed after the shooting concluded that the investigations were "clearly and seriously deficient" and that they left Fabrikant feeling he had been treated unfairly and had no opportunity for adequate relief. The board wrote:

> Our report is critical of the conduct of some individuals and some aspects of the university's practices and procedures. To a limited extent, therefore our criticisms can be read as bearing out certain of Dr. Fabrikant's allegations. But we do not intend to accept that these criticisms should be read as diminishing Dr. Fabrikant's responsibility for the tragedy, or as assigning such responsibility to the University or to any of its individual members.[7]

In short, there was some validity to Fabrikant's assertions, but his abrasive manner and bungling by the university obscured the underlying issues.

A few days before the shooting (August 21), a university lawyer sent Fabrikant a letter threatening severe legal and employment consequences if he did not stop his E-mail campaign. It was, in effect, as the summary of the case cited earlier noted, "a dismissal notice to a demonstrably unstable, armed man." The university had not taken any precautions to defend itself against him, and thus "was defenseless on August 24 when he came to campus armed and dangerous."[8]

The central defect in the handling of the threat posed by the professor was the lack of coordination between the academic and administrative sides of the university. The administrators correctly perceived him as a difficult disciplinary problem, whereas the academics took account only of his engineering expertise. While the administrators were trying to halt his abusive behavior, he was being rewarded with increasingly favorable academic posts. Moreover, as the second board of inquiry concluded, "on certain matters the university was too benign and passive with Dr. Fabrikant, while on others it may indeed have treated him harshly."[9] The inconsistency within the university community was self-defeating and ultimately encouraged his deadly outburst.

PART III

ALARMS, FALSE ALARMS, THREATS, AND PANICS

CHAPTER 8

The Case of the Dangerous Dreams

Bill Edwards had been reading meters long enough. After several years with the Anderson Valley Water District, he gave notice that he was leaving to take a job as a long-haul trucker. On his last day, he stopped by the office of Janet Belson in the Human Resources Department for an "exit interview." It was a routine practice. Whenever employees decided to leave, the district, which was concerned about turnover, liked to elicit their impressions of the employment experience.

What Edwards told Belson was more than mildly interesting. He said that several employees in the Metering Department had talked of having lurid dreams about Department Supervisor Pete Farmer. In the dreams, the meter men envisioned themselves committing violent acts against the supervisor, using knives, guns, axes, drill bits and broken glass. Edwards said to Belson that he was upset by what he was hearing and that it was an indication of severe morale problems in the department. He urged Belson to give it her immediate attention and added that if anything were to happen to Farmer, he would announce that he had warned the district in advance.

When Edwards had left her office, Belson began filling in the standard exit interview form, but she abruptly put down her pen and phoned her boss, Human Resources Director Larry Somerwell, to report Edwards's disturbing tale. Believing that urgent action was required, Somerwell convened a meeting of senior managers, including the district's general counsel and its director of operations. Unsure of the truth of Edwards's claims, the group decided to seek outside help. They contacted Business Security Services, headed by Jack Randall, a former policeman who was now a private investigator. Somerwell instructed Randall to look into "allegations that unidentified employees were verbalizing threats of harm" against Farmer.

Interviews Begin

Randall spent two full days in the Metering Department, interviewing more than 20 employees. He later said that he advised each of them that the interview was voluntary and that a report would be forwarded to management. When the report was filed, it summarized the interviews. Among the excerpts from the interviews were the following:

- "I have heard employees say, 'We should blow him away.' This was said as a joke. I have heard this from more than one employee. I have heard this a couple of times. The threats are just talk, there is no call for concern. I don't believe there is a real potential for danger, just employees who feed on one another."
- "People have dreams about killing him. People talk about killing him all the time. Most of this talk is joking. One guy has a machete in his desk, and he is the guy with the dream of killing. The dream is about cutting off Farmer's head."
- "One guy said he was dreaming of murdering Farmer. The dream was that he was driving a vehicle and ran over a bald head. The bald head was Farmer's. This has been alluded to by other employees, joking. Three people have made statements about coming in with an Uzi (machine gun)."
- "Employees have talked about taking the guy out. About five people are frustrated to the point where they can't sleep or say, 'I'll get him.'"
- "Randy has had dreams of killing Farmer. Ten of us were there when this was talked about. About 10 employees are having their sleep or health affected. Five people are dreaming of killing him. There is a lot of hopelessness."
- "I've aged 15 years in the last 5 years. I'm nervous. I don't smile. Many nights I can't sleep. About one month ago I had nightmares about work, nightmares about rushing around and not getting things

done. I'm dreaming things grotesque, like taking a brace and bit and drilling it into his head. One guy had a dream that all the buttons in the highway were Farmer's head."

- "We made a pact two years ago that the first person to get a terminal illness will take Farmer out. Approximately ten employees talked about this. Recently an employee got diagnosed with cancer and we kidded him about the pact and his responsibility to take Farmer out. About three or four employees have dreams about killing him. Examples: Taking a knife and killing him. Beating the hell out of him. Two people are at a level where they may actually do something violent in the workplace."

- "I have heard employees say things like tear Farmer apart limb from limb. There are approximately six or seven employees that think and say these things on a regular basis. Senior people are having violent dreams. If the situation remains unchecked, two people have real potential to do harm, due to stress at home and stress at work. Farmer is playing a dangerous game."

- "I've had feelings of killing him. I've had thoughts about committing suicide. I had a gun to my head about two months ago. The reasons were my medical condition. Farmer has pushed me to that limit. I thought about taking his head and shoving it into a CRT terminal and routing it around a couple of times. Farmer was pushing my button to see what I would do. He knows he is pushing to the extreme. He gets a kick out of doing that. Other employees say they would shoot Farmer in the head or take a machete to his head or show up on his doorstep and mow him down."

Randall also reported that members of the Metering Department held shooting practice, using a photo of Farmer as the target, at a local gun club. In addition, the investigator wrote, some members carried guns while at work.

The management team met several times, over a period of weeks, trying to decide how to respond to the Randall report. They consulted a forensic psychiatrist, Stephen Baldridge, who thought the situation was indeed serious, although he stopped short of recommending termination of any employee. Indeed, he advised against immediate discharge, on the ground that it might incite those who had been interviewed. The managers considered a variety of options, such as counseling and suspension. Finally, about a month after the report was submitted, the managers concluded that Farmer faced a serious threat. Three of the men whom Randall interviewed were considered to have engaged in a series of escalating actions that warranted discharge. Each was sent a letter, stating: "You have expressed unacceptable violent statements, thoughts and desires, graphically detailing physical harm, including death, you would like to cause your supervisor." In addition to firing the men, the district installed locks on unattended side and basement doors to the headquarters building.

When word of the discharge spread through the workforce, a crowd of employees gathered outside the headquarters building. They wore white ribbons in protest and claimed the district had given no reasons for its action. A reporter for the local newspaper arrived. The district issued a written statement: "The investigation revealed unacceptable actions and statements of a violent nature graphically detailing physical harm, including death, to a fellow employee. There were additional statements from those interviewed confirming that these statements were not considered jokes or hyperbole."

The union filed a grievance on behalf of the discharged employees, two of whom had been with the district for about 15 years, and an arbitration hearing was held, as called for in the collective bargaining agreement. At the hearing, the union presented its own mental health professional, Dr. Walter Jones, who testified that having nightmares did not indicate a potential for violence. He also said that the employer should have simply warned employees to stop talking about their nocturnal experiences, a measure that would have been more in keeping with the collective bargaining agreement, which states that the "primary objective of discipline shall be to correct and rehabilitate, not punish or penalize."

The Ruling

In his lengthy decision, the arbitrator held the discharge letter unacceptably ambiguous, because it "does not clearly state whether the grievants are being discharged for having dreams about killing" the supervisor, "making threats on his life, or something else." He ruled that employees could be discharged for making threats but that a dream is not tantamount to a threat. A dream, he said, is an "involuntary process over which the grievants have no control." In principle, employees might talk about their dreams in such a manner as to be threatening, but in the Randall interviews employees spoke in general terms. Many of the reported remarks were not attributed to an individual employee by name. In addition, some employees spoke about the dreams of other employees, so that the Randall report was largely inadmissible hearsay.

It was difficult for the arbitrator to see why the grievants had been singled out for discharge. Testimony about the so-called pact suggested that there were as many as ten members. The arbitrator wondered whether it "was really a serious agreement among the three grievants and seven other employees to kill [the supervisor] or whether it was some ill-advised and inappropriate talk in the lunchroom or break area." Even though one employee did contract an illness that could be fatal, the arbitrator noted, he showed no interest in carrying out the terms of the supposed pact.

One of the discharged employees had been fairly specific in the Randall interviews. He was quoted as saying that he had "thoughts of killing" Farmer: "I thought about taking his head and shoving it into a CRT terminal and routing it around a couple of times." Although the imagery was gruesome, the arbitrator held that the grievant told Randall only "what he thought. He never said he was going to do it. The arbitrator does not think that an employee can be fired for only having thoughts about doing violence to a supervisor."

The arbitrator believed that the employer had, in effect, engaged in a form of entrapment. It had sent Randall to ask employees what they thought about Farmer: "The employees responded that they didn't like him, that they were having horrible dreams about him and some of the dreams involved killing him . . . [T]his kind of conversation about dreams of violence is quite different from conversation among a group of employees where they are . . . whipping up anger" against the supervisor.

The three employees were ordered reinstated, provided that a psychiatrist certified that they posed no threat. (If the parties could not agree on a psychiatrist to conduct the evaluation, each side was to nominate a psychiatrist, and those two would pick a third and neutral psychiatrist.) Nevertheless, they were denied back pay, because the arbitrator believed that the grievants and the union were partly responsible for allowing department morale to deteriorate drastically. He thought that the union should have interceded with the district as a soon as it became aware of the widespread resentment of the supervisor.

Within a few months of the decision, the grievants had been certified and were back at work. But they brought suit against the district in federal court, charging defamation as well as a violation of their constitutional rights to free speech, privacy, and association. In their court filings, the employees contended that the investigator had misrepresented himself as a neutral and had told them that "the interview was part of a facilitation process" designed to address stress and morale issues. They claimed that he had promised that the "interview was absolutely and unqualifiedly confidential." The district was forced to mount a costly legal defense.

Critical Decision Points

Management Failure to Respond Promptly

The crisis response team that was charged with assessing the report about the Metering Department spent an entire month deciding how to respond. Had there been a serious threat, a delay of such length would have been irresponsible, especially if the team neglected to warn the alleged target of the conspiracy or transfer him to another department where he would be safe. The delay was most likely caused by the need of the human resources director to improvise a response team and a response protocol while the crisis was raging. There was no standing team, no established policies, and no proper training to allow a smooth, timely response. The lack of well-thought-out procedures also set the stage for the fumbles that ensued.

Failure to Investigate Completely

Neither the crisis response team members nor Dr. Baldridge bothered to speak directly with the three employees selected for discharge, and they interviewed no one else. They relied entirely on what they learned from the Randall report, which was replete with double hearsay and thus largely useless as evidence to prove just cause for discharge in the arbitration hearing. The team never determined whether any of the suspects had a history of violent behavior, which would have added weight to the report. Moreover, when the team decided to discharge the grievants, it did so without the support of its chief adviser, Dr. Baldridge. Although the psychiatrist regarded the situation as dangerous, he did not believe that anyone's discharge was warranted at that time.

Failure to Distinguish Dreams from Reality

From the outset, the employer's case was bedeviled by the failure to draw a distinction between thought and deed. Employees who described gory visions were considered to be threatening the supervisor. Yet, as the arbitrator pointed out, there was no necessary connection between dreams, which are spontaneous, and plots of revenge, which are deliberate thoughts or intentions to act. The crisis response team seemed to regard the graphic dreams as a kind of omen. Although they have figured in prophecy since biblical times, dreams cannot be equated with intent. Dr. Baldridge recognized that dreams are not reliable guides to future conduct. He chose to focus on more concrete behavior, such as talk about an Uzi and about suicide.

Singling Out Three "Offenders"

The employer was never able to explain adequately why it discharged only three employees. The purported plot would have had to involve many more members of the department, and eliminating a mere fraction of the plotters could hardly have eliminated the threat to the supervisor, had it been real. The employees of the department evidently were fantasizing en masse because of their dislike of the supervisor, and there was no logical basis for presuming that the behavior of the three was somehow more threatening than that of the other employees.

Failure to Ask the Obvious Question

Alarmed by the gruesome and disturbing content of the reported dreams, the crisis response team undertook to eliminate what it deemed to be the most serious "offenders," even though no concrete conspiracy had been uncovered. Management never asked: why are employees apparently consumed with hatred and rage toward Supervisor Farmer? Could something about his supervisory style provoke extreme revenge fantasies? Instead of further investigating the actual conditions in the workplace, the district team imposed the harshest of penalties—permanent separation from employment—and found it to be unenforceable. By seeming to act arbitrarily, the employer compounded the morale issue and fomented a labor relations and community relations crisis.

CHAPTER 9

The Case of the Battering Boyfriend

Betty Starbird was a service representative for the Mid-America Telephone Company, a job that entailed telephone and personal contact with the public. Although she had been a dependable employee for about ten years, her attendance had become erratic after she moved in with Steve Norman, a man with an explosive temper. He showed little respect for Betty's job obligations.

Betty received a final warning about her attendance and a three-day suspension to underscore the need for improvement. Unless she achieved four complete months without tardiness or absence, the company warned, she would be placed on Step 3 of the formal attendance control program, which was based on the principle of progressive discipline. Step 3 was the last step before discharge. Two instances of tardiness subsequently occurred. The company took no action—other than docking her pay for the time missed—because they were linked to bad weather that also affected other employees.

Betty's record began to improve, but then Steve had one of his violent outbursts. In a fit of rage, he attempted to strike her, injuring her hand as she deflected the blow. Betty notified her employer that she would need about a week off for reconstructive surgery and postsurgical outpatient treatment. The operation was performed, but because of complications she was out much longer than she expected. Her plastic surgeon sent the company a note, explaining that Betty was among the 30 percent of patients who have to enter a hospital after the procedure to prevent infection. He predicted full recovery within six weeks.

The weekend before she returned to work, Steve threatened Betty with a knife and a gun. On Monday, she was back at her desk, to the relief of her co-workers, but she seemed unusually subdued and troubled. The co-workers pressed to know what was wrong. Betty revealed that Steve was considering visiting the office—and that he might be armed. Betty's concern quickly spread. The notion of a violent intruder created alarm. At the urging of her supervisor, Kathy Miller, Betty spent most of the morning telephoning the authorities. The state police, as well as company security, were notified. Betty also consulted Kathy's friend Alice Almaden, a counselor with a doctorate in psychology who ran the company's Employee Assistance Program.

After lunch, the husband of the regular receptionist called Kathy to insist that his wife, who was pregnant, be taken off the front desk. He had heard about the morning's events, and he feared for her safety. Replacements were assigned to the desk—in pairs.

Toward the end of the day, the crisis atmosphere began to abate. The police had promised to protect Betty. Steve had calmed down and was staying with a friend. Kathy instructed Betty to resume her normal duties.

The next day, however, the menace of Steve loomed once more. He sent flowers to the office and twice telephoned Betty there. She told Kathy that she did not want to talk to him, then changed her mind and took the calls. Betty announced that Steve was near the company's offices and that she was trying to keep him calm. Her co-workers once again became fearful that the abusive partner might be considering a visit. The fear evidently was shared by Betty herself, because Steve had followed her home from work the previous night.

Later that day Kathy found Betty sitting at someone else's desk and directed her to return to her own desk. Betty burst into tears and complained that she was being made to sit beside a hostile fellow worker: "Must you seat me next to someone who causes me to be even more upset than I am?" she asked. "I can't take sitting there. I feel that she is watching me constantly."

Time Off Proposed

Kathy suggested that Betty take time off to deal with Steve. Given a choice of vacation time or unpaid leave, Betty opted for the latter. When she returned, ten days later, Kathy took her into an empty cubicle and formally cautioned her that "if there were any further disturbances in the office, it could involve disciplinary action, up to and including dismissal." Betty spent the next day at the hospital, having a surgical pin removed from her finger, and the following week she was on vacation.

When she returned to work, she neglected to bring a medical note, as the employer had requested, attesting to her ability to use both hands on the job. Nesting in her hair were two curlers, which Kathy considered a breach of the dress code. They were ordered removed.

The next day, the note was demanded again; Betty became agitated and left. Later that day she telephoned Kathy to explain that she was "under duress and could not work under existing conditions." Betty reported that she was receiving treatment of indefinite duration for anxiety and depression. A month later, she reappeared at the office, only to learn that she had been discharged.

Betty challenged the discharge through her union grievance procedure, and the dispute ultimately came before an arbitrator. At the hearing, the company argued that the discharge was for just cause, because Betty had been unreliable and had disrupted the office. For two days it had seemed that Steve might appear at any moment and cause harm.

Denying the allegation, Betty's union suggested that no disruption occurred except in the minds of Kathy and her co-workers, and that the grievant should not be held responsible for their reactions. The union argued that Betty did not intend to disturb others: it was not her fault that Steve called or sent flowers. She was merely a victim of an abusive boyfriend.

The company pointed out that it was Betty herself who pronounced Steve a threat, described him as armed with gun and knife, and speculated that he might appear at the office. Involvement of other employees was unavoidable. For one thing, everyone had to be instructed to divert Steve's calls to Kathy. (The union did not dispute that Steve was, in fact, a potential danger; its advocate referred to him during the hearing as "this nut.") The office staff could not help being distracted by the prospect of an intrusion by an armed and unbalanced outsider, the company maintained.

Several witnesses testified that the office routine was indeed disturbed during the initial days. Kathy described the scene as "just total chaos and commotion." In her estimation, "nothing was done in the office" as a result of the constant preoccupation with Betty's personal problems. The fear that Steve might harm Betty or her co-workers was pervasive, Kathy said. Hours were wasted briefing police and security officers or trying to reassure terrified staff and their families.

The Arbitrator Decides

Whether or not Betty had intended disruptive acts to occur, the arbitrator decided, the employer was justified in holding her responsible because she had allowed the turmoil of her home life to spill over into her work life. The preoccupation with Betty's personal problems diminished productivity, and there was no end in sight.

The decision was influenced by Betty's failure to maintain regular attendance. The union tried to show that each of Betty's lengthy absences (for a damaged hand and for psychiatric treatment) was a nonrecurring illness for which she could not be held accountable: Steve was the source of her unreliability. But the evidence established that absenteeism—she had missed 50 days in five months—was a chronic problem for her and not an aberration attributable only to the instances of abuse. Moreover, her attendance deficits were not medical in origin. Company records revealed that the medical department was asked to determine whether "special health-related issues are causing the employee attendance problems." The associate medical director concluded, after an examination, that they were not.

The arbitrator regarded the two illnesses, as well as the disruption incident, as part of a recurring pattern; personal difficulties eroded Betty's value as an employee. She was not in the office for much of the year leading up to the discharge. When she was present, she was a source of fear and distraction to other workers.

A Psychiatric Disability?

The union had also contended that Betty should not be held responsible for some of the days she lost, because she was suffering from a psychiatric disability and had been told by "a company doctor" to stay home. The reference was to Dr. Almaden, the EAP psychologist. In response to that argument, the arbitrator wrote: "It is well known in industry that EAP staff members are not line supervisors with authority to grant permission to take time off, nor are they authorized to certify an employee's medical status. An EAP is a confidential counseling and referral service; it does not grant amnesty from normal employee responsibilities or exemption from the disciplinary procedure." Betty had a specific reason to understand the role of the EAP. The evidence showed that in a conference call involving Betty, Kathy, and Dr. Almaden, the psychologist had emphasized that "management has a responsibility to make sure work is done."

The union asserted that Betty was not properly informed that discharge could result from her failure to return to work, even though Kathy phoned her daily. It was true that she was not confronted with an ultimatum: return or face discharge. But no prudent employee—especially one with her attendance record—could feel secure while staying away from work day after day without a documented medical excuse. Kathy had told Betty that she was not "paying her for the time off unless I heard something from [a physician]."

The grievant may have believed that she had been given "permission" by Dr. Almaden and that Kathy's calls merely indicated concern for her condition. If so, she was not heeding the supervisor's attempts to encourage her to return or provide a letter from a psychiatrist, certifying that she was suffering a stress reaction to the boyfriend's bullying. The employer no doubt was reluctant to recognize her as psychiatrically disabled before she submitted documentary proof of diagnosis, particularly since the treatment of her physical injury was unexpectedly prolonged and the time needed for recovery was undetermined.

Critical Decision Points

Failing to Adopt a Domestic Violence Policy

The employer was unprepared to deal with an employee whose domestic arrangements affected the workplace. Handling domestic violence threats when they intrude into the workplace, as they did in this case, is a complicated task for a manager, because it involves conflicting values. Each manager must ask: Do I intrude into the private affairs of my employee if I feel she is denying or mishandling a truly hazardous situation? Is it appropriate for me as an employer to get involved with police or courts if I feel my workplace is being threatened? Am I adding to the employee's victimization if I discipline her for personal problems that are impeding her work performance? Because of the complexity of the subject, the employer must thrash out the issues in advance and have in place policies to guide the initial response and the long-term management over time of a crisis with domestic implications.

Recognizing the risks of inaction, many employers have adopted a get-involved approach to domestic threats. Typically, their policies (see sample policies in the Appendix) do the following:

- Encourage or even require employees to inform the employer about any actual or possible domestic violence. Although some companies request notification only if a restraining order has been issued by a court, some go further, requiring employees to report any circumstances that might compromise workplace safety or affect work performance. Training programs and internal publications ensure that all employees are well informed about these requirements.

- Specify the actions that the company will take to protect the workplace and the employee. The company may give notice that it will take out a restraining order itself if conditions warrant, enter into close coordination with local law enforcement, or use private security services.

- Outline procedures, roles, and responsibilities for receiving and processing reported threats of domestic violence. As with other threats, they should not be handled at a department level but should be quickly brought to the attention of high-level decision makers, or the members of a crisis response team, who are trained and empowered to manage such a situation.

Preparation would have made a big difference in Betty's case. The terrified co-workers in her department and Kathy, the beleaguered supervisor, would have had the comfort and support of the whole company in the handling of this frightening episode. Betty herself might have kept her job, or at least have been spared weeks of uncertainty and anxiety as she attempted to handle her domestic crisis and her physical injury while keeping her employer satisfied.

In dealing with Steve, Betty often vacillated. She vowed to refuse his calls, then decided to take them, creating confusion about her attitude toward him. Moreover, she gave no sign that she would take decisive steps to end her relationship with him, which implied that the threats might continue indefinitely. Her uncertainty made it difficult for others to support her. In addition, she dramatized the danger—as when she speculated aloud that Steve might have a gun and might be on his way to the office. She wore down supervisors and co-workers alike, creating a form of "compassion fatigue." Once she had drained the well of sympathy, little stood in the way of her discharge. Because an employee may not always act consistently while under domestic threat, a firm, clear policy is an essential guide.

As Betty's case illustrates, employees being stalked or battered often are too frightened and traumatized to act decisively or wisely in their own behalf. They also may be reluctant to disclose details of their domestic life to the employer, fearing that admitting a problem could compromise their job tenure. It is the employer's responsibility to encourage disclosure of all details that may endanger the workplace. The employee must also be reassured that her job will not be affected by the simple fact that she finds herself in a painful situation.

Treating Attendance Issue in Isolation

It is common for female employees to suffer attendance and performance deficits as a result of an abusive domestic situation. In this case, Betty was particularly vulnerable because her attendance problems predated the acute episode of threatened violence. When Steve became an overt threat, her job was already in jeopardy. The company had repeatedly cautioned her about the likely consequences of continuing to be absent or late and had even suspended her to emphasize the point that she risked discharge.

The physical and psychological trauma that resulted from her relationship with Steve required her to take even more time off, for treatment or recovery. Because of her record, the employer was much less disposed to support her when she became a target of potential violence at work.

Betty's absences and erratic behavior were treated as a standard performance issue, to be dealt with by traditional means—progressive discipline "tempered" with compassion and referral to the EAP. Had her troubles been recognized earlier as symptoms of abuse, they would have been dealt with urgently as a matter of her safety and potentially that of the workplace. The crisis would not have dragged on as long as it did, and the employer would not have been drawn into "enabling" Betty's denial or allowing her to wallow in the role of victim.

Overlooking Option of a Restraining Order

As soon as the employer learned that Steve might appear at the workplace, the company could have taken steps to protect its employees by applying for a judicial restraining order against him—with Betty's knowledge and agreement, of course. Although employers generally try to keep a sharp boundary between employees' private and work lives, the boundary was effectively erased when Betty raised the alarm about Steve, creating enormous stress for her co-workers. Helping her obtain legal protection would have been eminently sensible and would have eased the fears of the rest of the staff when Steve began his campaign of telephone harassment.

Misreading Psychological Distress

There were tangible signs that Betty was beginning to suffer from the stress of being abused by Steve. She came to work with curlers, reacted in a defensive fashion to co-workers, and became upset and irrational when asked for a doctor's note about her surgery. It was difficult for the employer to recognize that a potential behavioral crisis was taking place, however, because Betty never provided proper documentation of her psychiatric diagnosis, and the company's own medical department could find no pathology underlying her persistent absenteeism.

Had company policy recognized Betty's situation as a case of domestic violence, she would have been encouraged to seek legal protection, take an extended leave, or obtain special counseling. Those options would have been more constructive than pursuing her for poor attendance—which at most was a symptom of her domestic crisis. So long as denial prevented Betty from recognizing the effect of Steve's violence on her life, she was unable to address the threat to her employment in a clear-headed manner.

Confronting domestic violence is a complex and frustrating process. The greatest barrier to prevention is the tendency to deny or avoid. "Respecting the employee's privacy" is a form of avoidance, as is treating the issue as a standard performance problem without looking beneath the surface. The employer, however, puts on blinders at its peril, because domestic violence may play out to a tragic conclusion in the workplace itself.

CHAPTER 10

The Case of the Fearful Foreman

The mechanics' break room at Eagle Airlines was known as the "Coffee Club." Its low prices and genial atmosphere attracted not only bargaining unit employees but also supervisors and even employees of subcontractors who worked in Terminal One at Sun Land International Airport. The refrigerator, which stood next to the coffee pot, was the center of attention, because it supported a monitor charting the progress of incoming flights that would require service. Private messages as well as official company notices were typically posted on the front and side of the appliance, where they could be perused while a worker was pouring coffee or spreading cream cheese on a bagel. There was a constant bustle around the refrigerator.

On a spring day, Chris Seeley, who was a shift foreman for the Eagle mechanics, received a phone call at home from Howard, another foreman, whose voice sounded unusually grave. Howard reported that he retrieved from the Coffee Club refrigerator a newspaper article and left it on Chris's desk. The article was about post office killings—and it had Chris's name written on it. Chris was flabbergasted. He arrived at work at about 10:30 P.M. and spotted the article tucked beneath his desk blotter.

It was a wire-service dispatch, torn crudely from a newspaper, and carrying the headline "Postal Service Pursues Changes." There was also a sub-headline: "Office Culture Blamed for Violence." The dispatch reported that the postal service was trying to change a "strict management style that may have contributed to employee rampages in which 32 people have died since 1986." The postmaster general was quoted: he termed the agency's management style "very authoritarian." The article also reported that "murder in the workplace is the fastest rising type of homicide." These passages were underlined in black ink, and some portions had also been highlighted with a yellow marker. Scrawled across the clipping in unfamiliar handwriting were comments, including "Read this Seeley!!! Try and understand it too!!!" and "Fuck Seeley."

Chris reacted viscerally to the clipping. He was disgusted and shocked, and he believed he was being threatened. After each paragraph, he put the article down to regain his composure. He said to himself: this is an article about killing supervisors. He felt hunted. Since he was the only maintenance foreman on that shift, he had to contain his emotions and work through the night. He put the article in his car for safekeeping and in the morning telephoned Pat Berman, the Terminal One maintenance manager, who was his immediate supervisor. He told Pat that he was the victim of attempted intimidation. The manager instructed him to call the police.

Chris went out to his car to get the clipping, so that he could read the exact wording to the police. He found a sticky, green, caustic fluid—a chemical used by mechanics in rebuilding engines—dripping from the roof. In his call to the police, he reported that he had been threatened and that his car had been vandalized. Detectives arrived at the Terminal One parking lot and took the article as evidence, promising to check for fingerprints and analyze the handwriting. Chris had no evidence of a connection between the car incident and the clipping, but the coincidence heightened his nervousness.

Following the maintenance manager's instructions, he stayed home during the next two shifts, resting in the suburban house that he shared with his wife and daughter. He also notified his village police department, as instructed by the airport detectives. The local police gave him some comfort: they pointed out that there was only one road in and out of his suburban housing development, and they promised to keep an eye on his house. Normally, a police car was never seen on his quiet street, but now a cruiser passed by every few hours.

While he sat at home, brooding about the article, he phoned contractors about installing a security system. He could barely sleep on either night. He wedged two-by-fours under the front bedroom door and broken pieces of broomstick in his window casements. His wife, to whom he had not mentioned the incident, demanded that he tell her what was making him so nervous.

When he returned to work, he reported to a different shift, handled administrative paperwork exclusively, and talked to as few people as possible. As he was preparing to leave for the day, he was approached by Jim Falkland, one of the mechanics on the night shift. "I need to talk to you," Jim said somberly.

Jim admitted putting Chris's name on the article. He also acknowledged that he was responsible for some of the comments and underlinings—but not all of them. When he came across the article on the refrigerator, he said, there was only the yellow highlighting. He said he had nothing to do with the car vandalism and meant no harm. He wanted to make amends.

Chris was astonished to discover that the cause of his unease was someone who had been an acquaintance for almost ten years and who had attended his wedding. They had been in the bargaining unit together before Chris became a supervisor. Resentment welled up in Chris. Jim had done something stupid and had disappointed him. Barely controlling his anger, Chris blurted out: "Do you realize what you have done? Do you know what you have put my family through?"

Jim replied with a litany of complaints about the way that Terminal One was managed. "Everyone here has his own idea about how to run the terminal," Chris said indignantly, "but that was no reason to single me out like you did." Rather than offering Jim forgiveness, he said that there was "nothing I could do" for him.

Chris hurried home to tell his family that they could relax and feel secure. Now that he knew who was involved in the incident, he was relieved. He had no fear of Jim. Yet the next day he told Pat that he could no longer feel comfortable working with an employee who had been so underhanded.

When Jim arrived for his shift, he was informed that he was being removed from service, pending an investigation. He was escorted to the parking lot and ordered to leave the terminal.

Pat conducted an investigation. He interviewed Jim, who said that he decided to reveal himself after learning that Chris's car had been vandalized, an action that he disavowed and deplored. "I always prided myself on being honest," Jim said, and he had no intention of causing grief to a person he had known for so long.

When he added his graffiti to the article, he said, he intended to send a personal message to a contemporary who happened to be a supervisor: "I figured a young person could make some changes in the style of management." Jim explained that he did not vent his feelings in person only because he and Chris were on different shifts and in different work areas: "You could go months without seeing him."

Pat tried to establish why Jim put Chris's name on an article about murder in the workplace. He could not fathom Jim's explanation—that he wanted to promote a change in management style—because most of his complaints could have been lodged through normal channels. Any management policies that were inappropriate would be corrected. He could not accept as a valid excuse Jim's apologetic statement that he been "driven by his emotions rather than his brains."

In his report of the investigation, Pat noted that Eagle did not "condone nor tolerate any individual being threatened for any reason. Given the impact that the employee's conduct had had on a foreman and his family, I conclude that he should be discharged."

Jim appealed through the grievance procedure established by the collective bargaining agreement, arguing that he never intended to threaten the foreman. At the arbitration hearing, the company contended that Jim's unsubtle message, combined with the subject of the article, amounted to a threat against the foreman, in violation of company rules. Even if others had posted the article on the break room refrigerator, Jim had embellished it with the handwritten exhortation: "Read this Seeley!!! Try and understand it too!!!" In the context of the vandalism incident, the message was naturally taken as a threat.

Witnesses testified that items posted informally in the Coffee Club typically drew more attention than official notices. The union president commented, "I just wish the membership at large would read my bulletin boards as avidly as they do the material posted on the refrigerator." Although management had attempted to keep the appliance free of inflammatory or derogatory material, there were, in the words of another witness, "degrading remarks and out and out profanity from one end of the spectrum to another."

Jim's characterization of the incident as an impulsive gesture was credible to the arbitrator. The employee was not accused of posting the article, after all; he merely reacted to seeing it on the refrigerator. His action was opportunistic rather than premeditated. No evidence contradicted Jim's assertion that when he put his pen to the article the only mark on it was yellow highlighting of the lead paragraph. By the time it was removed, the article had been further annotated with harsher comments by others, who were unknown. A reference to murder in the workplace, among other passages, had been underlined and a crude epithet ("Fuck Seeley") added. These later embellishments were in black ink, whereas Jim's message had been written in blue. In all, there were traces of four different writing instruments, including the yellow marker, on the article. Taking these factors into account, the arbitrator wrote:

> Here an article clipped from a general circulation newspaper and posted in the break room presented passers-by with an opportunity to goad the foreman about his approach to management. The grievant's ill-advised effort to seize the opportunity miscarried; along with other annotators, he caused the foreman to become concerned about his safety. The grievant was certainly inept, as he acknowledges, but the record does not establish that he intended to create an aura of physical danger. The absence of intent must be deemed a mitigating factor.

Another mitigating factor was the grievant's spontaneous admission that he wrote the message. It was far from certain that the company would have discovered the culprit had he not come forward voluntarily.

In light of these mitigating factors, the arbitrator held, just cause was lacking for a penalty as severe as dismissal, and Jim was ordered reinstated. But the arbitrator decided that the turmoil experienced by Chris and his family as a result of Jim's miscalculation relieved Eagle Airlines of any obligation to make him whole by restoring his back pay.

Critical Decision Points

Assessing the Threat

Although it was ultimately determined that a threat had not been intended, the appearance of the article on the refrigerator sent shivers through Chris and other managers. What is notable about this case is that it began with an act that was common at Eagle Airlines: the posting of an article. The Coffee Club had been a forum for robust self-expression for years. Employees routinely sounded off by leaving messages there, and no one had ever been disciplined for such an act.

Taking advantage of this tolerant attitude, Jim had voiced his dissatisfaction with management policies by writing on the clipping. Although he had no wish to frighten Chris, he blundered monumentally by putting the foreman's name on the clipping and omitting his own. It was the anonymity of the message, combined with its specific target, that bred a sense of menace; the grievant failed to appreciate the impact on the addressee of a hostile communication from an unknown source. Once the writer's identity was known, the foreman's terror evaporated: Jim was an acquaintance and was not considered dangerous.

Jim also failed to anticipate that a public expression of discontent might incite others to pen even more aggressive sentiments. The additions by unknown hands intensified the ominous quality of the posting, making him take blame for his fellow employees' feelings as well as his own. Less responsible than he was, they never came forward.

The way the company viewed the incident was obviously affected by the apparent vandalism of the car. But there was no evidence that the two incidents were related, and in fact there is no conclusive proof that the caustic fluid spill was an act of vandalism, as opposed to an accident. It was the coincidence that proved chilling.

Although the company believed that the grievant went beyond even the unbuttoned conventions of the Coffee Club, he never deliberately sought to instill fear in his onetime workmate—nor could he be held responsible for the purported vandalism incident or the most offensive of the scribblings. Nevertheless, the company was correct in its decision to treat the incident as a crisis and to take prompt action to investigate Jim's behavior thoroughly.

Imposing Discharge

Employers should value forthright behavior and encourage employees to take responsibility for their actions. In this instance, Jim confessed, at the risk of his job, although he was not even a suspect. Yet the employer gave him no credit for his contrition. It discharged him. The company believed that it was simply enforcing its policy of not tolerating threats toward supervisors, but the grievant, while misguided, clearly did not intend to threaten or intimidate the foreman. Chris was traumatized by Jim's clumsy attempt to offer management advice, yet the absence of genuine malice as well as Jim's remorse and readiness to acknowledge his misjudgment counted for something, as the arbitrator ruled. A severe penalty short of discharge could have been imposed without jeopardizing the company's tough stance against threats.

Recognizing Need for Systemic Improvements

The incident entailed important lessons that should have stimulated positive system change. If meting out severe discipline to Jim were the only response, the overall effect would be negative. First, other workers would have assumed that management feared criticism and challenges to its authority and that Jim was a sacrificial lamb. Second, the discharge would have conveyed an unhealthy message that open discussion of workplace morale issues was forbidden. Besides holding Jim responsible, therefore, the employer should have:

- Clarified—or created—a policy on threats, cautioning that none will be tolerated.
- Explored feelings of resentment toward management practices or other working conditions.
- Improved pathways for communicating with management, resolving disputes, and correcting sources of workplace stress.

In short, the employer should have asked itself why an employee who was critical of management found it necessary to resort to an anonymous message to express himself. His act implies that there was fear of retaliation for bringing up problems and a need for safe mechanisms to ventilate feelings about morale and stress issues. (See Chapter 19, "Designing a Violence Prevention Program.")

CHAPTER 11

The Case of the Muttering Mechanic

Bill Lawson had been a mechanic in the pressroom of the *Harbor City News* for more than 25 years. A divorced man in his mid-fifties, he was more than six feet tall and heavyset. He held himself stiffly, as if to say: "I have had my share of troubles; don't push me too far." Although he had few friends among his fellow mechanics, Bill had been active in the union. "I like to stick up for the little guy," he had told a co-worker during a stint as a shop steward.

The *News*, a family-owned daily for generations, was purchased by a conglomerate that altered the paper's management culture. Increasingly, production depended on advanced technology, but the pace at which the technology was being introduced sparked resistance. Some line employees and their immediate supervisors, who had themselves risen from the ranks, were resentful and mistrustful of the new managers and the unfamiliar practices they tried to impose. Tasks that had previously been done with tools now had to be accomplished with a keyboard and computer screen. A formal grievance had been filed, seeking a more gradual, less autocratic introduction to the new equipment and work standards.

Bill was required to use a computer as part of his job and to report to a new manager, Gene Trimble, a much younger man. Bill became openly resistant to the new regimen and began to incur discipline for poor performance. Gene confronted Bill about his deteriorating work. During the conversation, Bill became agitated and angry. According to a report that the manager later filed, Bill complained of "management harassment" and twice made reference to "how this place could turn into a Post Office if you continue to do this to people."

Gene reported the statements to a superior. The next morning, decision makers in the company met to consider the manager's disturbing report. At the meeting were executives representing key company departments: Operations, Employee and Labor Relations, Legal, and Health. They became aware of other remarks attributed to Bill, referring to guns and "getting even" with people at work. They also heard rumors of violence in his personal life. Bill seemed to fit the so-called profile of the violent employee they had all read about: a divorced white male in his fifties who was a loner with an interest in guns.

Albert Dean, the vice president of Employee and Labor Relations, was a seasoned professional. He had worked in the field more than 20 years and had a taste for tough negotiations. He never backed down in difficult situations. He now faced what appeared to be just such a situation: a potentially dangerous employee walking around the plant.

Seeking expert guidance, Albert consulted the in-house Employee Assistance Program. The EAP supplied the name of a local psychiatrist. In a call to the Harbor City Police Department, Albert also explored law enforcement options for dealing with threats. An independent legal opinion was sought from an outside attorney. All three—the police, the psychiatrist, and the attorney—gave the same advice: obtain a court order for an emergency psychiatric examination to determine if the employee was dangerous.

After hearing the company's description of what Bill was alleged to have said, a judge granted the order. The next day, a Friday, Bill was suspended with pay and barred from the plant. The police came to the Lawson home, served him with the order, and took him to a nearby hospital, where he underwent an evaluation by Dr. Hillary Grundwall, a staff psychiatrist. Bill was released immediately after the examination.

On Monday morning, Dr. Grundwall called the company to report that Bill represented no threat. The call was followed by a written opinion from the psychiatrist, confirming that the employee was "not dangerous by virtue of mental impairment."

Outraged by the indignity he had suffered, Bill contacted his union, the Harbor City News Employees Association, and his personal lawyer. Furious at what he considered high-handed treatment of a member, the union's administrative director demanded immediate reinstatement. A letter to the company from the personal lawyer hinted at possible legal action.

In the executive offices, Albert Dean fretted. Far from helping to resolve the crisis, the compulsory examination had aggravated it. The psychiatrist's brief, carefully worded opinion offered few specifics and little reassurance. Albert faced a dilemma. Returning the employee to the workplace seemed ill advised; in all likelihood Gene Trimble would be unable to manage Bill, who might well be dangerous and who was now angry, confused, and mistrustful. At the same time, the union was aroused and determined to defend the rights and the dignity of its member.

Albert interviewed several other employees and learned that they were fearful for their lives. They believed that Bill had the potential for violence. Several months earlier, Albert discovered, anonymous postings had appeared on the machine shop bulletin board. One explicitly discussed post office violence; another was a bulls-eye riddled with bullet holes. Albert's investigation also confirmed the rumors about Bill's personal history. While his divorce proceedings were pending, Bill had been convicted of destruction of property and possession of a pistol without a permit. He had discharged a full clip of ten bullets into the car of his wife's lover. Once these facts came to light, the company arranged to have Bill placed under surveillance.

The psychiatrist the company had consulted initially recommended a systematic risk assessment performed by an outside psychologist, because the psychiatric exam at the hospital was insufficient in itself to assess whether the employee posed a threat in the workplace. He had explained that an examination is based mainly on a personal interview and is "designed to meet certain legal criteria but is separate and apart from the more thorough assessment you would want to follow up with."

Obtaining a referral from the National Institute for Occupational Safety and Health, Albert retained Dr. Bryant Nelson, an organizational psychologist, to undertake a thorough risk assessment. The assessment would entail an interview with Bill himself, as well as a review of all reports about possible threats or behavioral problems and Bill's entire employment record. It would also require interviews with Bill's current and previous co-workers.

If Bill were judged not to be dangerous, the company would still have to fashion a return-to-work plan that would be acceptable to fearful employees and managers. In addition, Dr. Nelson cautioned Albert, the investigation might identify problems with management style or policy that needed to be addressed. The vice president agreed to consider seriously whatever suggestions emerged from the inquiry.

Dr. Nelson spent two days at the *Harbor City News* studying records and conducting interviews. He talked to the executives on the original response team, along with Gene and other managers in Bill's work area. He met with the shop steward and the president of the union local. Not surprisingly, they were suspicious of Dr. Nelson's professed neutrality and remained convinced that he was there to build a case for discharging Bill because of his union activism.

No workplace risk assessment would be complete without an interview with the employee at the center of the case, but Bill contended that he had already passed a psychiatric examination and should not be subjected to another. The company pointed out that Dr. Nelson was a psychologist, not a psychiatrist, and that the company was trying to complete a workplace risk assessment, not administer another psychiatric examination. The company ordered Bill to meet with Dr. Nelson, informing the mechanic that he could be terminated for insubordination if he failed to do so. When Bill remained steadfast in his refusal, he was discharged. The union filed a grievance on his behalf. The dispute ultimately went to arbitration, as provided in the collective bargaining agreement.

The issue presented to the arbitrator was: "Whether the suspension and subsequent termination of the grievant were for just cause and, if not, what should be the remedy?" During the hearing, the company took the position that the grievant's failure, after clear warning, to cooperate with its outside expert justified his dismissal. The union, which deemed the company's actions a witch-hunt and persecution, contended that managers who resented the grievant's union activities concocted the story about alleged threats. The union insisted that Bill justifiably declined to meet with Dr. Nelson, since he had already successfully undergone a psychiatric evaluation. Absent a provision in the collective agreement, the union added, an employer's right to require an employee to submit to a psychological examination is severely restricted.

Gene testified that Bill had complained about his lack of computer training and twice threatened to create a "Post Office situation." Contradicting Trimble, Bill testified that what he actually said was, "The way you keep on harassing people around here, it's a wonder it doesn't end up like the Post Office." He said that the remark was not meant as a threat but as a simple observation. The shop steward, who was present at the interchange, had heard the grievant say, "It's a wonder someone around here doesn't go off, like at the Post Office."

Dr. Grundwall, the hospital psychiatrist, was called as a witness on behalf of Bill. She asserted that it had been an abuse for the company to secure the court order when there was no credible evidence, in her view, of a severe psychiatric illness. She "made a diagnosis of adjustment disorder, which is a mild psychiatric condition that occurs in individuals who are subject to a significant but not extreme amount of stress." In Bill, that had produced "a moderate degree of anxiety, unhappiness, [and] depression."

Although the psychiatrist regarded Bill as open and honest, management was able to show that the mechanic had not told her about his conviction for riddling a car with bullets. The psychiatrist acknowledged that if she had been aware of this "fit of rage" and of the gun that Bill kept at home (it was not mentioned in the interview), she would have been more concerned about the potential for violence.

After considering the hearing record, the arbitrator ruled that the discharge was for just cause. He found that the company correctly decided, after consultation with experts, that a comprehensive risk assessment was necessary and was not duplicative of the psychiatric evaluation. The arbitrator was persuaded that, in view of the grievant's lack of candor during the Grundwall interview, the psychiatric evaluation was an unreliable measure of the risk Bill posed in the workplace. The grievant therefore had a duty to cooperate with Dr. Nelson's investigation and could be discharged for refusing.

The arbitrator also stated that employers, who have an obligation to provide a safe work environment, may properly require an employee to submit to a psychological examination that is essential to a safety-related investigation. He ruled that the employer acted reasonably in terminating Bill, since it had given a clear warning of the dire consequences of failure to cooperate in its investigation. The arbitrator also found unpersuasive the grievant's claim that he did not mean to convey a threat.

Company executives believed that they had won. But had they? Although an arbitrator had agreed with the company that it had a right under the collective bargaining agreement to discharge the grievant, there was more at stake than that narrow principle. Despite its ostensible triumph in the arbitration forum, the company had actually suffered twin defeats:

A Labor Relations Defeat. The grievance-arbitration process and its outcome further damaged a labor-management relationship that was already in low water. Relations with the union clearly were less than optimal when the episode started. The union was not brought into the information-gathering and decision-making process that Bill's perceived threats set in motion. When the union came upon the stage, it was as a committed adversary, and that role never changed. The union ignored the employer's attempt to conduct a comprehensive investigation, depriving the process of an important source of information and legitimacy. The company was unable to convince the union that managers' worries about Bill were genuine. Until the end, union leaders maintained that the company was operating in bad faith and ascribed the discharge to anti-union animus. The episode thus represented a lost opportunity to improve labor relations and adopt a collaborative approach toward an issue—workplace safety—

in which there was a demonstrable mutuality of interest between labor and management. An opportunity for productive partnership had been squandered.

A Defeat for Safety and Security. Safety was the most important value at stake, and ironically the employer's approach failed to make the newspaper a safer place to work. If Bill was a threat to the workplace, the mere fact that he no longer worked there did not mean that he stopped being a threat to the company or to individual co-workers. Even persons without authorized daily access to a plant may pose a danger.

For the supervisors and co-workers who felt threatened by Bill, the news of the arbitration decision was not comforting: "Sure, the company has won its case," they thought, "but what about us? How will Bill react now that he has lost everything?" Indeed, Bill had even more reason to be resentful. His obvious and growing distress at work had been compounded by the humiliating, at times frightening, experience to which he had just been subjected. Suspicions about the company's true motives were confirmed, and the grievance process did nothing to cure the sense of injustice. The union's insistence throughout the arbitration that Bill had been singled out for his union activities validated his anger and added to his sense of victimization. The nasty spectacle of a 25-year employee losing his job for devious reasons might even have engendered hostility in other employees.

Critical Decision Points

Failure to Prepare for New Technology

The roots of the incident are to be found in broad organizational changes that new ownership had set in motion, along with the introduction of computerized production methods. The demands on employees, the conditions of work, and the patterns of interaction throughout the company were all affected. In many respects, the old ways persisted as a kind of underground culture. Bill was not the only employee to react adversely to computerized work methods, as indicated by the grievance concerning the introduction of technology. The grievance should have forewarned the employer that some employees were being stressed unduly by the pace of change.

Although expressing his own personality, Bill's remarks to Gene were also symptomatic of the unhappiness, resentment, and mistrust that prevailed on the shop floor. Gene's fearful response to Bill reflected the general insecurity of middle management. "We are not in control of our employees," the middle managers seemed to be brooding, "and they are angry and sullen. What might happen next?"

Dr. Nelson's investigation was later to reveal the extent of the dissension, but at the time of the incident upper management was unaware of the seething mistrust and of the safety and morale problems that plagued the unit. As a result, they could not read the signals when the threat-of-violence episode erupted and were unable to place the reports about Bill in their proper context. If the top leaders had been aware of the tensions in the unit, they would have moved more circumspectly when Gene reported a threat.

During the arbitration hearing, the union argued that Bill's difficulty in dealing with the sudden arrival of the computer age should be taken into account. The company responded that training opportunities had been ample. At that point, of course, the company was deeply mired in an adversarial process and could only adopt a defensive posture. It was too late to pay attention to the larger issue of technology on the job, and the company could not afford to acknowledge that the pace of change might have prompted Bill's expression of feelings. Earlier, however, the employer could have more readily adopted a listening stance and taken the objections seriously.

The technology grievance had been a distress signal that the company failed to read—a signal that employees needed more help adapting to changing work conditions. When employee dissatisfaction surfaced, however, it was seen by management as just one more union demand to be resisted. There was no recognition that rapid change might have traumatized the workforce, including line-level supervisors. Ideally, management and labor should have worked jointly to smooth the adjustment. Systems for support, communication, and early response to signs of stress should have been essential components of the transition.

Failure to Connect with the Employee

The employer's first responsibility is to determine whether a real threat exists, and the employee himself is the primary source of information. The abrupt, coercive way in which the employer sought to obtain information from Bill thoroughly alienated him. What prevented the employer from approaching the employee directly and asking for an explanation? Certainly not security considerations: Bill had not displayed a weapon, nor had he voiced any specific intention to do harm. Yet the employer reacted as if there were an emergency, requiring Bill's immediate removal from the workplace.

Fear of violence is natural. Unless the possibility of harm is imminent, however, responding to a crisis on the basis of fear, rather than reliable evidence, often precludes an effective investigation. Pushing the panic button prematurely blocks access to the prime source of information for evaluating a perceived threat—the employee himself.

Maintaining contact with a possibly violent employee does not mean adopting a "soft" or lenient approach. Quite the contrary is true: a decisive, swift response is called for, including whatever disciplinary or administrative action may be dictated by company policy if an infraction has been committed. But decisiveness must be distinguished from precipitate action. In this case, the employer too hastily abdicated its responsibility to talk directly to the employee.

As the arbitrator later ruled, the company had the right to require Bill to cooperate fully in an investigation of the allegations. Inexplicably, it neglected to exercise that right at the beginning of the episode: the employer failed to ask him for an explanation. Instead, it sent Bill to Dr. Grundwall, who was unfamiliar with the employee, the demands of the work situation, or the circumstances surrounding the remarks at issue. The employer subjected him to compulsory psychiatric examination without fully appreciating its limitations and found itself in the embarrassing position of having to repudiate the very medical opinion it had itself sought.

Those who are at risk for violence typically feel invisible, powerless, and cut off from others. Under all but the most extreme circumstances, the surest way to reduce the immediate danger is to maintain close contact. The same is true of an employee who, without actually uttering a threat, emits a distress signal that others find ominous. The cause is often some form of severe or increasing stress involving personal ties or relationships that have become frayed. Strengthening the quality of the employee's social bonds counteracts those sources of stress, yet co-workers and supervisors often become distant—as if to say, "Don't confront that person. It might push him over the edge!" Although understandable, such a response is misguided. A sense of invisibility is the problem; reconnecting with the employee will tend to pull him back from the edge.

Ordering a Psychiatric Assessment

Believing that a crisis was at hand, managers resorted to what they considered to be the appropriate medical/mental health approach: the standard psychiatric assessment. A psychiatric assessment addresses a broad spectrum of questions about emotional and cognitive functioning. Asked to examine an individual, a psychiatrist or other mental health professional (such as a psychologist or clinical social worker) will take a "snapshot" intended to provide quick answers to a handful of crucial questions. These questions will relate to the individual's ability to think clearly and to function safely in various aspects of life. The professional may go beyond those questions if circumstances warrant, and he or she may attempt to evaluate the risk of violence. But an assessment limited to an office visit or outpatient clinic protocol will not satisfy the requirement of an employer faced with a possible threat of violence.

A thorough evaluation requires additional questions to be asked: What is the record of discipline for past problems? What is the record of performance problems, or claims for medical disability? What else is going on in the subject's life? In other words, what is the total psychosocial context of the behavior under investigation? Without consulting with other employees, without a thorough knowledge of the context gleaned from interviews with management, union, other employees, and records, the professional cannot answer the crucial questions. And until these questions are answered, no violence risk assessment can be considered complete or reliable. Any recommendation for intervention, treatment, or administrative action is premature.

When they compelled Bill to undergo the psychiatric assessment, the managers did not fully grasp its limitations. At they time, they were casting about for a response in an ad hoc and somewhat disorganized fashion. Their information depended on whom they happened to telephone and what they happened to hear from the workforce. They were also influenced by the popular belief that a dangerous person can be identified by being matched to a standard "profile"—a belief that has no scientific validity (see Chapter 17). Given the randomness of their information input, it is hardly surprising that the managers' initial response was ill conceived.

Belated Use of Independent Consultant

The decision to hire a consultant to investigate the risk of violence represented an attempt by the company to break a logjam. Unfortunately, the decision came too late. Even though the company commissioned Dr. Nelson to act in a neutral capacity, rather than to support a particular outcome, Bill was in no mood to cooperate with such an inquiry. No doubt he believed that his was a no-win situation: the company would arrange to have him declared dangerous if he allowed himself to be questioned by the consultant and would discharge him for insubordination if he refused.

The News Employees Association also was unwilling to cooperate with the investigation. Its reluctance was understandable. Union leaders had been frozen out of the decision-making process until then, even though the union, too, had an obvious interest in preventing violence. Management made a good faith effort in hiring Dr. Nelson but never convinced the union that its intentions were honorable. The company's failure to explain at the outset that the compulsory psychiatric assessment would not be the only examination contributed to the union's suspicions when Dr. Nelson arrived. Had the company implemented a violence prevention policy before the incident and invited the union to be part of the planning, the collective bargaining partners could have agreed upon a procedure for investigations; the questions about Bill might have been resolved in an atmosphere of mutual trust.

Resort to Arbitration

As the company representatives and lawyers prepared to enter the arbitration hearing, a little voice should have whispered to them: "You can't win in this dispute! If the arbitrator rules against you, you will have to return an angry, emboldened employee to a workplace where he is feared and resented by his managers and co-workers. On the other hand, if you prevail, and Bill ceases to be your employee, you will lose all control over a man whose potential for violence remains unknown and who is angrier and more desperate than before. You face an unknown danger—the very problem you had when the incident first surfaced."

The employer might say: "Wait a minute, we told the employee what the consequences would be for refusing to cooperate with our investigation, and he chose this course. It would be wrong for him to prevail, a loss for order and discipline. Sure, we could have handled this a bit better, and we will learn from our mistakes. We were not perfect, but we should not be punished for taking a threat seriously."

The employer's rationale is predicated on a false framing of the question. The primary issue is not the employer's ability to command obedience, enforce rules, or validate its rights under the collective bargaining agreement. The issue is preventing violence. Confronting such a risk requires a dispassionate and fair-minded inquiry, involving all stakeholders. A complex interaction between human coping behaviors and a variety of environmental factors must be explored. An adversarial proceeding such as arbitration, however, stifles dispassionate inquiry, encourages polarization, and exacerbates tension. By the time the issue of Bill's remarks had reached the arbitration stage, it had degenerated into a duel over each party's contractual rights.

Going into the arbitration, the employer had no reason to be confident of the outcome. The company first compelled a psychiatric examination and then declared the outcome inconclusive. Some arbitrators might not have allowed the company a second bite of the apple—that is, they would not have upheld a discharge for failing to submit to examination by yet another mental health professional. Such a requirement might have been viewed as a form of double jeopardy or harassment. Although it had broad discretion to investigate, it could be argued, the company must accept the consequences of its own blunder in choosing an inadequate investigatory technique. Court-ordered compulsory examination is a drastic measure, and the company in a sense deserved to be held accountable for choosing such an extreme response when other approaches promised to yield more useful or complete information.

Moreover, another arbitrator might well have determined that there was no compelling evidence of a threat. The statement about the post office was at least open to interpretation, and the grievant did not speak about taking action personally. Nor did he single out a specific target.

Although the company vindicated its contractual right to discharge the grievant, not everything that is permitted by the contract is wise or just. There are other standards by which a company response should be judged, such as enhancement of safety. Responding to a reported threat of violence with ill-considered unilateral measures, top executives created a stand-off that prevented the incident from ever being fully explored and that left them vulnerable to accusations of bad faith and conspiracy. If the question were whether the employer had made the workplace safer, the answer would have to be no. In an arbitration, one side walks away a "winner," the other a "loser." But when the subject is violence prevention, a loss for one side is usually a loss for both.

Afterword: When the Violence Alarm Sounds

The incident at the *Harbor City News* is, unfortunately, not uncommon. Disputes often erupt because management overreacts to a reported internal threat of violence and alienates those whose cooperation is needed to get to the bottom of the problem. In large part, the overreaction is due to misinformation and the absence of established policies and procedures. The newspaper's executives were unprepared to respond and had to cast about desperately for an ad hoc strategy. As a result, they made critical mistakes. Although they would have known how to respond to a fire alarm—because fire drills and evacuation plans are worked out in advance—when a violence alarm was sounded, they could only improvise.

Perhaps the most important lesson to be learned from this case is that the resolution of the issue of a threat of violence in the workplace is not about winning disputes with unhappy employees. There is a risk that the very systems that have been developed to resolve disputes, respond to injuries and emergencies, and preserve safety will themselves contribute to a climate of frustration, helplessness, and alienation.

CHAPTER 12

The Case of the Ejected Engineer

Managers are often accused of bullying and harassing subordinates. But sometimes intimidation and terror are directed upward. This is a story of abuse by a subordinate, a case in which a verbally and physically aggressive employee ultimately ended the career of a gifted manager. In the process, a multinational corporation lost a valued executive-grade employee because it failed to protect her from a pattern of overt threats.

Donna Ward was a 36-year-old African American who had worked for seven years at the Turbo Systems Corporation, which designed power-generating equipment for utility companies. She was appointed the supervisor of a group of mechanical engineers working on a project for Mid-Basin Power and Light Company, an important client. Donna was a bright, ambitious engineer who welcomed the added responsibility. Heading the Mid-Basin project signified that she had found a route to success in a company and profession dominated by males in hard hats.

Shortly after she took charge of the project, Donna was warned by her superior, George Marley, that an engineer in the group, Rajiv Patel, was unhappy about his new supervisor. Rajiv resented having to report to a woman. George advised her to do what she could to ease any tension that might arise between them.

Born in Bombay, Rajiv studied engineering at an American university, a background that was similar to that of several other company engineers, including a vice president. His technical skills were good, but he had a tendency to miss deadlines.

Donna found Rajiv difficult right from the start. He looked for opportunities to confront her, grumbling about work assignments and scheduling. Donna tried doggedly to improve the relationship, paying extra attention to Rajiv in order to win his cooperation.

Her strategy seemed to be succeeding—until she heard from others in the group that Rajiv had been making disparaging remarks about her. After she had been his boss for six months, Donna had to prepare a periodic performance evaluation. She conscientiously reviewed Rajiv's work, noting several aspects of his performance that needed improvement. At a meeting arranged to discuss the evaluation, Rajiv became hostile and aggressive, demanding that she assess him more favorably and recommend him for a promotion. She refused.

In the next few months there were unpleasant incidents. When Donna passed along a request from George for calculations on generator output levels, an aspect of the project for which Rajiv was responsible, he became upset and used an obscene epithet. He also blurted out: "I'll get my gun and blow his head off." Several other engineers complained that Rajiv was surly and uncooperative, interfering with their ability to get work done.

Noting the proximity of the completion deadline, several engineers appealed to George to curb Rajiv's disruptive behavior. George recorded the complaints and requested that Donna discuss them with Rajiv. When she called Rajiv into her office, he angrily protested that his relationship with the other engineers was "none of her business." Donna replied that she had the right to speak to him about issues that directly affected group performance. He rose from his chair and shouted, "If you call me a slave again, I will kick your ass." Donna abruptly ended the meeting and phoned George. Yet no action was taken by management to respond to Rajiv's outburst.

A Blowup

Donna herself received an excellent evaluation and a promotion. Although she kept quiet about the rise in grade, Rajiv heard about it from his contacts in "the Penthouse," the company's top-floor executive suite. He told her that the word from the Penthouse was that she been promoted only because she was black and a woman. On another occasion, when he was resisting an assignment that would require him to work outside the office once a week, Rajiv became angry at Donna. Shortly afterward, he approached her in the corridor with a look of rage in his eyes. He passed her by, jabbing his elbow into her ribs. "Look out," he shouted with mock alarm. "Somebody could get hurt."

Frightened, Donna reported the incident to George, who warned Rajiv that he would be terminated if he threatened her. She was advised to keep a log, recording any further incidents. For the next several months, Rajiv stayed away from her, but she began to dread another attack. The department secretary revealed that on several occasions Rajiv had asked her where Donna was. Twice Donna observed Rajiv loitering in the company garage, where she parked her car. Another engineer, an old friend of Rajiv's, shared with Donna his concern that her subordinate might be schizophrenic or psychotic.

When Donna delivered Rajiv's next periodic evaluation, she made sure that George was in the room. Even so, Rajiv became agitated. He protested that Donna was intentionally undermining him and warned: "You won't get away with what you are trying to do to me."

To Donna, it was the last straw—the culmination of 18 months of persistent intimidation. She began crying after the session. George advised her to go home. Afraid to enter the parking garage alone, she had to be escorted to her car. That evening, George called Donna at home and informed her that Rajiv would be removed from the Mid-Basin project—as soon as the company found another assignment for him.

Donna returned to the office two days later, accompanied by her husband, and announced that she no longer felt safe at work. George met with his immediate superior, Ed Smethers, vice president for operations, stressing the need to remove Rajiv from Donna's group at once. About two weeks later, Donna learned that Rajiv had been transferred to another project. But he had not been disciplined and was still in the company's headquarters complex, albeit in a different building.

Dave, another engineer in Donna's group, warned her that Rajiv was "out to get her, no matter what it took." He advised her to be careful. Helen, a supervisor on the project, reinforced her sense of foreboding. She told Donna that Rajiv had voiced a threat in her presence, saying that "he would not go down alone" and that "he would do whatever he had to do to ensure that." Helen urged Donna to be wary of Rajiv, who she believed was determined to do physical harm. Helen was unwilling to share her impression of Rajiv's intentions with management, however, for fear that Rajiv would retaliate against her as well.

Donna insisted that action be taken against Rajiv. Ed Smethers consulted with human resources and legal executives at corporate headquarters. He told her that nothing could be done unless the co-workers came forward to attest to Rajiv's threatening behavior. Without their evidence, the company would leave itself open to a suit for wrongful termination if it discharged him. If she had "officially documented" the jabbing incident, Ed remarked, it would also have helped prepare the ground for a discharge. Donna replied that she had in fact documented the incident—by reporting it—and reiterated her concern about her safety.

The next day Donna failed to appear at Turbo Systems. When George called her at home, she explained that she was so distraught she could not work. After two days at home, Donna received a call from George and Ed: they had arranged for her to see a counselor from the EAP to help her "deal with the stress." Accompanied by her husband, Donna met with company executives instead and explained that Rajiv's hostile behavior had begun to affect her health. She was experiencing headaches, upset stomach, and sleeplessness. Unless something were done to make the job safe, she emphasized, she could not return to work. The company still refused to terminate Rajiv.

The Resignation

Ten days later, Donna resolved the impasse by resigning from the company herself. In a letter to George, she wrote:

> For the past year, while on the Mid-Basin project, Rajiv has been very hostile, obstinate and violent towards me. . . . During this time, he has made many statements using vulgar language, made threats to me, hit me on the arm, attempted to assassinate my character professionally and told a project team member of his intent to do physical harm to me. These incidents have caused me to fear for my safety in the work place and have made it extremely difficult to function effectively because of the unsafe work environment.
>
> As you know, these incidents have been reported to the proper project and functional managers. However, the proper action was not taken against Rajiv to ensure this type of behavior would cease. Therefore, this situation got increasingly worse and unbearable for me. No employee should be confronted with threatening comments and gestures in the work place. Yet this was allowed to happen to me. Given the options available to me at this time, I have no other recourse than to terminate my employment to ensure my safety and well being.

Donna's resignation jolted the company, finally attracting the attention of the higher echelons of management. Ed asked her to reconsider, offering her a generously paid leave of absence. The executive assured Donna that "the incidents described in your letter are issues which the company has treated very seriously." He wrote: "Given the information available to your management, action was taken and alternatives and/or solutions were discussed with you in an effort to resolve all of your concerns. In addition, Rajiv was counseled and given a verbal warning subsequent to the elbow incident, and he was removed from the project and reassigned to a project located in another building."

Ed also announced the hiring of a team of independent experts, headed by Dr. Alexander Cosgrove, an industrial psychologist who specialized in violence issues. Cosgrove and his assistants spent three days interviewing at the company facility. They asked to see Donna, but she refused to cooperate, asking the company to accept her resignation. The company agreed, informing her that the Cosgrove investigation had been "unable to identify any evidence that a threat exists toward you or any other member of the project team."

Donna hired a lawyer and filed a lawsuit against the company for discrimination, intentional infliction of emotional distress, failure to maintain a safe work environment, and negligent hiring, supervision, and retention. The original petition stated that "the defendant breached this duty [to provide a safe work environment] by either intentionally or negligently permitting Rajiv to engage in an ongoing pattern of misconduct." Both sides took depositions.

In a declaration prepared for the lawsuit, Dr. Cosgrove said that Donna had been "unwilling to participate even with a home interview." He concluded that Turbo Systems' management evinced a balanced and appropriate concern for the rights of both employees and provided his team with prompt access to all employees who might have potentially useful information. Dr. Cosgrove also found no evidence to support the premise that Rajiv was a threat to Donna or any other employee.

To Donna's consternation, a court granted the employer's motion for summary judgment, ending the case without trial. The judge ruled that Donna failed to provide evidence that she suffered an adverse employment action or discrimination because of gender or race. The judge found no merit in the claim that the employer was guilty of negligent supervision or retention of Rajiv, and also found no evidence that Donna had suffered emotional harm. The ruling was a disastrous end to what had been a promising career with the company. Donna had been maneuvered out of a job that she cherished, her tormentor had gone unpunished, and her legal recourse had been exhausted.

Critical Decision Points

Failure to Adopt an Appropriate Guiding Policy

Management's weak response to Donna's complaints stemmed from the absence of a suitable standing policy coupled with a failure to improvise a suitable response when basic standards of conduct were being clearly violated. Donna's inability to gain protection at work may have been an indication of a corporate culture that emphasized self-reliance and tacitly tolerated the irresponsible and abusive behavior exhibited by Rajiv. Clearly, the corporation was unprepared to recognize reports of harassment and threats—even though they emanated from multiple sources. George was a witness to several of the outbursts that frightened Donna, had heard some of the same warnings from co-workers, and was himself the target of a menacing remark. He knew that her concerns were far from imaginary. Yet, even with his corroboration, management refused to take her complaints seriously.

Operating in Discipline Mode Instead of Safety Mode

The company's reluctance to respond illustrates the difference between the "disciplinary" mode and "safety" mode. When employers operate in disciplinary mode, substantial proof is required to support an allegation of misconduct. The employer waits for informants and complainants to come forward with accounts that will withstand cross-examination. The fact that Helen refused to repeat on the record what she heard from Rajiv caused the company to wash its hands of the matter; since it had no witness, it did nothing.

Similarly, the company failed to respond firmly to the jabbing incident because there were no witnesses to corroborate Donna's account. Management professed to need "documentation." Donna's own report that she had been jabbed in the ribs was not considered sufficient, even though she was entrusted with supervisory authority over Rajiv. If the company relied on her reviews of his performance, why would it not believe her assertion that he had attacked her?

Ed was loath to act without a clear signal from corporate headquarters, which seemed to be primarily concerned that Rajiv would sue them successfully for wrongful termination if he were dismissed without solid evidence. Headquarters ignored Rajiv's prior performance problems, which would have buttressed the company's case should he bring an action.

In contrast to disciplinary mode, safety mode is active. It addresses problems at the earliest possible stage. Maintaining a safe workplace is assumed to be the employer's paramount obligation, and management acts forcefully whenever safety is in doubt. Rather than remaining paralyzed while waiting for "evidence," a company in safety mode takes immediate steps to allay the fears or concerns of its employees. The search for facts is not ignored or deferred, but the need for more facts is not allowed to inhibit a prompt response to a potential hazard.

Donna's case demonstrates the value of going into safety mode when a threat is perceived. In waiting for evidence of misconduct, management allowed a potentially dangerous situation to go unattended. The company was preoccupied with gathering evidence for a future disciplinary action against Rajiv; the more immediate question of Donna's safety was ignored. It was management's duty to investigate the reasonable suspicions that Donna brought to them and determine whether the work environment was safe or not. In this case, the company evaded its duty and displaced the burden onto Donna by instructing her to keep a log to demonstrate the threat. It should not have been her duty to determine the significance of the chilling reports she was receiving or to assess the degree of danger. The primary issue—Donna's growing fear that she would be harmed—was never the subject of discussion among managers until she had resigned in desperation.

By limiting its response to considerations of discipline, the company effectively acted as if it was sure that no threat existed, a position that could hardly be justified by the facts at hand. A surly, disruptive employee, who believed that he was being unfairly evaluated, should not have been ignored merely because he could not yet be disciplined.

An employer operating in safety mode would launch an investigation based on the reports that suggested danger. It could employ outside experts for the purpose. In this instance, outside experts were called, but they arrived too late—when the employee had already resigned—and they were used for self-justification rather than self-analysis.

Had management been more sensitive to signals of distress at an earlier stage, the tension between Rajiv and Donna might have been amenable to a problem-solving approach, relying on conflict resolution principles. Some companies have teams of peer mediators pre-positioned in the workforce to detect and deal with incipient conflict. Rajiv's obstructive behavior could have been addressed by such a team. The communication barrier between Rajiv and Donna might have been breached by consensual means, a strategy that could have precluded the need for any discipline.

Regrettably, there was no protocol for involving co-workers in an effort to resolve the tension between Donna and Rajiv. There was also no mechanism for addressing the racial and gender prejudice in which Rajiv's resentment was apparently rooted. It is possible that his relationship with Donna was influenced by traditional attitudes toward women in his native country—an expression of culturally based intolerance. He may also have believed that he had support in the upper echelons of the company because some of the top engineering executives had immigrated from the same part of the globe. Since the tension between Rajiv and Donna amounted to a clash between two ethnic minorities, it might have been resolved by the process that community relations mediators use to settle volatile interethnic disputes.

In any event, passively awaiting proof of dischargeable misconduct squandered an opportunity for intervention that might have remedied the discontent underlying the threatening behavior. Indeed, the company's failure to act may well have been interpreted by Rajiv as tacit acceptance of his behavior, encouraging him to continue intimidating Donna.

Referral to EAP Counseling

Referring Donna to the EAP was a misuse of counseling services and a classic example of blaming the victim. Instead of decisive administrative action, beginning with an investigation of Rajiv's aggressive behavior, there was a feeble offer of a palliative. The company shifted responsibility for the friction from Rajiv to Donna, saying to her, in effect, "The problem is in your reaction to these events." Rather than attempting to help Donna tolerate the stress of her job, the company should have confronted the chief source of that stress.

Belated Reliance on Outside Experts

Hurt, frustrated, and alienated by the employer's inept response, Donna had already distanced herself emotionally from the workplace by the time the experts arrived. The strain of dealing with Rajiv had taken its toll. The employer was finally saying, "You have our attention. We can solve this problem together." But she was saying, "It's too late. I don't trust you any more," even though she had once taken great pride in her workplace.

The timing of the call to Dr. Cosgrove thus raises questions of credibility and good faith. Dr. Cosgrove and his associates were brought in after the damage had already been done. In addition, the doctor's compliment to the company for its cooperation with his investigation was gratuitous; the executives naturally were eager to cooperate once Donna had departed so that they could be vindicated. But their alacrity after the fact contrasts starkly with the denial and neglect that caused her to leave. Although the focus should have been the company's actions *prior* to Donna's resignation, the investigation omitted any consideration of the company's response during the 18 months in which she supervised Rajiv. In their report, the experts implicitly criticized her for not allowing herself to be interviewed. In so doing, they ignored the fact that her refusal was the direct result of the company's disregard of her complaints.

The purpose of the investigation quite obviously was to erase the memory of earlier mistakes and protect the company from the appearance of wrongdoing. Genuine self-examination and learning for the future were not among the goals. The inquiry thus served to support the company's flawed response and to ensure that it did not learn from its mistakes. The subsequent "victory" in court allowed the company to congratulate itself, but it was a Pyrrhic victory. Instead of being able to take pride in having an African American woman in a leadership role, the employer ignominiously forced out a pioneer. It was setback for the engineering profession as a whole as well as defeat for the company.

Afterword: Underestimating Psychological Trauma

The Case of the Muttering Mechanic (Chapter 11) demonstrated the perils of overreaction to a perceived threat of violence. The Turbo Systems case illustrates the damage that may result from underreaction to a threat of violence. Here, a corporation failed to prevent psychological injuries to an employee. The employer ignored a pattern of threats and outright assault, undermined the authority of a manager, and avoided confronting possible issues of race and gender.

As in the Case of the Downsizing Dissenter, which follows in the next chapter, an adjudication process shielded the employer from liability. Applying the doctrine of employment at will, the court deferred to managerial prerogative. The employer did not have genuine cause to celebrate, however, for the legal victory blocked any learning that might have flowed from Donna's resignation. Undue reliance on the law as an insulator is a mark of the crisis-prone organization.

The company failed to take Donna's complaint seriously because it feared that Rajiv would accuse the company of invasion of privacy, discrimination, or wrongful dismissal. But that legal risk had to be balanced against the risk that Donna's story might be true. In the end, the company avoided a legal penalty but paid a greater price—the needless loss of a talented employee and the chance to become a diversity pacesetter in its industry. The injustice was surely obvious to the remaining employees, who could hardly have been unaware that a professional with leadership potential had been casually sloughed off. Morale undoubtedly suffered, particularly when the other engineers realized that the obstructive Rajiv would remain on the job—now virtually immune to corrective measures. Such a disquieting outcome shakes confidence in managerial competence.

Faced with the task of evaluating whether a threat existed, the outside experts had no access to the most important body of evidence—the perceptions of the person who felt threatened. The company had waited until she left the workplace before calling for outside review. Without Donna's input, the experts could glean only one side of the story and were unable to gain a thorough understanding of events. The report was essentially a whitewash. Rather than rendering an impartial opinion, the experts were drawn into collusion with the company, which sought to reconstruct the episode in a light favorable to itself.

The employees who had reported Rajiv's threatening behavior to Donna either did not speak to the experts—or told them a different story. Her co-workers may have chosen to keep silent because they perceived the outcome as foreordained; they understood that supporting her allegation of harassment was not a prudent career move. Who, then, would dare to raise the alarm at the next instance of abuse or threat?

The investigating experts found no evidence "to support the premise that Rajiv posed a threat of harm" to Donna. Since they rendered that opinion without interviewing Donna and without reference to the full record of the Rajiv-Donna interaction, their conclusion was suspect. It was based on accounts from the alleged threatener and employees who probably were fearful that candor might cost them their own jobs. Donna herself no doubt would have provided a far different account of the events. The experts helped the company disguise what had happened, but Turbo Systems itself was primarily responsible for this violation of workplace safety and neglect of basic human values.

CHAPTER 13

The Case of the Downsizing Dissenter

In today's workplace, downsizing has become a fact of life—and often a traumatic experience for individuals and for the workplace as a whole. At a time of downsizing, trust and communication are the first casualties. To assuage anxiety, employers offer assurances about the future: "No more cuts!" they proclaim. And they believe it, desperately hoping that wholesale job losses will end. But promises about job security are often broken, causing the remaining workers to doubt the credibility of the boss. Once seen perhaps as benevolent, fair, and honest, company leadership may now be perceived as unscrupulous, unfeeling, and untrustworthy. An ethos of teamwork and a feeling of security may be replaced by fear, rage, and resentment. Who will be the next to go? Whom and what can you believe?

In this climate of mistrust and insecurity, tolerance of "otherness" begins to break down. Behavior that was ignored in the past is now seen as dangerous or sinister. There is worry that a homicidal worker may act out the anger that is felt throughout the organization. Suspicion tends to fall on workers who do not fit the conventional mold—such as an employee with a flamboyant manner of speaking. Parallels to the past become disturbingly apparent as the phenomenon of witch-hunting makes an appearance in the modern workplace.

A case in point occurred at National Communications—known as NatCom—a company that provides telephone service to a five-state area. Some years ago, an employee had carried out a threat to kill a co-worker. Although the murder was not committed at the workplace, company executives moved quickly to develop a violence prevention program. A policy was drafted, training materials were produced, and representatives of the Security, Human Resources, and Health and Safety Departments were designated as the team responsible for managing crises. Despite these initial steps, however, the policy was not implemented. The "team" never met or developed plans for responding to a threat or an act of violence. The policy was not publicized or brought to the attention of management personnel.

In the early 1990s, deregulation of its industry had forced NatCom to downsize significantly. Repeated thinning of the ranks had engendered demoralization and resentment. The loss of many colleagues left the survivors burdened with increased work responsibilities and unsure about their own futures. The line and mid-level managers in particular had begun to mistrust the company and felt out of touch with their superiors. At the same time, upper-level managers sensed that their subordinates had become remote. Tension in most departments ran high.

Joyce McCarthy was a 24-year veteran at NatCom. An energetic, outgoing woman in her late forties, Joyce had advanced from an entry-level job to a line management position. Joyce was a colorful, outspoken person who was unafraid to make references to sex and violence in her everyday speech. Even her friends would shake their heads when Joyce expressed herself in a particularly uninhibited manner. Although she had been talking that way during the entire quarter century that she had been with the company, it was her turn of phrase that ultimately led to her downfall. Here is a week-by-week account:

Week One

Wednesday, 3 P.M. During a conversation with co-workers, Joyce remarked that she would "blow away" the manager who had presided over many of the staff cuts if he "got in my face." The remark was overheard by three women who worked in the department. Aware of the tension in the office and having just seen a television program about workplace violence, the women felt that they should report what they heard. They told Ron Smith, who headed the department, about Joyce's remark.

Thursday, 9 A.M. Ron took the report seriously but, owing to the obscurity of company policy on such matters, was unsure of what to do. He had received no instructions or training. Ron called the medical director for advice. Finding him unavailable, Ron talked to Donna Logan, a social worker in the Medical Department. Donna advised Ron to have Joyce assessed by Psychological Associates, a firm that had contracted with the company to perform mental health services. Donna's advice was predicated on a belief that a "fitness-for-duty" evaluation was supposed to be administered whenever a behavioral or physical condition might impair job functioning

Thursday, 1 P.M. At Ron's request, Cathy Perkins, who was Joyce's friend and supervisor, had lunch with her. The supervisor let Joyce know that certain co-workers, who went unnamed, had been frightened by the remark about shooting a manager. As a result, Joyce would have to submit to a psychological evaluation in order to determine if she posed a threat. Cathy assured Joyce that she considered the charges ridiculous and hoped that her friend would cooperate. Joyce agreed to the evaluation.

Friday, 10 A.M. The receptionist at Psychological Associates handed Joyce a stack of forms to complete. They included a four-page personal and medical history questionnaire and a document authorizing release of information to her employer. Joyce was taken aback; she had not been warned that the evaluation would entail such a sacrifice of her personal privacy. She refused to sign the release but was interviewed anyway. Psychological Associates notified the company of the refusal and omitted the results of the interview. Joyce also was unaware of the results.

Week Two

Monday, 10 A.M. Joyce reported to work. She was summoned to the Security Department, where she was charged with threatening a member of management. Joyce protested that her remark was a jest, that she intended no harm, and that her extravagant turns of phrase had never alarmed anyone. She was unaware of any policy prohibiting loose talk. Nevertheless, she was suspended for refusing to complete the forms at the psychologist's office. She agreed to sign the release and to complete a standard psychological test, the Minnesota Multiphasic Personality Inventory (MMPI).

Wednesday, 9 A.M. Joyce returned to Psychological Associates and took the MMPI. By now confused and anxious, she waited to be informed of the results and to be called back to work.

Thursday, 4 P.M. Although a written report was not yet available, a social worker from Psychological Associates told Donna that there was no evidence of Joyce's being a danger to the workplace. For some reason,

Donna made no attempt to notify Ron or any other manager about that determination.

Week Three

Monday, 11 A.M. Ron met with Jane Hicks, the security manager, who had transferred from the Accounting Department two years earlier. Jane recounted a few rumors about Joyce that had been relayed by other employees. They portrayed her as highly emotional in general and particularly unstable in the immediate aftermath of cancer surgery. There were reports that she talked about bringing a knife to work.

Since Donna had not passed the word along, both executives were unaware that the evaluation by Psychological Associates revealed no signs of danger. Ron's meeting notes read: "We still do not have a report on the threat of violence from the evaluation." In the absence of any information to the contrary, Ron and Jane concluded that Joyce might be mentally unbalanced. They saw reason to take her threats seriously. They were supported by the Human Resources Department, which believed that the *lack* of an evaluation argued in favor of suspension: "Since Joyce has not completed the evaluation, it's in our best interests, until we know, to remove the employee from the workplace; to secure the workplace for the other employees."

By the time the meeting was held, Joyce, who had heard nothing from the employer since her second visit to Psychological Associates, was experiencing crying spells and loss of appetite. In the afternoon, she called the psychologist's office and was informed that the results of the MMPI were "satisfactory."

Wednesday, 10 A.M. Ron suspended Joyce for three weeks without pay "due to the seriousness of her statements." As a condition for return to work, Joyce would be required to attend a class on getting along with others. Ron cited the company's workplace violence policy as the reason for the suspension, although he admitted that the policy had never been shared with the employees.

Joyce's emotional condition deteriorated rapidly. She suffered dramatic weight loss, uncontrolled crying, and severe depression. She began seeing a psychological counselor of her own for treatment.

Week Five

Joyce's primary care physician wrote to the company that she was experiencing extreme stress and that he would not release her to return to work at the end of the suspension. Joyce filed a claim for disability based on her emotional condition. The company, meanwhile, had finally received the formal report from Psychological Associates. It stated that Joyce was not a danger, was mentally normal, and was able to work. On the basis of the report, the company asked Joyce to return to Psychological Associates once again—this time to verify that she was qualified for the disability benefits that she now claimed.

Week Six

Joyce's physician wrote the company that she was totally disabled and that she "might never recover from the emotional trauma she has experienced." The company offered Joyce a disability retirement, which she accepted.

Week Twenty-Five

Six months later, Joyce was still being treated for depression. Barely able to leave her home, let alone work, she brought a legal action against NatCom, claiming constructive dismissal (i.e., that she was forced out of the job). The legal papers listed eleven claims for relief under federal employment regulations; the alleged violations included harassment and discrimination on account of a perceived disability—namely, emotional instability. Joyce also asserted that the company was negligent in the way it investigated the purported threat and used psychological testing. She faulted the company for failing to disclose its violence policy to employees, and her lawyer wrote that the company "breached its fiduciary duty to plaintiff as a long-term employee to understand her personality, interview fully her coworkers and supervisors, treat her with the respect she deserved, and maintain her dignity as a hard-working, loyal twenty-four year employee."

The case was submitted to binding arbitration. Ten days of hearing took place over three months. The arbitrator found for the company, asserting that the evidence had failed to demonstrate that the company violated antidiscrimination statutes.

Critical Decision Points

Failure to Implement the Workplace Violence Policy

In order to be effective, a workplace violence policy must include two components: (1) clearly defined criteria—an exact specification of the behaviors and situations that the policy covers, and (2) a set of procedures, including roles and responsibilities, to guide the actions of company personnel in responding to a perceived threat. The first component clearly was lacking in the NatCom policy. The kind of behavior that would be considered threatening or intimidating had not been explained at all or, in the words of several arbitration witnesses, communicated "poorly." The second policy component, that of procedures, also was absent. The informants who reported Joyce's troubling remark were motivated by a television program and were not complying with established company procedures, which were unknown to them. The company's uncoordinated response painfully illustrates that managers, too, were unaware of how to react in a manner that protected both the safety of the workplace and the rights of the suspect employee.

Although NatCom had taken an initial step toward preparing itself for a threat of violence, the company failed to follow through with crucial implementation steps. As a result, NatCom displayed two classic characteristics of a crisis-prone organization: reactivity and a leadership void. The impetus for a workplace violence policy was in itself reactive; the policy—a few barebones guidelines—was prompted by a murder. Many companies benefit from a bad experience, treating it as a "wake-up call." But without perseverance, policy initiatives fall flat. Although a crisis response team composed of Medical, Legal, Security, and Human Resources staff was supposedly standing by, the mechanism proved rudderless. When Joyce became an issue, no one knew who was responsible for activating the team.

Failure to Involve Upper-Level Management

Responsibility for responding landed haphazardly in the lap of Ron, who was only a middle manager and who had to improvise at every stage of the crisis. Deprived of adequate guidelines, Ron delegated responsibility downward, to his subordinates, without alerting upper management. Responsibility was dispersed among a number of individuals who failed to act in concert and allowed critical information to fall between the cracks.

At the Medical Department, Joyce's case was fumbled by a junior professional employee who was not a manager and who lacked specific experience or training in violence issues. In the Security and Human Resources Departments, similarly, inexperienced persons failed to assess the possible risk accurately and to disseminate the Psychological Associates report in a timely fashion. Consequently, basic errors were made—such as the failure to interview Joyce immediately and get her account of what she meant by her remark.

Distancing the Employee

A crisis-prone organization typically fails to give due weight to human concerns and to stay close to an employee whose risk level is being assessed. Although NatCom may have been justified in ordering a psychological evaluation, the employer should have helped Joyce feel comfortable with that often intimidating process. Rather than explain to her the nature of the allegations and the evaluation process, Ron shunted the matter to Medical, which in turn created even more distance by entrusting it to outsiders (Psychological Associates) .

For the employee, the investigation thus began as a mystifying and threatening experience, which cut her off from the persons to whom she normally reported. Although she was asked to cooperate with the psychological evaluation, its purpose was never explained to her face-to-face. Unless there is an acute situation (e.g., when a weapon is present or a specific intent to harm has been articulated), an employee should be approached directly before the need for evaluation by outside professionals is determined.

Failure to Obtain Informed Consent

Given the paucity of explanation, it is hardly surprising that Joyce, confronted with a raft of documents at Psychological Associates, refused at first to sign the consent form. No one had explained to her the distinction between a standard counseling or health care contact, the purpose of which is therapeutic, and an evaluation for the purpose of determining whether the workplace is endangered. In the latter, the results are not confidential. Had a proper explanation been given, she might not have balked when confronted with a release form. She would have been prepared to give "informed consent," a crucial element in danger assessment. In fact, NatCom's rules for "fitness-for-duty" examinations provided that informed consent must be obtained *before* the employee reports for the examination.

Reliance on a Conventional Medical Assessment

It was the junior professional employee in the Medical Department who largely shaped the company's response to the possible threat posed by Joyce. Donna concluded that the appropriate step was a form of fitness-for-duty examination, a conventional occupational health assessment—in this instance focusing on the employee's mental status. Such an assessment is well suited to determining if an employee who has been ill or injured has recovered sufficiently to resume job duties. When the company asked Joyce to visit Psychological Associates in Week Five, for example, it was to evaluate her claimed disability—in principle a proper use of a fitness exam. A fitness examination, however, is not adequate to evaluate a perceived threat, because the issue is not the employee's health status but the safety of the entire workplace. The inquiry requires consideration of many nonhealth-related factors.

If the statements attributed to Joyce were in fact uttered and if they suggested a possible danger, she should have been informed that company policy required a professional risk assessment the results of which would be shared with the company. Since these steps were omitted, however, the employee was kept in the dark, where she became alienated and eventually traumatized. In this instance, the company was fortunate, because the employee was not dangerous. Had Joyce really posed a threat, the delays and miscues would have significantly *increased* the risk of violence.

Failure to Consider the Results of the Evaluation

Once the evaluation was completed, there were fateful gaps in the transmission of the results. Crucial information was not shared among decision makers in a timely fashion. Although Psychological Associates thoroughly explored the question of danger and found that Joyce did not pose a risk, the results of the evaluation somehow failed to reach key decision makers for weeks.

A suspension was imposed, therefore, under the erroneous assumption that the level of risk remained unknown. As a result, the company shattered the career of a long-service employee without benefit of the assessment that it originally considered essential. The news that the psychologist found no grounds for concern did not reach the employer for another month, by which time the trauma of job loss had overwhelmed Joyce.

Mishandling of the Security Investigation

The Security Department as well as the Medical Department was a weak link in the chain of decision making. Security Manager Hicks had no experience in law enforcement or violence risk management. Her preparation consisted of two weeks of orientation after her transfer from Accounting.

Owing to inadequate background, her approach was riddled with inadequacies. For example, there was no effort to find out if Joyce had any history of violent or threatening behavior, even though that is among the most important considerations in assessing potential for violence. Since the company managers clearly were aware of rumors about ominous behavior, it was incumbent on them to find out the facts. The security manager's answers revealed her unfamiliarity with violence-related issues and the extent to which her decisions were based on flimsy premises. The effect on the case was profound, because Human Resources often deferred to Security. When they could not answer a question at the arbitration hearing, Human Resources representatives would typically reply that "Security was handling that."

Afterword: The Lessons Learned

When she said she would "blow away" the manager, Joyce was voicing a rage silently felt by employees throughout the company because they viewed downsizing as a betrayal of loyal workers. Managers were well aware of that sentiment. A plausible explanation of the outcome of her case is that it expressed managers' unconscious fears that the rage would some day erupt into violence.

Such free-floating fear tends to focus on a person who seems to deviate from the mainstream. In seventeenth-century Massachusetts, demonic powers were ascribed to persons who were perceived as deviating from religious orthodoxy. Today, demonic qualities, linked to a potential for violence, are sometimes attached to persons who exhibit mood swings, unusual exuberance, or momentary outbursts. Just as the "witch" became the embodiment of what was feared in Salem (Satan), Joyce became the embodiment of what was dreaded at NatCom (the wrath of employees outraged by downsizing). Because of worry that an employee may run amok, such behavior can be wrongly interpreted as a "red flag" that merits expulsion or punishment.

In a calmer time, Joyce's tendency to give vent to her feelings was treated as a mere idiosyncrasy. In a stressful period of economic dislocation, however, it attracted suspicion and triggered extreme measures. Once identified as a potential danger, Joyce became stigmatized and ostracized. She was kept at arm's length and fobbed off on strangers (the outside psychological consultants). Unverified rumors were readily accepted as fact, and sanctions were invoked without anyone's bothering to read her psychological evaluation. The most persuasive pieces of evidence, the favorable psychological assessment and the absence of past violence, were neglected, as was the finding that her customary outspokenness had never gone beyond mere talk.

NatCom's managers were not motivated by personal animosity toward Joyce, nor did they intentionally target her for termination. Their unintentional blunders prevented her from shedding the suspicion that she was dangerous and regaining the employer's trust. Because of an exaggerated sense of danger lurking in the workforce, Joyce was not treated with the respect and concern that normally would be accorded an employee whose 24-year career was at stake.

Regrettably, the company had learned nothing from the fatality years before and was no better prepared when Joyce's alleged threat surfaced. Indeed, the earlier incident may have heightened the feeling of insecurity and eased the way to the suspension.

The arbitrator's decision should have been of little comfort to the company. The arbitrator ruled that the treatment of Joyce violated no laws. But there can be little doubt that Joyce's downfall violated the sensibilities of the surviving employees. NatCom not only lost a good employee needlessly, but it also heightened the demoralization linked to the downsizing.

The only safeguard against witch-hunting is a well-established set of procedures that ensure fairness, adequate gathering of facts and informed decision making. The procedures must be well known; an obscure memo will not do in a time of emergency. Teamwork arrangements, including coordination with outside service providers, must be made well in advance and diligently monitored during a crisis. It is also crucial that an employer implement programs to help employees at all levels deal positively with organizational change so that they are less resentful and their leaders less edgy.

CHAPTER 14

The Case of the Menacing Mortgage Broker

Scott Southwell had worked in the small mortgage department of Pequot National Bank for somewhat less than two years. He had been a so-so performer—clearly capable but erratic. He was considered touchy by co-workers.

The bank had been striving to increase the volume of mortgage business, and the department was called upon to speed up the pace of application processing, a task that involved complex and painstaking calculations. There were signs that the workload intensification was getting to Scott, a single man in his late thirties. He complained of being pushed too hard and seemed to create needless delay. Several of the other clerks in the department, who were mainly young women, felt uncomfortable in his presence. In fact, when the deadline for the department's annual report was approaching, he flew into a rage. Dorothy Hotchkiss, a fellow member of the department, reported the incident to Julie Braden, the bank's human resources director, saying that he often behaved that way when he was stressed by the workload. But this time he seemed more frustrated than usual, and blurted out: "If you see me come in one day with my Uzi, you'll know to run for cover."

Wary of Scott's temper, Dorothy asked that her report be kept confidential. Julie agreed. At Scott's periodic performance review a week later, Julie

referred obliquely to "inappropriate interaction with peers that was causing a tense environment." She explained that his attempts at humor could
be considered out of keeping with a business environment. Scott was upset and puzzled by her comments.

A few months later, Scott returned from a weekend trip, during which
he had been stranded by a car breakdown. He was angry and on edge. In
the cafeteria at lunchtime, he recounted his experience to a group of co-
workers that included John Evans, who was in charge of building maintenance. Trying to cheer him up, John told a similar "horror story" involving a car.

Scott apparently felt that he was being ridiculed by John. He said nothing in the lunchroom, but as he was leaving the building that evening,
he encountered John in the elevator. Scott lost control and pinned John
against the wall. With a wild look in his eyes, Scott announced that he
would kill the maintenance man if he ever talked to Scott like that again.

John's account of the run-in reached Julie the following day, prompting
her to call a friend, Dr. Barry Peters, a consulting psychologist. "Oh, by the
way," Julie said in concluding her description of Scott's behavior, "he often
wears military fatigues and dog tags to work," testing the limits of the relaxed company dress code for employees whose jobs entailed no direct
contact with customers. She did not think he had been in the military,
however. "And he's a loner," Julie said. "Doesn't that fit some sort of profile? Should we be worried?"

On the basis of his behavior alone, Dr. Peters told the manager, Scott
gave cause for concern. He advised her to respond to Scott's conduct directly and immediately, but he reserved judgment about whether any
danger existed. He would need to determine systematically whether Scott
posed a genuine risk. In addition, the bank would have to reassure the employees who were frightened by Scott. Dorothy and John had to be told
that an investigation was under way, that their safety was paramount, and
that they would be notified if, at any point in the process, Scott was deemed
a threat to their safety.

Laying the Groundwork

Julie asked Dr. Peters to meet with Scott at once to assess whether
he was dangerous. But the psychologist insisted that Julie first explain to
Scott why his behavior was unacceptable.

When Scott was called to Julie's office, the bank's security officer was
stationed discreetly in an adjoining room. Julie told Scott that they had
received reports of his menacing behavior. She described the incidents,

and explained that verbal or physical threats were a serious breach of the bank's rules, regardless of whether he intended to harm his co-workers. He was advised that disciplinary action could result but that a decision was being withheld, pending the outcome of an investigation. As part of the investigation, Dr. Peters would interview him and other employees. Given the seriousness of the reports and the potential risk, he was warned, his continued employment was predicated on his cooperation with the investigation.

Scott's reaction was curious: he was mystified and surprised. He had no memory of talking to Dorothy about an Uzi or threatening John. Scott seemed calm, engaged, and accepting of the need to pursue these reports. He agreed to meet with Dr. Peters, who had been called to the bank.

Dr. Peters had already spoken with Scott's co-workers, who painted a picture of a socially uncomfortable and immature man. He took offense easily but generally suppressed his anger—until it erupted in unpredictable outbursts. Although they did not consider him capable of violence, the co-workers worried about his emotional volatility and feared that he might "snap."

The Interview

Scott walked into the meeting with Dr. Peters mistrustful and guarded. He was slightly built and looked considerably younger than his actual age. Dr. Peters quickly made it plain his main purpose was to listen to what Scott had to say; others would decide whether Scott would keep his job. Dr. Peters expressed interest in the employee's background, experience at work, and life outside of work.

Scott relaxed and became quite forthcoming. Typically, employees in his situation acknowledge the statements attributed to them but assert that they were taken out of context or too literally. They may also claim that they were misquoted or their words distorted. Scott, however, continued to insist that he could not recall the incidents that had been described. Dr. Peters believed him and suspected that some kind of psychological or neurological condition might be at work, producing uncontrollable emotional states or explosive episodes that were dissociated from his consciousness.

Scott's description of his earlier life provided another clue. A history of failures at school and parental disapproval suggested an undetected learning disability. The associated neurological and psychological impairments might have contributed to chronic problems with stress, relationships, and handling anger or frustration.

Dr. Peters asked if there were any history of violent behavior or thinking, or if Scott had been exposed to violence and abuse at home or elsewhere. Did he have violent thoughts or plans? Did Scott have access to weapons? Had he experienced depression, suicidal or irrational thoughts, or auditory hallucinations (hearing voices)? Had he ever been treated for psychological symptoms? He answered all those questions in the negative.

Dr. Peters ventured that Scott may have been struggling for most of his life with learning and intellectual performance deficits that caused him stress at work. The unrecalled outbursts might be related to that long-term syndrome. Scott reacted to the Peters diagnosis as if a light had been turned on in a dark room. He welcomed the doctor's insights and felt comfortable about his sharing them with management.

Dr. Peters told Julie that there was little risk of violence. But Scott's apparent inability to control or even recall his moments of rage clearly created an ominous atmosphere in his work group and lowered morale. The psychologist recommended that Scott be granted paid medical leave, an option in the bank's health benefit package, in order to undergo a full medical-psychological assessment at a nearby university hospital that specialized in identifying cognitive and neurological impairments. The assessment would provide complete personality and vocational aptitude studies. The benefit plan did not cover such studies, but the bank would agree to pay for them anyway. A decision about possible discipline or discharge would be deferred, pending the outcome of the assessment.

Dr. Peters arranged to meet with Scott periodically so that he could provide support, monitor his condition, and collaborate with the specialist performing the assessment. When the assessment was completed, in about two to four weeks, Dr. Peters would interpret it for Scott and discuss with him the recommendations that would be made to the bank.

Julie informed the other mortgage department employees that Scott would be absent for a while. Scott's privacy was being respected, they were told, but any information that involved their safety would be communicated to them at once. Management would ensure that they were not exposed to any danger while working at Pequot National.

Results of the Assessment

The results of the psychological and career assessment confirmed Dr. Peters's preliminary diagnosis and illuminated the source of Scott's difficulties on the job. Scott's brain functioning was markedly deficient in the areas of memory, information processing, and recognition of facial expressions and emotional cues. In effect, Scott suffered from a learning disability. It had affected a wide range of cognitive tasks since childhood but had escaped notice.

In the opinion of the psychologist, Scott's deficit interfered with his ability to function in the mortgage department, a job that called for good memory and high-level information processing. Although he had managed to compensate for his limitations, they often produced sheer frustration and unbearable stress, particularly on occasions such as the bank's drive to increase mortgage volume. Over time, his deficits in understanding interpersonal cues had contributed to severe unease with people and a crushing sense of inferiority.

Scott's susceptibility to job-induced stress had combined with his difficulties in social interaction and his low self-esteem to produce the outbursts that had alarmed his workmates. Dr. Peters concluded that it would be in Scott's interest to resolve through counseling the emotional issues that resulted from the learning disability. In the meantime, the psychologist recommended, he should reevaluate his career path in the light of his condition.

After considering the assessment and Dr. Peters's interpretation of it, the bank decided that Scott would be unable to reintegrate into the department. The decision meshed with Scott's own determination to take time away from the demands of a job and reevaluate his life and career plans. He returned to his family home in a neighboring state, enlightened about his own condition, and better prepared to make the choices that would set him on a successful path.

Critical Decision Points

Delayed Confrontation

When the Uzi remark was brought to Julie's attention, the human resources manager acquiesced in Dorothy's wish to remain anonymous. Although a well-meaning decision, it was dangerous and misguided. Scott should have been immediately confronted and told in unmistakable terms that his conduct was unacceptable. Julie's cryptic reference to "humorous comments" served only to confuse him; he could not fathom the meaning of her remark. Inasmuch as Scott's memory was impaired, offering him only vague hints rather than specifying what troubled his co-workers did him a disservice and delayed treatment of the underlying condition.

Julie assumed that Scott meant to be funny when he talked about bringing his Uzi to work. But since he had never been asked about the remark, there was no basis for that assumption. In fact, the official record of

Dorothy's complaint noted that she was frightened by Scott's words because he looked serious and angry, "as though he really meant it." Had Scott's behavior resulted in actual violence, the bank would have been negligent for failing to respond vigorously to the first hint of threatening behavior.

By minimizing the seriousness of the Uzi incident, the bank left itself open to more serious episodes. Dorothy's report should have been considered a distress warning, and she should have been told that in the course of protecting possible targets of violence it may not be possible to hide the identity of complainants. Safety is the primary concern once the employer is notified of menacing behavior, and common sense dictates that no one, including an informant, is safe when a disturbing report is buried or handled ineffectually.

Once informed of a possible threat or danger, the employer must take action proportional to the seriousness of the report. This principle should be enshrined in company policy, leaving no room for ambiguity or "judgment calls."

Seeking Help from a Behavioral Specialist

Given the worrisome nature of Scott's behavior, the employer wisely called for outside help. Still, Dr. Peters's intercession was merely a chance occurrence, stemming from the acquaintanceship between Julie and the psychologist. The company lacked an EAP or any other regular access to mental health or specialized medical care. Luck therefore played a large role—too large, in fact. Like many other employers, the bank had no contingency plan. The bank's executives began searching for sound advice only when they found themselves facing a crisis. They were fortunate to find the help they needed; many employers are not so lucky.

Preparing for Behavioral Assessment

It was important for the employer to prepare Scott for the meeting with Dr. Peters. Fairness required that he be notified of the suspicion, that he be given an opportunity to respond, and that he be informed about the investigation process. The notification should have occurred as soon as the Uzi incident came to light. But concern for Scott's rights was not the only reason for notification. All too often, employers faced with a possible threat of violence abruptly force the suspect employee into an intimidating encounter with a stranger. The employee typically feels confused and insecure in dealing with a consultant from outside, leading to several untoward results.

First, a sense of isolation, mistrust, and helplessness is conducive to violence. Employees who are at risk for violence or behaving in a threatening manner need the reassurance of direct contact with the employer. Second, distancing the employee puts out of reach the most important source of first-hand information, whereas careful and considerate treatment maximizes the chances of candor and cooperation. The employee's response when confronted with direct questions about allegedly threatening behavior may provide insight into his or her attitudes and relationships with coworkers. Simple misunderstandings may be quickly resolved. The employee's immediate response is usually less self-conscious than the story later presented in a behavioral assessment, when the person's mental health, dangerousness, and overall fitness to remain on the job are explicitly at issue. The employee is likely to treat that session as a test, not as an opportunity for dialogue.

The employer should make the assessment as nonforbidding as possible. The employee should be informed of the purpose of the interview, the safeguards for privacy, the extent to which the information will be shared, and the decision-making process that will ensue. Because of its hesitation when Dorothy first complained, Pequot National found itself at a disadvantage.

Informing Other Employees

While the assessment of potential danger was underway, the concerns of other bank employees had to be addressed. They were told exactly what they needed to know: that their fears about safety were being taken seriously and that they would be kept informed as the assessment progressed. The assurance minimized anxiety and maximized confidence in management.

Management also displayed admirable fairness by balancing Scott's claims to privacy against his fellow workers' claims to safety. The bank could thus justifiably say that it had carefully protected his rights while satisfying its obligation to inquire into a potential threat. Other employees could take comfort in the awareness that their privacy and dignity would be respected similarly should they be accused. The employer's actions were significant because qualities such as credibility and loyalty are tested during a crisis generated by a threatening employee.

Taking Control of the Assessment Process

A crucial ingredient of the amicable outcome was the employer's willingness to pay for a specialized assessment that the normal health care benefit structure did not cover. By investing in a thorough medical exploration of the employee's condition, the bank assured itself adequate information on which to base a decision about Scott's future. It also won the employee's cooperation, because he, too, had something to gain—insight at last into a condition that had plagued him all his life. Because the employer remained connected to him at every stage of the process, Scott understood what was happening at all times and had a stake in the outcome. He felt protected, rather than threatened, valued rather than rejected. The process remained nonconfrontational, and the employee acquiesced because there was a mutual interest in probing his condition.

Afterword: Promoting Safety and Self-Awareness

Although accused of making threatening statements in the workplace, Scott left feeling grateful to his employer. Yet here was a case that seemed at first the classic employer's nightmare. An employee had made two direct threats. His behavior was erratic and frightening. He was a white male, isolated and with few, if any, social or family supports. Many employers would have terminated Scott immediately.

Had Scott been discharged in that way, there would have been troublesome consequences. Employees would have been fearful that Scott, potentially violent and unstable, might seek revenge on those responsible for his firing. Albeit rare and unlikely, the scenario would play vividly in their minds: a threatening employee is sent out the door—only to burst back through it with a spray of bullets from an automatic weapon. The fear would not be limited to his immediate circle. Rumors would spread the story from department to department. What was really known about Scott? Was he not capable of anything? Did he not fit the profile? Even the most frightening version of the tale might seem plausible, because the employer would have known little about the man it had unceremoniously put onto the street.

By the same token, when the encounter with John Evans was reported, the company could delay no longer. Julie could not afford to repeat the mistake of months earlier, when she failed to confront Scott about the Uzi remark. This time management was prepared to take action. To their credit, company officials paused to secure guidance from an authoritative source. Even more to their credit, they were willing to invest the time, the resources, and—most important—the personal attention to Scott that was required for a positive outcome.

Ultimately, the bank achieved its primary goal, which was assuring the safety and health of its employees. When the evaluation was complete, there were ample grounds for feeling confident that Scott represented no threat and would not become vengeful. In the process, the employer performed an invaluable service for Scott, helping him toward self-understanding and career renewal. The moral is that immediate discharge may seem the most prudent course, but the safest and most constructive approach for the long term is to take the time to understand a feared employee.

CHAPTER 15

The Case of the Ambiguous Alert

The monthly grievance meeting was being held in the principal's office at Orchard Valley High School. Jack Jason, the superintendent of the school district, was present, along with chemistry teacher Elliott Speth and Elliott's friend Randolph Nevins, who was the head of the Orchard Valley Education Association, the local chapter of the state teachers' union.

Elliott, a chemistry teacher for nearly 20 years, had filed a grievance, protesting that the school authorities were compiling a secret dossier on him. At the meeting, the superintendent acknowledged that several letters had been received from female students, complaining that Elliott had persistently paid inappropriate attention to them. He would hold their hands, play with their hair in the lunchroom, and insist on dancing with them when he was chaperoning school functions. He was also said to have invited females to the movies and made suggestive comments. In one instance, he came uninvited to a girl's home.

After reviewing the complaints, he tried to explain his behavior, asserting that, "You guys don't understand." But he became frustrated. He put the letters down, stood up, and said, "Forget it . . . I can't take any more of this." He stalked out of the room.

Elliott drove home and ran up the stairs to the bedroom without bothering to take off his overcoat. His wife, Anne, who was an English teacher at the high school, heard him rummaging about in the drawers of a dresser. He came out of the room muttering about the school authorities, and hurried back down the stairs and out the door. He sped away in his car. Anne was alarmed, because she knew that her husband, who worried about break-ins, kept several guns for self-defense, including .44-caliber and .22-caliber revolvers, a .357 Magnum, a 9 mm Browning semiautomatic pistol, and an AK-47 assault rifle. Sensing his anger, she decided to follow him to the high school in her own car to make sure that he did not do anything foolish.

But first she phoned the regional headquarters of the statewide organization to which OVEA belonged and asked to speak with Phillip Inglesby, the union representative who served the Orchard Valley district as well as several others. Phillip was out of the office. He was 35 miles away, at the Spirit Lake School District office, negotiating a new contract for its teachers. The secretary promised to try to reach him with a message about Elliott.

The secretary dialed his cell phone number. When he heard the ring, Phillip was sitting at a table with the Spirit Lake officials. It was an inopportune moment, because the negotiators were just about to strike a bargain about pay for afterschool activities, one of the teachers' key demands. He said he would call back shortly. A few minutes later, with the deal made, he asked to be excused and phoned the secretary to clarify the situation at Orchard Valley.

The secretary relayed the message from Anne. Phillip decided that he had to warn the superintendent. He called Jack and told him that Elliott was angry and might be coming back to the school. After hanging up, Jack remarked that Phillip had "suggested that Elliott was going to do some harm to me" and that he "basically made a threat." Phillip had cautioned: "If I were you, I'd leave the office and see what happened."

About five minutes later, Elliott burst into the office and pulled a semiautomatic pistol from the inside pocket of his overcoat. Randolph tried to calm him. "You don't need to do this," he told the enraged teacher. Later Randolph recalled that Elliott had a "cold, determined look in his eye."

Elliott fired four shots into Jack's abdomen and also wounded Randolph and the principal, albeit less severely. When his ammunition clip was empty, his wife arrived. Elliott reloaded the gun and pointed it at her. Anne, along with Randolph, who was still conscious, begged her husband to put the gun down. Randolph appealed to the 13-year friendship that had existed between Elliott and him. Eventually, Elliott did relinquish the gun. With preternatural calm, the chemistry teacher walked to one of the school's science laboratories and sat down at a desk as if nothing had happened. Anne began giving first aid to the superintendent.

The office staff called the police, who found Elliott sitting in a laboratory, quietly reading papers. The superintendent had died, and Elliott was charged with murder. He was also charged with two counts of assault with attempt to do great bodily harm as well as three counts of possession of a firearm during commission of a felony. His lawyer argued at the trial that Elliott was not guilty by reason of diminished capacity and had no ability to conform his actions to the law. He told the court that Elliott was being treated by a psychiatrist for clinical depression at the time of the shooting and was taking the antidepressant Prozac.

Elliott was convicted, however, and received a mandatory sentence of life in prison without parole. "I do not hate you, I do not pity you, I fear you," the judge said. "It's important that you never set foot in this community free again."

But the legal consequences of the attack were not confined to the criminal sphere. After Elliott had gone to prison, the teachers' union was sued for civil damages. The widow of the murdered superintendent brought the action on behalf of Jack's estate, alleging that the union—and Phillip in particular—had been guilty of negligence.

Mrs. Jason alleged that the union was aware of Elliott's intention to attack the superintendent. She accused the union of downplaying the immediacy and lethality of the threat in order to protect a member from possible professional and/or criminal culpability. Her lawyers argued that a variety of duties arose from the "special relationship" between a labor union and an employer. Among those duties, they claimed, were the following:

- A duty to warn of impending danger without delay.
- A duty to refrain from unnecessary discussion and conferencing within the union before taking action.
- A duty to provide an adequate, complete, and detailed warning, clearly explaining the fact that Elliott was armed and conveying a sense of urgency to the people in the principal's office.
- A duty to train its members in the proper handling of threats of violence.
- A duty to maintain a policy of placing the personal safety of employers at a higher value than the labor-related interest of the union members.
- A duty to contact law enforcement as soon as it learned of the danger.

The union argued that it was blameless: it had warned the superintendent, and he failed to heed the warning. Many years of litigation lay ahead. A key issue would be whether Phillip should have specifically mentioned in his warning call to the superintendent that Elliott had a gun. The union representative insisted that he was unaware of any gun. But the attorneys for the estate claimed that those who were in the room with Phillip when he received the call from the union secretary were prepared to testify that he spoke about a gun. The case was dismissed at the trial court stage, but the estate vowed to press on with appeals.

Critical Decision Points

Feeding a Delusion

This case is unusual in that a union rather than the employer was asked to accept blame for the alleged negligence of an employee. But clearly much of the incident was beyond the ability of the union to change. As in the Hartford lottery incident (see Chapter 5), the violent employee was someone who was receiving treatment for clinical depression, unbeknownst to the union, yet lived with a working gun collection. Long before she decided to sound a warning about her husband, Anne should have reduced the size of the home arsenal or at least kept it under lock and key so that it was not readily available to him when he was in an agitated state.

In addition, the employer allowed the student complaints to accumulate without confronting Elliott. It was Elliott who initiated the meeting at which the complaints were revealed, triggering the lethal reaction. The complaints were telltale signs that something had changed for the worse—he had taught for nearly 20 years without incident—yet the school authorities never inquired into the teacher's changed behavior. In fact, their very reluctance to act promptly on the complaints fed Elliott's paranoid delusion that they were conspiring against him by building a dossier.

Creating a Conflict of Duties

The suit presented the union with the possibility that it might be caught in a conflict of legal obligations. The union, which had a duty to provide the employee with fair representation, might find itself with a countervailing obligation to warn others about the same employee. Many union officials are hesitant to take action against a member, even when that person threatens the safety of other members of the union, as the

Royal Oak incident demonstrates (see Chapter 3). The source of the dilemma was Anne's decision to phone the regional headquarters of the union, rather than the police or the school. No doubt she felt comfortable talking to the union because she was a teacher herself, but her message had to be routed via a secretary to a union representative who was preoccupied with negotiations in another district. The message may have lost clarity, given the circumstances, or the representative may have been too immersed in his immediate task to appreciate the potential gravity of the situation in Orchard Valley.

Failure to Notify Police

Distracted by his bargaining duties, Phillip neglected to call the police and failed to impress upon the superintendent the imminent danger he faced. However, the union representative did suggest that the superintendent leave his office, which should have signaled that the threat was serious, even if Phillip did not specifically mention the gun. Notifying the supervisor that Elliott was armed might have been tantamount to spreading panic recklessly if Phillip were genuinely uncertain. Clearly, the most prudent course of action for the representative would have been to err on the side of safety by alerting law enforcement and by exaggerating rather than downplaying the degree of danger. It is conceivable that his failure to do either was influenced, perhaps on an unconscious level, by a conflict of obligations.

Failure to Be Prepared

This case underscores the importance of policies to direct the actions of key players whenever there is a possibility of violence. Had members of the school administration noticed signs that Elliott was becoming unstable? Did they give him a wide berth because he was intimidating, or because they were reluctant to confront him? An agreement between stakeholders about how to act in special circumstances would have removed the "burden of ambiguity" in this matter. School and union officials both would have been clear about their obligation to respond to warning signs and to act diligently in case of an actual threat.

If the parties had been better prepared, they would most likely have initiated a coordinated intervention into Elliott's case earlier in the process. School administrators, in cooperation with the local union—led by Elliott's friend Randolph—could have paid direct attention to Elliott's behavior and approached him in a nonadversarial context. Inquiries into his emotional state might have yielded important information, and, with his permission, the union or the employer could have contacted his wife or his psychiatrist. Had information about Elliott's paranoia and his gun collection come to light along with his risky behaviors at school, action could have been taken to protect him and others from the disaster that ensued.

PART IV

BENEFITING FROM EXPERIENCE: STRATEGIES FOR PREVENTING VIOLENCE

CHAPTER 16

Understanding Violent Behavior

To understand violence in the workplace, it is necessary to look at the individual in the context of the system in which his or her behavior is occurring. Type III workplace violence—in which an employee or former employee acts in a threatening or destructive manner toward fellow employees, superiors, or the property of the workplace—is always the result of the interaction of violence-prone individuals and a system that provokes them and allows their proclivities to become manifest. Unfortunately, there is a tendency to focus on only one of these elements—the employee. An employee's behavioral background or history of violence are crucial elements, but they are not the whole picture. It is necessary to examine the contextual factors, especially in a "crisis-prone" organization.

Most explanations have focused on the causes of violent behavior. That narrow focus unnecessarily limits the inquiry. A more significant question must be asked: how well does the system deal with the symptoms of stress in an individual? Rather than focusing on cause alone, we should examine the capacity of the organization to respond to the signs of stress or potential trouble, whatever the possible causes.

Imagine yourself walking down the street with a young child in your care. Suddenly, a stranger appears, pushes you away, and attempts to run

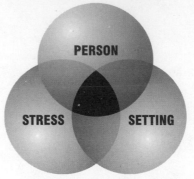

Figure 1. Sources of violent behavior

off with the child. Will you use all the physical force you can muster against this aggressor? Think about someone striking a loved one, or imagine being subjected day after day to abuse, hardship, or humiliation by a bully, and imagine what it would take for you reach the limits of your restraint. Violence is a natural human behavior, an attempt to respond to an unbearable stress. Each of us would resort to it if pushed to the limit.

Generally speaking, violence is most likely when three factors are conducive to it: the personality, the stress, and the setting or social context, as shown in Figure 1. The intersection of the three circles represents the danger zone.[1]

The Personality

Although unbearable stress can have a variety of outcomes, including serious or chronic physical illness, emotional breakdown, and suicide, for some persons violence is the most likely result. What personality factors determine that violence will be the outcome when stress is applied? The most important have to do with the individual's interpersonal functioning—the way that he sees himself in relationship to other people:

- Do his behaviors and styles tend toward understanding the point of view of others and reaching agreement, or do they involve control, manipulation, and intimidation?
- Is he able to take responsibility for what happens to him, or does he blame others or "the system" for his life problems?
- Is he capable of feeling guilt and shame, or is his sense of right and wrong determined by what he thinks he can get away with?

- Can he control his impulses, or does he act first and think later?
- Is there a history of violent behavior?
- How have his attitudes about the acceptability of violence been shaped by his cultural background or family experience?

The answers to these questions will all bear on the person's ability to withstand stress and to find acceptable, useful ways to deal with pressure and conflict. One set of answers will suggest that a person has basic skills for dealing with life's minor and major stresses, and that, in the face of challenges, he will remain connected to vital sources of support and will preserve positive means of coping. But if the answers tend in a different direction, a person will be apt to descend into deeper depression, social isolation, and helplessness. Taken together, these qualities increase the risk of violent or self-destructive behavior — or both.

The Stress

The risk of violence increases when a person with a predisposition for — or history of — violence is subjected to stress. In the workplace context, the most serious forms of stress usually have to do with loss of employment or income, humiliation, or isolation. The most potentially dangerous stresses are those that reduce or remove the underpinnings of the individual's physical, financial, and social well-being. Stress is typically associated with events such as loss of employment at mid or late career, injury or illness leading to a loss of self-esteem or control, and domestic or family problems.

When evaluating the potential for workplace violence, one looks in particular at the effects of stress on the individual's connection to interpersonal and organizational supports and on his sense of power and effectiveness. Some persons begin to be at risk for violent or threatening behavior when they feel powerless. They are struck by an overwhelming sense of desperation and an increasing sense that nothing can be done to change their situation. They are poorly equipped to maintain positive supports when things begin to go wrong.

Because he cannot easily understand his own contribution to his misfortune and instead blames others, the person at risk for violence progressively alienates those around him and uses up the resources and good will that might have supported him. In these situations, you will often hear managers or co-workers declare, "We are exhausted by this guy! There is really nothing more we can do for him." A union, exhausted and disgusted by never-ending appeals for help, may limit itself to perfunctory responses. That, in turn, leads to greater isolation and intensified feelings of desperation and depression.

The Setting

When an individual with a predisposition to violence is stressed beyond his ability to cope, two crucial ingredients for violence are present. But in order for the violence to occur, there must be a third factor: a failure of the workplace to recognize the signs of stress-related breakdown and to interrupt or retard the process. In other words, violence cannot occur unless it is allowed to occur. As the case studies demonstrate, in every story that ends in violence, there are several points at which intervention could have changed the outcome. The failure to stop the downward spiral contributes directly to the violent outcome.

An employer has little sway over the first circle, that of personality. Predisposing characteristics may be undetectable or inchoate at the time of hire. The employer may or may not have control over the second circle—the stress—because it may be intrinsic to the production process or the economic cycle, or it may involve factors—such as family issues, illness, or crime in the community—that are largely beyond the employer's ken. A *potential* for violence is generated by the interaction of the first and second circles, which may be beyond workplace control. But the potential can be realized only where they overlap with the third circle—the setting—and there the workplace does exercise considerable control.

Effective violence prevention depends, therefore, on the ability of the social or institutional setting, in this case the workplace, to recognize warning signs and to mediate the effect of stress on an individual at risk. In some cases, the workplace itself may be the source of the stress, so that modifying the setting may be particularly crucial in altering the outcome.

Figure 2 illustrates how the employer can make a difference in that third circle, the setting, through early awareness of a reaction to stress. At the left side of the diagram is the employee who is affected by one or more of several possible stresses. Depending on individual factors, he or she may respond by exhibiting any of the behaviors listed. Here are the warning signs, and here is where the crisis-prone and crisis-prepared organizations diverge.

The bottom portion of the chart demonstrates the disaster scenario, in which violence occurs because signs of distress are met by no response or the wrong kind of response. A crucial point of intervention, in which early symptoms might have been recognized and defused, has been missed or

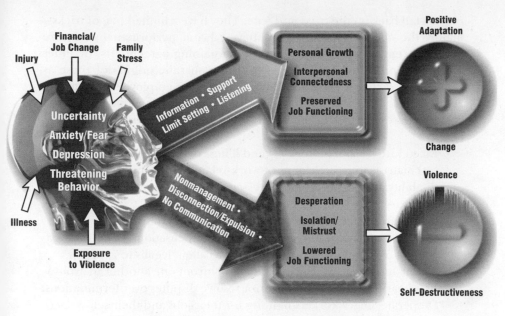

Figure 2. The effect of intervention on violence potential

mishandled. The at-risk individual moves, through increasing mistrust and isolation, to the violent or self-destructive finale. Having missed the opportunity to change the outcome, the organization is reduced to reactive measures. The alternative, shown in the top portion of the diagram, demonstrates how intervention can profoundly alter the outcome. Note that the outcome of "positive adaptation" or "change" may involve a separation from the workplace, just as "personal growth" in the intervening step may involve a painful confrontation with discipline or other responses to unacceptable behavior. The journey to a nonviolent outcome may be far from "warm and fuzzy" for all parties.

In the third circle in Figure 1, and in the crucial first response in Figure 2, is where the workplace can make a difference. The "violent employee" can be anyone. He or she has already been hired. Prevention lies in recognizing the need for a prompt and effective response as soon as signs of distress appear.

The Effect of Inertia

The primary barrier to effective response is the tendency to do things the way they have always been done. When there is a question of threatening behavior or when an act of violence has been committed, employers fall back on the tried and true. They have a limited bag of tricks—mainly the classic responses to behavioral and performance issues required by employment law, collective bargaining agreements, or illness and injury procedures. The legal and bureaucratic origins of these arrangements dictate the form and style of employer-employee relationships around these issues. Employer and employee are set against each other, and that paves the way for a disaster. Here are some prime examples:

- Faced with a claim of work-related illness or injury, employers engage psychiatrists to refute claims of work-related stress and psychological disability, turning an already stressed, unhappy employee into a legal adversary.
- Corporate legal departments appeal to worker compensation boards to deny or delay employees' claims for compensation. A complicated issue of occupational stress turns into a callow, legalistic struggle.
- Union and company representatives confront one another in arbitration hearings because they cannot resolve disputes over terminations. Desperate, angry workers fighting for their jobs and their self-respect are treated like pawns in struggles between warring parties.

These scenarios are not the exception, and they are not even unusual. They are, sadly, the normal and accepted methods for dealing with safety, behavioral, disciplinary, and health issues at work. They reflect fundamental legal principles underlying employment practice in the United States. In organized workplaces, union-management disputes are typically carried out in an atmosphere of mutual mistrust and strict control over information. In many organized and nonorganized settings, employers are advised by their attorneys to treat claims of psychological injury as potentially fraudulent. Occupational health procedures are designed to contain costs associated with medical care and lost work time. All of these practices and attitudes result in a distancing of the employee from his or her employer at a time when qualities of personal attention, careful case management, and enlightened compassion are most needed.

The result is that the employee whose life may have been ripped apart is relegated to the sidelines of an adversarial struggle that bears little relevance to his or her real issues. The languages of law, medicine, and government regulations do not speak to the reality of the employee's experience. These approaches do not provide the tools to understand and resolve the particular human problem that has produced the threat of violence. Indeed, remote, formalistic modes of dealing with problems actually exacerbate the conditions that breed violence and ensure that violence-inducing stress reactions are not detected in time to avoid casualties.

The post office shooting at Royal Oak, Michigan, provides a searing demonstration of this point. Thomas McIlvane, the letter carrier who killed four supervisors and then himself in 1991, spent eight years at the facility before being discharged. During that period, as McIlvane's threatening behavior escalated, the focus was on the collective bargaining agreement, federal disability statutes, and state and local laws governing criminal complaints. While argument flared around these issues, an already unbalanced individual, faced with a system that left him feeling increasingly powerless, was transformed into a man focused only on revenge. The persistent signals of danger were ignored. A dysfunctional employee was permitted to exploit the adversarial standoff between union and management. No one confronted the emerging menace. In effect, well-meaning persons paved the way for McIlvane's self-destruction and the destruction of others.

The Predictive Profile

A cartoon in the *New Yorker* magazine pictured a CEO notifying his deputy of a downsizing: "We've got to get rid of some people, Cosgrove," the executive barks at the surprised deputy. "Who are the least likely to come back and shoot us?" The scene is meant to be humorous, but it accurately portrays the mentality of those who believe in a "profile of the violent employee."

Prediction is an attractive concept that matches the current enthusiasm for screening. But the possibility of predicting which persons will commit violence has never been proved scientifically.[2] Nevertheless, the notion that violent individuals exhibit common characteristics has entrenched itself in popular mythology. The best-known profile—the white male loner who is a military veteran and gun enthusiast—is based on retrospective analysis and is too broad to have predictive value. The perpetrator of the Royal Oak postal massacre fitted that description, but so do millions of workers who are entirely peaceable. Multiple killers Matthew Beck (Hartford) and Arturo Torres (Santa Ana) both collected guns, but that is hardly an unusual passion in the land of the Second Amendment. As a labor neutral has pithily observed: "Most of us have had arbitrations where half of the work force would fit the profile, at least around deer hunting season."[3]

Profiles also raise serious ethical concerns. They could be used to weed out likely union supporters, identify potential whistleblowers, or even stigmatize groups on the basis of social or ethnic characteristics. In some versions of the profile, a personal history of labor-management disputes or low socioeconomic status is counted as a risk factor.

The American Psychiatric Association has argued, in a brief filed with the United States Supreme Court, that psychiatrists' predictions of future violence should not be relied upon in making legal determinations about the fate of a convicted defendant. As Justice Harry Blackmun observed, "The APA's best estimate is that two out of three predictions of long-term future violence made by psychiatrists are wrong."[4] According to John Monahan, a prominent student of predictability, clinical research "indicates that psychiatrists and psychologists are accurate in no more than one out of three predictions of violent behavior over a several year period among institutionalized populations," whose past behavior is well documented.[5] There is even less chance of correctly predicting the behavior of non-institutionalized persons, such as workers. Indeed, a group of medical and legal experts, writing in the *Journal of Forensic Sciences*, has concluded that "no professionally competent and ethically bound forensic psychiatrist or psychologist would ever claim a level of absolute certainty and confidence in the determination of either short- or long-term future violent behavior."[6]

In 1996, James J. McDonald Jr. and Paul R. Lees-Haley, a lawyer and psychologist respectively, published an article titled "Personality Disorders in the Workplace: How They May Contribute to Claims of Employment Law Violations."[7] The authors argued that many employees suffer from conditions such as Borderline Personality Disorder and Anti-Social Personality Disorder when they are hired and that these conditions can "cause an employee to misperceive the words or actions of supervisors or coworkers as malevolent." The upshot is claims of harassment and discrimination, say the authors. The logical inference from their argument is that psychological screening could be a means of precluding litigation against the company. Yet, apart from occasioning an unprecedented intrusion into the psyche, such screening would yield little benefit, because extreme behavior on the job is more likely to be the result of workplace stress than of pre-existing tendencies. In the Case of the Dangerous Dreams, for example, it is clear that the employees who exchanged fantasies about the supervisor were not delusional when they joined the utility company but developed bizarre ritual discourse as a strategy for coping with an unsympathetic manager.

Elite organizations that have traditionally hired according to a well-defined profile of supposedly desirable traits have not been immune from workplace violence. The highly selective Swiss Guard, the 100-man security force that has protected the Vatican since the sixteenth century, recruits according to strict guidelines; for one thing, only Roman Catholic males of Swiss nationality in their twenties are eligible. Yet in 1998 a corporal "embittered over a formal reprimand" used his service pistol to murder Lt. Col. Alois Estermann, the commander of the guard, along with the officer's wife. Another incident, involving a gun-brandishing renegade guardsman, occurred in 1959.[8]

Some proposed profiles are unduly mechanistic in their approach to what is, after all, a human phenomenon. Martin Blinder, a psychiatrist who practices in San Francisco, has constructed a profile "by which management can identify well in advance those employees most likely to engage in lethal acts of revenge."[9] He postulates that there are 18 traits conducive to lethality and that a person exhibiting "any 10 or more" should give rise to concern. Some of the traits on the Blinder list undoubtedly are associated with troubled personalities of certain kinds: for example, if an employee is convinced of being "surrounded by 'enemies'," or if he tends to "make co-workers . . . anxious." Other traits on the list, however, are dubious indicators of propensity for physical aggression. Many nondangerous persons "daily make mountains out of molehills" or express "approval of . . . capital punishment."

Belonging to a fringe rightwing group is considered a risk factor by Blinder, but membership in a fringe leftwing group carries no stigma in his eyes. Should we fear followers of the Aryan Nation but not the Red Army Faction, a group known throughout the world for politically inspired terrorism? The Blinder profile is an example of the futility of trying to predict violence "by the numbers." A rigid catalog of supposed predictive traits is no substitute for the exercise of informed and nuanced judgment.

A profile would be of scant benefit where the threat is from nonemployees, such as customers, whose access to the workplace cannot be controlled through psychological screening. Training supervisors to recognize profiles is therefore of little use as a countermeasure. Indeed, it is a "quick fix" solution that misleads by offering false assurance.

A more effective approach would be to train managers to recognize signals of distress in workers and customers as a complement to a well-planned system for early response to imminent crises. Managers could also be alerted to the significance of "flags"—changes in status that might betoken violent responses. The revenge of the deadbeat dad in Watkins Glen might have been forestalled had there been recognition that the garnishment of his wages was likely to spark an intemperate reaction. In the Hartford lottery incident, the return of the employee from a stress leave should have warranted close monitoring, especially since it was known that his failure to win promotion still rankled.

As we have seen earlier in this chapter, three conditions are necessary for violence: personality, stress, and setting. It makes more sense to use resources to ameliorate the stress and improve the setting than to exclude personalities that are presumed—on very little evidence—to be dangerous. The profile that is needed—the violence risk profile—focuses on the systemic failings, rather than on the flaws of individuals.

Psychiatric Disability

A relatively new concept is the notion of the worker with a "psychiatric disability." In the Case of the Menacing Mortgage Broker, had Scott not agreed to leave voluntarily, he might have been able to claim protected status under the Americans With Disabilities Act as a worker with a psychiatric disability. Guidelines issued in 1997 by the Equal Employment Opportunities Commission (see Appendix B) define a psychiatric disability as a "mental impairment that substantially limits one or more of the major life activities of [an] individual."[10] The impairment must be a psychological disorder or emotional or mental illness of long standing, typically one of those that are cataloged in DSM IV, the latest edition of the *Diagnostic and Statistical Manual*, a standard reference.

If Scott could show that his learning disability, memory lapses, and emotional outbursts amounted to such a disorder, he might be able to claim successfully that the employer was obligated to make a reasonable accommodation so that he could continue his employment with the bank. According to the guidelines, an employer must "provide a reasonable accommodation to the known physical or mental limitations of a qualified individual with a disability unless it can show that the accommodation would impose an undue hardship."[11] Of course, if Scott's condition were such that he would seriously disrupt the operations of the bank by continuing to have "rages," then the employer could plausibly argue that no reasonable accommodation was possible.

Some employers might argue that the risk of such a claim should make an employer wary of evaluating an employee like Scott. Certainly, an employer should avoid quick, irresponsible, and unprofessional speculations about an employee's mental state. Here, however, the employer was faced with behavior that was clearly disturbing. There had been no quick "lay diagnosis," and the employee had agreed to the evaluation. The risk that the employee would challenge the employer under the ADA was minimal, because he stood to gain real benefits and self-enlightenment. Furthermore, if challenged, the employer could have cited the duty to preserve safety.

According to the guidelines, employers can refuse to hire an applicant with a history of violence "only if the employer can show that the employment of the individual poses a direct threat." The employer must specify the behavior that poses the direct threat and assess the likelihood of violence occurring. Many employers have opposed the guidelines on the grounds that they might be held liable if the employee became violent again; it could be claimed that the employer had prior knowledge of a propensity for violence.[12]

A few *causes célèbres* have particularly alarmed employers. In one dispute, litigated in the federal courts of Florida, an employee was discharged for bringing a loaded gun to work, in violation of an employer policy prohibiting weapons. He was later hospitalized and found to be suffering from a "chemical imbalance." In his defense, the employee argued that the imbalance "caused him to exhibit poor judgment, but that his poor judgment was clearly a symptom of a mental or psychological disorder," entitling him to reasonable accommodation by the employer. He asked for the termination to be delayed while he underwent treatment.[13]

Commenting on this case, in which the employer ultimately prevailed, the EEOC opined that it has

> consistently maintained that an employer may hold all employees . . . to the same conduct standards. . . .This would certainly include rules prohibiting violence or the threat of violence in the workplace. Although an employer may be required to provide reasonable accommodation (when requested in advance) so that an individual can meet conduct standards, an employer would not be required to rescind discipline for misconduct. Therefore, it appears that this employer could terminate the employee for bringing a loaded gun onto company property, assuming it would impose such discipline on employees without disabilities.[14]

The employee would have been on firmer ground had he discussed his need for accommodation and treatment before the fact. But undiagnosed or untreated mental illnesses are common. It has been reliably estimated, for example, that about 100,000 persons with schizophrenia nationwide receive no treatment.[15]

In the popular imagination, mental illness is firmly linked with violence, but the research data suggest that the link is an overblown stereotype and an artifact of sensationalized journalistic and entertainment media. A group of experts assembled by the National Stigma Clearinghouse in New

York and the MacArthur Foundation reviewed numerous empirical studies and issued a "consensus statement":

> Serious violence by people with major mental disorders appears concentrated in a small fraction of the total number, and especially in those who use alcohol and other drugs. Mental disorders—in sharp contrast to alcohol and drug abuse—account for a minuscule portion of the violence that afflicts America society.[16]

Further research, supported by the foundation and published several years later in the prestigious *Archives of General Psychiatry*, confirmed that conclusion. A study of a large sample of patients released from mental hospitals in Pennsylvania, Kansas, and Missouri found that they were no more likely than their neighbors to be violent so long as they did not abuse alcohol or drugs. The prevalence of violent incidents was about 18 percent, which, the researchers note, was "statistically indistinguishable from the prevalence of violence among others in the neighborhood without symptoms of substance abuse."[17]

The few mentally ill persons who do commit violence are likely to be those with the severest forms of illness, experiencing acute symptoms of psychosis. But a person beset by hallucinations or delusions usually would not be in the workforce, carrying out normal duties. Matthew Beck, the Hartford multiple killer, was imprudently permitted to return to work from a medical leave despite suffering from acute depression and having recently attempted suicide. The disastrous lapse should be ascribed to a poor system for reviewing return-to-work status. Fortunately, such mistakes are relatively rare.

Antipathy toward employees with mental illness, however unjustified, may be exacerbated by clumsy attempts to comply with ADA accommodation requirements. Professor Sheila Akabas of the Columbia University School of Social Work, who studies the on-the-job experiences of persons with mental diagnoses, has drawn attention to what she calls "over and inappropriately accommodated" workers. She lists three adverse effects:

- Resentment from co-workers because of what they perceive as special unwarranted privileges for the person with a disability.
- Fear from the individual accommodated who does not want to seem ungrateful by rejecting the effort.
- Anger from the supervisor who notes that, despite extensive accommodation, the job performance of the person with a disability remains inadequate.

Akabas gives as an example the case of a landscape maintenance employee who suffered from a panic disorder. When he seemed upset, his overprotective supervisor assigned him to a job in which he could work alone. But being on his own and unsupported actually increased his feeling of panic. Meanwhile, other employees, who preferred working solo, considered his assignments plum jobs and resented his special access to them.[18]

Straining to accommodate an employee on the ground that he has a mental illness diagnosis could cause co-workers to become concerned about his stability—and their safety. In addition, as a corporate disability manager has pointed out,

> it undermines the integrity and consistency of work rules if one individual is treated differently because they have a "difficult personality," are "too spacey," or are simply viewed as "crazy." Often, difficult people are treated with "kid gloves" by their supervisors because they fear a recurrence of past disruptive or abusive behavior . . . and their behavior is excused, ignored, and otherwise tolerated.

In the end, attempts to work around one employee who is viewed as difficult and overlook his improper behavior could lead to exasperation and dangerous levels of stress on other employees, possibly causing a resentment-driven outburst.[19]

CHAPTER 17

Assessing the Risk of Violence

When a threat of violence is reported, assessing the risk is the first order of business. As with any allegation of possible misconduct, such as sexual harassment or breach of safety, a violence risk assessment requires meticulous investigation. The personal and psychosocial context of the behavior must be fully understood before any decision about intervention or administrative action can be made. Caution is necessary. Mistakes committed in haste or panic can be costly to the employer and damaging to the rights of individuals.

It is advisable to have a violence risk assessment performed by a qualified mental health professional—a psychiatrist, psychologist, or clinical social worker—whenever any of the following conditions exist:

- An employee has actually threatened to commit violence.
- Co-workers are fearful of an employee because of menacing behavior, such as displaying a weapon or habitually talking about violent acts.
- Worrisome behavioral changes are observed in an employee who is being subjected to an unusual stress, such as a disciplinary penalty, the possibility of job loss, or other significant pressure, on or off duty.

One must proceed with due diligence. Determining whether an unacceptable risk of violence exists and whether an employee presents a danger to others involves more than just an examination of the employee who is thought to represent a danger. In order to be useful, the assessment must take into account a wide array of information and indicators. Moreover, the inquiry must not be allowed to degenerate into a witch-hunt: even-handedness is essential.

The employer or crisis response team must balance competing obligations. On the one hand, there is a need for prompt and firm response to possible danger. On the other hand, the employee's rights and dignity must be maintained. Weighing the two obligations, the team has to find a middle ground that results in a fair and careful process.

Finding the Right Expert

Finding a suitable mental health professional is the first step. Here is a conversation that is all too familiar in our experience: an employer receives a report of a threat and phones Dr. Jones, a local psychologist with a good reputation, to seek an assessment of the employee. Dr. Jones readily agrees to meet with the employee at his office and to render a prompt opinion. Such an offer would not be worth accepting, because the assessment must take the work environment into account. To evaluate the subject properly, the assessor should become familiar with the work site and gather direct as well as collateral information from many sources, including managers and fellow workers. He or she should review medical and personnel records, obtaining informed consent from the employee at issue so that the details of the case can be shared with the employer or crisis response team in the interest of consensual decision making.

It is advisable to begin the search for a reliable expert assessor before a crisis is at hand and to establish in advance the ground rules for information gathering and information sharing. Credentials as a forensic psychologist or forensic psychiatrist may be useful, because they signal familiarity with legal issues, such as criminal behavior or mental competency. But expertise in the workplace context and on work-related issues may be even more pertinent.

At all times, the team must retain "ownership" of the investigative process and remain appropriately involved, choosing the response to the alleged threat. The responsibility should not be delegated to the outside expert, although the team obviously can take advice from that source. Ideally, the team should assimilate the expert's findings along with information drawn from a wide range of other sources, including the Human Resources, Security, Legal, and Health and Safety Departments. The immediate supervisor of the employee in question should be involved, and so should the union if the employee is a member of a collective bargaining unit.

Determining the Danger

Determining whether an employee poses a danger to the workplace represents a significant challenge. It is necessary to understand the individual and the context in which the purported threat was made. Among the questions that must be answered are:

- Has an intent to harm or a plan been expressed?
- Does the employee have the means to carry out the threat?
- Has the employee displayed or practiced with a weapon?
- Has there been talk about guns or bombs?
- What is the record of discipline for misconduct?
- Are there documented performance deficits?
- Have there been claims for medical disability?
- Is there turmoil in the employee's personal life?
- Has he considered harming himself or attempted to do so?
- Have there been significant changes in the workplace?
- Is there a morale issue or persistent complaints about the work unit?

Threats can never be treated casually, because many are carried out, as happened at the Royal Oak postal facility. Yet, as the Case of the Muttering Mechanic and the Case of the Dangerous Dreams demonstrate, there is often a dispute about whether a remark or gesture should be regarded as a bona fide threat. Michael J. Gan, a lawyer who represents union members, discerns an "unprecedented harshness in the discipline" imposed on employees who are perceived as threatening. He observes that "the scope of what is considered violent has been expanded to include nonphysical verbal threats, many of which are not uttered with the seriousness with which they are taken, or minor physical contact. Now a taunt or a touch, in many places, leads to summary discharge."[1]

Indeed, not everyone who voices an ostensible threat actually poses a threat. It may be just talk, albeit imprudent and thoughtless talk. Conversely, there may be employees who are, in fact, threats to others but who do not make overtly threatening statements or otherwise telegraph their hostile intentions. Such was Matthew Beck, the Hartford lottery killer. Although he was evidently seething with resentment, he threatened no one before opening fire. Similarly, John Miller, the Watkins Glen shooter, argued with a social services supervisor the day before the shooting but stopped short of actually articulating a threat.

As a rule, a targeted threat—which specifies the intended victim—engenders more fear than a generic threat. The National Institute of Justice, a research arm of the U.S. Department of Justice, has sensibly recommended careful analysis of the targeting of threats as a means of assessing the potential for danger. The following questions should be asked:

- Are potential targets identifiable, or does it appear that the subject, if considering violence, has not yet selected targets for possible attack?
- Is the potential target well known to the subject? Is the subject acquainted with a targeted individual's work and personal lifestyle, patterns of living, daily comings and goings?
- Is the potential target vulnerable to an attack? Does the targeted individual have the resources to arrange for physical security? What might change in the target's lifestyle or living arrangements that could make attack by the subject more difficult or less likely (e.g., is the targeted individual planning to move, spend more time at home, or take a new job)?
- Is the target afraid of the subject? Is the targeted individual's degree of fear shared by family, friends, and/or colleagues?
- How sophisticated or naïve is the targeted individual about the need for caution? How able is the individual to communicate a clear and consistent "I want no contact with you" message to the subject?[2]

Obviously, the fact that an employee has put forward a name does not always signify the possibility of harm. In the Case of the Fearful Foreman, scribbling a supervisor's name on a posted clipping created panic. In the Case of the Downsizing Dissenter a casual remark about an executive destroyed the company's trust in a long-service employee. In both cases, a sense of terror gripped the workplace, because employees had attached a name to their anger. Yet in reality they were expressing dissatisfaction with management style as a whole.

Goals of the Assessment

A comprehensive assessment should achieve three goals: ascertaining the level of risk, uncovering the causes of the crisis, and determining the possible responses.

Level of Risk

A violence risk assessment is an incremental process that should be undertaken by the expert. When a possible threat is examined, the first question should be: Is anyone in imminent danger? This preliminary inquiry rarely yields a clear-cut "yes or no" answer. Risk is a matter of degree, which can best be expressed by a "traffic light" analogy:[3]

Red Light: There is imminent danger that the employee will carry out a plan to harm others, and protective measures must be taken at once. Among them are contacting law enforcement, securing the plant or office, notifying potential targets, and arranging for surveillance. Given the specificity of the threats and the employee's background, the Royal Oak facility should have been considered in red light status while the arbitration case was pending.

Yellow Light: No immediate risk is evident, but there is a *potential* for violence. That risk must be eliminated or at least diminished. The assessment should begin to specify the underlying causes and suggest remedial measures. If no action is taken, the situation could worsen and become acutely dangerous. In the Case of the Dangerous Dreams, the arbitrator refused to put the grievants back to work without a psychiatric examination (which they eventually passed) because the evidence suggested that departmental morale was poor and many employees resented the supervisor—an indicator of yellow light status.

Green Light: There is no evidence of danger now or in the foreseeable future. A green light often means that a report of a threat stems from a misunderstanding, a misperception of an employee's behavior, or a deliberate misrepresentation. A green light is not necessarily the end of the inquiry. Even in the absence of a finding of acute risk, the crisis response team may have to deal with behavior that for some reason engenders fear in fellow employees. In the Case of the Fearful Foreman, once the identify of the employee who scrawled the frightening message was known, the terminal reverted to green light status because it was clear that he posed no danger. Yet it behooved managers to discover why that employee had such a jaundiced attitude toward them.

The traffic light system of classification does not yield precise answers, but it represents a rough guide to determining the danger level.

Underlying Causes

As discussed in the preceding chapter, violence typically results when elements from the setting and a particular stress interact with personality features. To be useful, therefore, an assessment process must go beyond the individual and explore the interpersonal and organizational context of the crisis. For example, an employee may have a low tolerance for stress and a history of violent behavior, but it may also be the case that poor labor-management relations have raised tensions, blocked the lines of communication, and thwarted commonsense problem solving in that employee's bargaining unit. There may be diversity-based conflict in the unit, or the individual may suffer from severe marital, health, or financial troubles, exhausting his ability to cope.

Fashioning the Correct Response

Naturally, each of these findings would trigger a different response from the crisis response team. Changes in the workplace might be indicated or interventions to address the non–work-related issues. The team would have a range of options, such as moving the employee to another work location, correcting a management practice, or arranging for a medical or disability leave.

A common response to a reported threat is immediate suspension of the offending employee. As some of the case studies in this book clearly show, however, such a reflexive response is often unwise, because the suspension can seriously disrupt the process of fact-finding and impede the ultimate resolution. In order for assessment to be successful, it is essential that the bond between the employer and employee be preserved. Therefore, it is generally preferable to defer disciplinary decisions; the employee being investigated may be removed from the workplace *with pay* as an administrative measure if there is a question about safety while the investigation is underway. Deferring discipline precludes disputes about a "rush to judgment" and may obviate a union grievance. Without prejudging the matter, the employer establishes a "time out" period in which fact-finding and decision making can take place. Union-management polarization around this issue should be avoided in the interest of safety.

Most employers, however, deal with employees who have threatened violence by suspending them pending examination by a doctor. Cut off from the workplace, the employees feel, correctly, that they are "fighting for their jobs," even if they are still receiving pay. They have little incentive to be candid about the source of their anger. Placing such employees in an interim, nonpunitive status, on the other hand, allows them to participate in the process of fact-finding without feeling embattled, and without the sense that they have already been tried and found guilty in advance.

Encouraged by their national headquarters, many postal districts, in cooperation with unions, have developed alternative ways to respond to alleged threats of violence. Under these arrangements, discipline is deferred pending the results of fact-finding conducted by joint union-management teams. In the past, union-management disputes over disciplinary actions in cases such as Royal Oak have blocked violence prevention efforts. In the alternative arrangements, management retains its right to administer discipline and the union its right to defend a member against charges. But discipline is no longer the sole possible response when threats are perceived. A "time out" allows a range of other options to be explored, including counseling, dispute resolution, job accommodation, and changes in management practices. Employees suspected of committing violence or making threats welcome the opportunity for nondisciplinary approaches, and the typical labor-management tug of war is avoided.

It is a crucial—and at times fatal—mistake not to involve the employee directly in the process of assessing the risk. Unfortunately, the assessment process tends to distance the employee rather than engaging him or her. Out of fear, employers avoid contact with a worker suspected of violence potential. In almost all cases, however, that approach is misguided. The great majority of reported threats present themselves as allegations or suspicions, rather than as overt behavior. An allegation calls for diligent investigation rather than instantaneous reaction unless the danger is palpable. Any willingness on the part of an employee to answer questions or cooperate will quickly evaporate when unwarranted assumptions are made. As soon as a disturbing situation comes to light, the "suspect" at the center of the case ought to be included in the fact-gathering process.

The most common mistake is to send employees outside the workplace for interviews instead of talking to them immediately on site. The fear that confronting such employees directly about the allegations or reports will "push them over the edge" is rarely justified. On the contrary, persons who are perceived as threatening usually have been unable to make themselves visible or their feelings known. They crave contact and communication above all else. Keeping connected to the employee is the single most important factor in dispelling tension, de-escalating feelings, and thereby reducing the likelihood of dangerous outcomes. In fact, investigating a reported threat typically provides the first and best opportunity to establish contact with an employee who is probably feeling isolated, frightened, and angry. For this reason, the crisis response team should begin by meeting with the employee, his or her manager, and perhaps a more senior manager or human resources staff member. If there is to be an assessment by a professional, the nature and purpose of the assessment should be made clear. The use of the results and the limits of confidentiality should be fully explained. Only then should assessment by an outside professional proceed.

The crisis response team benefits in several ways from following these guidelines. If the team approaches the employee in a firm but collaborative way, reaffirms the principle of "innocent until proven guilty," and does not immediately impose discipline, the employee will be less likely to refuse to cooperate.

The first step in the assessment process should be at the work site, not in an unfamiliar clinic or medical office setting. Employees should feel that they are participating in a neutral and open investigation process, of which meeting with a professional is but one part. In this way, there may be some positive outcome even when the ultimate result is the employee's separation from the workplace, as was illustrated in the Case of the Menacing Mortgage Broker. There, the investigation uncovered cognitive problems that had dogged Scott all his life and that the employer was now prepared to have diagnosed at its own expense.

Limits of Conventional Approaches

When a potential for violence is suspected, conventional occupational mental health approaches cannot be relied upon. Each has severe limitations when used in such a case. The main techniques and their shortcomings can be summarized as follows:

Counseling

A mental health consultant, psychologist, or Employee Assistance Program may receive the following request: "We have an employee who is alleged to have threatened another employee. People in his unit are afraid of him. They say he is 'stressed out.' Can you give him some counseling?" The wise employer is always ready to facilitate employee access to mental health treatment. Yet, when risk of violence is the issue, safety, not treatment, must be the priority.

Counseling, a form of supportive therapy, is the wrong response to bullying or intimidating behavior. Appropriate limit setting might have corrected the behavior long ago. Informing the employee plainly that his or her conduct is unacceptable would be more to the point than counseling. Indeed, a referral for counseling could be considered tolerating potentially injurious behavior—a form of negligence.

At the same time, an employee who is being abused by a supervisor should not be counseled for stress. It is disingenuous for an employer to refer to counseling an employee who is struggling with unacceptable working conditions that may be within the employer's control. "The Case of the Ejected Engineer" exemplifies the inappropriate—and in that case injurious—decision to use an EAP referral as a solution to an abusive work relationship.

Fitness for Duty

When an employee has left the workplace because of an illness or injury, a "fitness-for-duty" (FFD) evaluation is typically required in order to determine if the recovery has progressed far enough to allow the person to return to work. Usually, the FFD is performed by the company medical department or outside physicians. A return-to-work date is established, as well as any limitations on present or future work assignments. It is also appropriate to use an FFD to evaluate psychological fitness in case of suspected mental illness or stress-related emotional problems.

Increasingly, however, an FFD is used to determine whether an employee can return to work after being removed for threatening behavior—a purpose for which the technique is ill suited. In threat-of-violence cases, job performance is not the question. Rather, there is the far more complex and high-stakes issue of whether such employees are a danger to themselves or others. A proper FFD results in an opinion about a person's ability to work, not about the likelihood of his or her becoming violent.

Furthermore, the FFD is governed by standard policies on benefits (how a person is compensated for time off the job), discipline (if it is a matter of rule breaking), job accommodation (if a temporary or permanent disability is involved) and reimbursement for medical treatment when a third party (insurer or HMO) is involved. Issues like these must not be allowed to influence the immediate response to a threat. Given the urgency of a threat assessment, for example, it is impractical to worry about third-party reimbursement. The FFD certainly has a bearing on the employment status of an individual. But the prudent employer will suspend questions of fitness to work until the circumstances of the alleged threat are accurately determined through a more comprehensive inquiry.

Standard Psychiatric Exam

A standard psychiatric examination consists of a broad spectrum of questions about emotional and cognitive functioning. These include:

- Is the employee in touch with reality? For example, does he think he is someone else or respond to "voices" that only he hears?

- Is she in command of her emotions so that she can function in the world? For example, can she control her anger and aggressiveness? Is she so depressed that she cannot carry on normally at work or at home?
- Is he organized enough in his thinking to able to care for himself on an everyday basis?

The psychiatrist must report promptly whether the employee is a danger to himself or others. She will attempt to elicit answers to the most important questions and probe further if there are specific concerns. For example, if the referral states, "This man has threatened his supervisor, and we want to know if he is dangerous," questions will be asked about his violent feelings and about his intention to express them through actions. The goal is to determine if the employee has a concrete plan to harm his supervisor and the means to carry out the plan. The psychiatrist will take into account the employee's motivations and history of violence. Is this an impulsive person—or can he think about consequences, control himself, and deal with frustration or anger? Does the employee have a firm sense of right and wrong—or does he readily trample on the rights of others?

These questions are certainly relevant when a potential for violence is suspected. But the usefulness of the answers may be limited by the conventions of the clinical interview, a model developed in medical practice. The limitations are threefold:

Subjective Factors. The practitioner's findings are based solely on his observations of the employee and on the facts that the employee chooses to report. Both elements may be influenced by the attitude of the subject. How does the employee perceive the practitioner? Is she seen as a caring professional, intent on helping, or as being in league with a persecuting employer? Is the examination viewed as a test that the employee must pass in order to preserve his job? Owing to these factors, the information elicited may be scanty and unreliable. A defensive employee most likely will omit or minimize any actual symptoms that he may be suffering in the belief that no employer wants a worker who is distressed.

An employee also may make management style an issue, attempting to persuade the practitioner that he has been wronged and unfairly burdened by inhumane supervisors. Yet the need is for an objective evaluation, not for the practitioner to take sides in a struggle between the employee and the employer.

A novel approach to this dilemma emerged in the Case of the Dangerous Dreams. Under the terms of the conditional reinstatement ordered by the arbitrator, the three grievants were to undergo a psychiatric evaluation to ensure that their return did not create a risk. Each party—union and management—nominated a psychiatrist, and the two doctors in turn agreed upon a third, neutral psychiatrist. In that way, both sides could have confidence in the outcome.

Lack of Workplace Context. Behavior takes place in a context, but a standard clinical assessment may be performed without any knowledge of the realities of the workplace. No matter how skilled the practitioner, she is often unaware of the background to the alleged threat. Other employees may not have been interviewed about the allegation. The practitioner may not have scrutinized company records or familiarized herself with working conditions before issuing her report. At best, the report is no more than an instantly developed snapshot of the employee's mental functioning, as gauged in the clinical setting—not the full of album of images that represent his working life as a whole.

Privacy Considerations. Mental health practitioners are governed by laws of privacy as well as codes of professional ethics pertaining to patient-doctor confidentiality. Under these rules, the results of examinations may be communicated only to the patient. A crisis response team may find that frustrating when attempting to preserve workplace safety. No one should naively assume that access to information about employees is unlimited. In the absence of prior and specific agreements with practitioners and subjects of examinations, confidentiality remains safeguarded, a condition that typically constrains the effort to answer the crucial question: Is there a danger? Before an examination to settle the issue of risk is initiated, steps ought to be taken to ensure that the results will be available to the crisis response team.

The assessment of risk represents a litmus test of a commitment to health and safety for employers, unions, and crisis response teams. In no other area of violence prevention are conventional disciplinary and occupational health approaches challenged so fundamentally. As the case studies demonstrate, employers and unions often stumble profoundly, because they are locked into standard responses. Preparation is the key to proper risk assessment. Employers and unions should plan jointly to ensure that they

- Create and train a standing crisis response team.
- Select qualified risk assessment experts as consultants to the team.
- Secure access to essential information about an employee being assessed.
- Maintain contact with the employee throughout the assessment process.

CHAPTER 18

Ethical and Legal Dimensions
of Violence Prevention

Many employers rely on their attorneys for advice about how to deal with employees who are perceived to be troublesome or dangerous. Since employees may claim damages for improper use of personal information and for discriminatory treatment at work, the goal uppermost in the lawyer's mind may be protecting management clients from liability. The protective zeal of attorneys can, however, prevent employers from dealing effectively with threats of violence.

The privacy principle, deriving from values deeply rooted in our individualistically oriented culture, conflicts with an equally compelling and valid set of norms pertaining to the duty to provide a safe workplace. This so-called duty of care can also give rise to liability. The challenge for employers is to balance these conflicting principles. The balance is often difficult to achieve, as is illustrated by this account of the experience of a consulting psychologist:

The safety director of a construction company called me regarding a worker on an extended leave after he had been injured by a fall. When the company had determined that he should have sufficiently recovered to return to work, requiring that Workers Compensation payment be stopped, he claimed that he was unable to return because of psychological stress caused by the accident. The company argued that the claim for psychological stress was new and that the two-year "statute of limitations" had expired. Since he had refused to undergo recommended surgery on his back, the company argued, the law did not require further compensation.

For more than two years, the employee, a man in his forties who had long been divorced and was now living in an unstable relationship with a woman, had litigated against the company. He had been hospitalized for depression a number of times and had been treated unsuccessfully for a variety of physical conditions that he claimed were connected to the original injury. The company's lawyers, believing that they had the better case, refused to consider a lump sum settlement proposed by the employee's lawyer. They reasoned that with an employee who was not being paid, a waiting game was the best strategy.

On the day I was called, the company had just been informed that the employee had threatened to kill representatives of an insurance company (which was denying his claim) and "take out" the people at the construction company. I was asked to evaluate how dangerous the situation was and to recommend a plan of action.

When I asked John, the company lawyer, to let me see the employee's personnel file, which included reports of medical and psychological evaluations, he responded: "That's protected information. I can't let you see it without a release from the employee." John was only doing his job; he feared a possible suit for violating the employee's privacy. I pointed out to John that we had to evaluate whether a risk of violence existed. In my role as an expert, I needed the information in order to help the company decide how to protect the safety of its other employees. Assuring a safe workplace, I reminded John, was also mandated by law: the duty of care required that an employer protect employees from a possible threat to health or safety. Now that the company had been made aware of a threat of violence, there was an obligation to take steps to respond to the possible danger. Was John prepared to take responsibility for the harm that might result if the company failed to take prompt corrective action?

John recognized the dilemma. There clearly was a conflict between safeguarding privacy and simply safeguarding employees. Like most of the management lawyers I had encountered in these kinds of situations, John was focused on defending against claims that a right, such as privacy or nondiscrimination, had been violated by the employer. This defensive posture results in paralysis. Owing to fear of litigation, the employer may, for example, decline to ask an employee's physician for information relevant to the assessment of the risk of violence.

John's reluctance to cooperate with my investigation was a good illustration of the danger of the defensive legal posture. While the impaired employee remains isolated and insulated, possibly growing more dangerous, the employer deprives himself of the information needed to respond to clear signals of danger. The lawyer's defensive posture might protect the employer against one sort of exposure: to liability. But it fails to consider another, potentially much more serious, exposure: to physical harm.

I told John, "Suppose the employee were to carry out his threats. Which lawsuit would you rather be defending: his claim that you released his records without his permission, or the claim of the family of a dead or injured co-worker that you did not protect their husband or son, even after having been warned about a threat of violence?" Even if no actual violence ensued, I pointed out, "you have to consider that you already have some employees that are quite frightened about what they have heard. They could claim that they have suffered stress as a result of your failure to ensure their safety."

John began to see the potential for disaster, and we agreed on a limited release of records that I judged to be relevant to my investigation as well as 72 hours of surveillance. Even if no violence ensued, John realized, he could justify the record release and surveillance as protective measures.

In order to make sound decisions in confronting threats, it is necessary to weigh the competing principles underlying the law and then to find a balance based on a realistic assessment of the relative risks. John's reluctance to hand his employee a cause of action exemplifies the tendency to be overly sensitive to the threat of litigation even when it increases the risk of violence. A realistic assessment of the relative risks requires that all the conflicting legal, ethical, and security issues be taken into account. There may not be a "right" decision, but diligently collecting information, consulting knowledgeable experts, establishing a rationale, and documenting each step is the responsible course. The most prudent option, from both legal and practical standpoints, is not inaction or undue caution but a well-documented and reasoned consideration of all factors.

The requirements of the Americans with Disabilities Act, state and federal antidiscrimination statutes, and employment law create a minefield of confusing and potentially conflicting decisions for the human resources director or risk manager. Even frivolous or far-fetched lawsuits can be costly. It is understandable that companies have become extremely reluctant to expose themselves to liability. Fear of litigation can lead to absurd results, however.

A case that has been much discussed in employer circles involved a worker who had been absent often and made numerous errors. When he was dismissed, he claimed a violation of the Americans with Disabilities Act, asserting that the employer's real motivation was a belief that he suffered from an emotional problem. As evidence of his assertion, he cited the employer's suggestion, during the disciplinary process, that he consult the Employee Assistance Program to determine if family stresses accounted for his poor performance. As a result of that case, some employers have been advised by counsel to refrain from encouraging employees to use the EAP. A recommendation of that sort would be counterproductive, since it would remove one of the strongest social supports for troubled workers, leaving them more at risk for extreme behavioral crisis. EAPs enhance workplace safety by offering distressed employees advice on dealing with problems constructively.

The Duty of Care

The duty of care consists of two components: the federal law that created the Occupational Safety and Health Administration and the law of negligent employment torts.

The OSHA Act

Under the General Duty Clause of the Federal Occupational Safety and Health Act of 1971, the employer is charged with eliminating any condition that represents a hazard to the life, safety, or psychological well-being of employees. Under the broad scope of the act, an employer is responsible for injuries or illness resulting from a wide range of workplace conditions, including violence, threats of physical harm, or the creation of a hostile work environment. The employer has broken the law if it allows such conditions to persist and fails to take action against the individual employees or managers who are responsible. In 1992, the Occupational Safety and Health Administration affirmed that the General Duty Clause applied to violence, and in the following year the agency issued its first violence-related citation. The recipient was a psychiatric hospital that failed to protect staff members against patients suffering from psychosis.[1] OSHA also promulgated comprehensive workplace violence prevention guidelines—recommendations for employer action rather than enforceable rules—for the health care industry in 1996 (see Appendix C) and the late-night retail industry in 1998.

Negligent Employment Torts

Broadly speaking, there are three varieties of negligent employment torts:

Negligent Hiring. In the civil courts, an employer may be liable if it fails to show reasonable diligence to avoid hiring an employee who might present a danger to others in the exercise of his or her duties. The nature of the job is a central consideration. For example if the employee were to have access to private dwellings, an employer would have to take pains to ensure that the worker did not have a history of assault. In one case, a man who had been convicted of forcible entry to commit rape was hired as a caretaker of an apartment complex. When the caretaker used his key to enter an apartment and sexually assault a woman, the employer was held liable. A second type of negligence involves ignoring or failing to consider information that would indicate an obvious risk. For example, a company that had fired a man for stalking and threatening a fellow employee rehired him some years later. He proceeded to stalk and kill a female employee whom he met during his second spell with the company. An employer must keep this tort in mind while screening a potential new hire, even though there are legal restrictions on the kind of questions that may be asked in order to protect prospective hires from discrimination.

Negligent Retention. A company commits the tort of negligent retention if it fails to take action with respect to an employee, already hired, who may threaten or pose a risk of harm to fellow employees, customers or clients, or members of the public. As soon as an employer acquires information that would lead to suspicion or belief that that anyone is put at risk by an employee, investigation and corrective measures must ensue. Failure to act immediately when there is evidence that the employee is the cause of injury, illness, or an unsafe working environment exposes the employer to liability claims brought by individuals who have been harmed. When a danger or possible danger comes to the employer's attention, it can be pursued *without* compromising the legal rights of employees, if the employer exercises common sense. Of course, if an employee is covered by a collective bargaining agreement with a "just cause" provision, the employer must be prepared to support a disciplinary decision to discharge the employee with concrete evidence that a threat exists. The evidence must be more than mere speculation or rumor.

Negligent Supervision. The employer is obligated to correct employees who act in an inappropriate, unprofessional, or harmful manner. According to the doctrine of *respondeat superior*, the company is responsible for the behavior of its employees and their managers when performing job duties. An employer must evaluate the performance of its employees, including its management staff, to determine whether they adhere to the standards of behavior prescribed by law and by company policy. The fact that employees or managers are productive does not amount to a sufficient reason to retain them if they endanger others.

Achieving a Balance

Given that the duty to guard employees against violence may be at odds with other obligations to workers, how can the employer strike the correct balance among competing legal obligations? Here are some recommendations:

Seek Permission. Most employers, cowed by privacy concerns and skittish about dealing directly with health care professionals, have forgotten or ignored this obvious option. An employer who wants records opened or wishes to talk to a psychiatrist or therapist should simply ask the employee for permission. If the employer has wisely enlisted the employee's cooperation at an early stage, the permission usually will be granted—as it was in the Case of the Downsizing Dissenter. Employees are generally eager to clear their names and are relieved that the employer cares enough about their welfare to talk to the doctor. Only if the employee has denied the privacy waiver—or if circumstances make it impossible or impractical to obtain it—should the employer act unilaterally to gain access to protected information.

Limit the Information Sought. The employee should be assured that only necessary medical information will be sought. In the case of a threat of violence, the request should be limited to the doctor's opinion about the person's ability to work safely and any evidence supporting that opinion. Details of current personal life, history, and psychiatric or medical diagnoses *may* be relevant to the question, but if they are not, the employer should refrain from seeking the details.

Observe the "Need to Know" Rule. The information flow should be restricted and monitored. If private records or medical data are obtained from an outside source, the employer or crisis response team should share the information only with the violence specialist whose opinion is being sought and with those personnel who must participate in the decision-making process. Other employees can be interviewed without being given more information than they need to permit them to be helpful. They should be asked to help protect privacy by keeping their knowledge confidential while the matter is under investigation. Any sharing of information with persons other than the subject of the investigation and the decision makers should be carefully documented.

Safety First

Good crisis management requires sound judgment, teamwork, reasoned decision making and respect for the individual who is at the center of the issue. It also requires the crisis response team to find a way to balance the need to protect privacy and the need to protect against physical harm. A collaborative information-gathering process can be helpful, because issues of consent and information control can be settled through negotiation, mediation, and consensus building.

It must never be forgotten that the primary responsibility is to protect employees from harm. Many of the cases described in this book are examples of the ways safety is slighted when workplace decision makers remain immobile in the face of danger or take ineffective action. The desires to protect privacy, avoid discrimination, prevent litigation, and maintain good relations with a collective bargaining partner are important considerations. But, at the end of day, they cannot be allowed to compromise safety.

CHAPTER 19

Designing a Violence Prevention Program

Some workplaces are more likely than others to experience violence. As outlined in a previous chapter, the difference has been conceptualized by crisis management specialists as a polarity between "crisis-prone" and "crisis-prepared" organizations.[1] Transforming a crisis-prone organization may require profound changes in policies and perceptions. Most employers—65 percent, according to the American Management Association survey of 500 human resource managers cited in Chapter 1—lack policies specifically designed to deal with actual or potential violence originating within or outside of the workplace.[2] They rely mainly on conventional disciplinary procedures. As the Royal Oak episode demonstrates, conventional, unilateral disciplinary approaches do not effectively prevent crises and in some cases make matters worse. A collaborative problem-solving approach is more likely to succeed.[3] The absence of a clearly enunciated violence prevention policy, accompanied by a collaborative problem-solving mechanism, also increases risk by depriving employees of a recognized nondisciplinary channel for reporting incipient crises. Reluctant to trigger discipline, supervisors, fellow employees, and union representatives do not reliably report warning signs, thereby precluding early intervention and allowing volatile situations to persist.

Each workplace should have a violence prevention plan that articulates the rules against harassment, threats of violence, intimidation, and violent or disruptive behavior. The rules must be applied fairly and should become as well known as the fire evacuation plan. Employers should not act precipitately, without addressing the cause of hostile or unsettling behavior. Nor should they avoid action for fear of pushing possibly unstable employees "over the edge." Ignoring threats reinforces the objectionable behavior and increases the risk that the threats will be carried out.

Unions have a crucial role to play in defusing dangerous situations and in responding to possible threats. Unfortunately, the adversarial labor relations climate that prevails in so many organized workplaces militates against unions' taking a positive role. According to a survey of union officers, "where union leaders feared that workers could seriously harm him/herself and others, they were caught in a terrible quandary: should they—in violation of deeply held beliefs and, perhaps, their duty of fair representation—take their concern to management?"[4] A system of early, nondisciplinary intervention by a joint crisis response team could spare the union such a quandary. Moreover, the ability to call on the team would help shield the union's members from victimization by nonemployees. Unions can ill afford to allow a reflexively adversarial stance to thwart a mode of collaborative problem solving that could be its members' best protection.

Implementing a successful violence prevention program often requires profound changes in the culture and practices of an organization. Traditional ways of handling labor relations, injury management and discipline may have to be jettisoned. The following steps are essential:

- Form a crisis response team, representing all stakeholders.
- Construct a violence risk profile for that workplace.
- Develop policies and procedures to guide the team.
- Train team members and supervisory staff.
- Arrange for easy, nonpunitive access to medical and mental health expertise.
- Promulgate clear, commonsense disciplinary rules.

There must be an unambiguous sign that the highest levels of the organization support the changes needed to make the team effective. Visibility on the part of top leadership will help ensure that the program does not become a meaningless set of rules or procedures that are forgotten—until a crisis erupts. The best designed and conceived training program will fail to produce the desired outcome unless there is tangible support from the upper echelons.

The Team

The team will guide the process from design to initiation to on-going implementation. It must be composed of stakeholders who are in leadership positions, who represent a range of functions in the organization, and who are empowered to make decisions. Often a single person, perhaps a mid-level safety or training manager, is saddled with the task of developing a violence policy or a training program. That is a prescription for failure, because the expertise of the departments of Health and Safety, Legal, Employee Relations, Employee Assistance, and Operations is needed to make policy effectively. If there is a union, it should be included in the planning. A high-ranking executive actively engaged with the team is also an asset, at least in the beginning. The executive might move to an ex officio status once the plan and the team are in place.

The team should begin by drafting the violence prevention plan. The team can grow and evolve with the plan as it changes over time. After the plan has been crafted, the team should present it to the rest of the organization in training sessions. Designated members of the team then can begin receiving and processing reports of tension or threat. Over time, the group will continue to oversee the program and learn to coordinate smoothly in the event of a crisis.

Violence Risk Profile

In order to craft a useful policy, the team must know the organization's violence risk profile. This profile is nothing like the unreliable predictive personality profile discussed above. The violence risk profile focuses on the organization as whole, rather than on individuals, reflecting the results of a systematic audit that provides specific data about past experience, current exposures, and possible warning signs. Outside consultants typically prepare the audit, which can be structured in a variety of ways. It should provide the following information:

Employee Opinions and Concerns. This information can be obtained through a combination of written surveys, interviews, and focus groups. Although all these methods yield crucial information, the information gained from focus groups is particularly valuable. These groups tend to yield the fullest, most candid picture of employees' fears and vulnerabilities. Focus groups also reveal the best information about the important systemic issues, such as safety or security concerns, union-management problems, or workforce diversity. (In the Case of the Dangerous Dreams the employer assigned an investigator to interview employees, but the information gained was used for—ultimately unsuccessful—disciplinary measures, rather than to assess morale deficiencies.)

Past Experience with Violence and Conflict. Interviews with key personnel and a review of records will yield information not only about the frequency and nature of incidents, but the stories behinds these occurrences. How did the episode begin (warning signs heard or not heard)? How did the system respond (well or poorly)?

Current Policies and Systems That Relate to Violence Prevention Capability. A careful review will indicate which policies and structures need to be modified. For example, do employees know where to go to report a threat or a feeling that a co-worker is unduly stressed?

Framing a Policy

Once the team has developed and analyzed the violence risk profile, it can set about developing the policy. The policy process is as follows: (1) define workplace violence, (2) set forth a conduct standard and range of specific consequences for failing to meet that standard, (3) specify the reporting procedures, and (4) ensure safety and nonretaliation for reporters. It is up to the team to fill in the blanks with the specific list of behaviors and situations that are covered by the policy.

No policy should be promulgated until the team and the violence risk profile are both in place. Without a team, there will be no general stakeholder support and locus of expertise. Without the violence risk profile, the policy will not reflect the specific risks the organization faces or the behaviors it needs to control.

There are two basic approaches to framing a policy: the general and the specific. In some organizations, the preference is for a general definition of the prohibited conduct. The DuPont Corporation, for example, states its policy in the following terms:

> [C]onduct creating an intimidating, hostile, offensive, or threatening working environment through unwelcome words, actions, or physical contact will not be tolerated. Those violating this practice may be subject to disciplinary action up to and including discharge.

The Wells Fargo Bank policy is also general in its definition of the offense, but it anticipates the possibility that a threat-of-violence assessment may be necessary and specifies a reporting procedure:

> Threats of violence, bodily harm or physical intimidation by employees will not be tolerated and may be grounds for immediate termination. In instances

where this type of behavior is exhibited, the company reserves the right to request an evaluation by a mental health professional to determine fitness for duty. Likewise, threats or intimidation of employees in the workplace by individuals outside the company will not be tolerated. If you receive a threat, notify your line personnel officer and the Security Department. You may also call Employee Assistance Services if you want to discuss your concerns.

In the public sector, the federal government's Office of Personnel Management recommends a general policy that includes some examples of prohibited conduct:

Violence, threats, harassment, intimidation, and other disruptive behavior in our workplace will not be tolerated; that is, all reports of incidents will be taken seriously and will be dealt with appropriately. Such behavior can include oral or written statements, gestures, or expressions that communicate a direct or indirect threat of physical harm. Individuals who commit such acts may be removed from the premises and may be subject to disciplinary action, criminal penalties, or both.[5]

Another example of the general approach is the policy adopted by the federal government's Centers for Disease Control in Atlanta when it was headed by Dr. David Satcher, who later became the U.S. surgeon general. The policy stresses personal responsibility for avoiding conflict:

Violence and threatening behavior will not be tolerated. . . . All members of the workforce are responsible for their own behavior and are expected to interact responsibly with fellow employees and supervisors. To help prevent problems, employees and supervisors should participate in training in conflict resolution and stress management and seek the help of Employee Assistance Program Counselors. Preventing problems originating from non-employees requires a combination of restricted access and employee vigilance.[6]

Unions have suggested including in collective bargaining agreements general statements that obligate employers to safeguard employees from aggression. Here is sample language drafted by the Service Employee International Union (SEIU):

The employer shall develop written policies and procedures to deal with on-the-job assault. Such policies must address the prevention of assault on-the-job, the management of situations of assault, and the provision of legal counsel and post-traumatic support to employees who had been assaulted on the job by clients or the public.

Other organizations have opted to provide an illustrative list of specific behaviors that are not tolerated. An example is the model policy framed by CMG Associates, a Massachusetts-based consulting group. The policy focuses on the concept of harassment, which it defines as:

Any form of unsolicited, and/or unwarranted, verbal or physical deprecia-
tion of person;
Explicit derogatory statements;
Use of profanity, when linked with physical and/or psychological aggression;
Any actual, implied or veiled threat, made seriously or in jest;
Discriminatory remarks made by someone in the workplace which:

- Are offensive to the recipient.
- Cause the recipient discomfort or humiliation.
- Interfere with the recipient's job performance.

Another variant of the specific policy, also crafted by CMG Associates, offers an even more detailed catalog of offenses. Prohibited are:

Violent or threatening physical contact (e.g., fights, pushing, physical
intimidation).
Direct or indirect threats.
Threatening, abusive or harassing phone calls.
Possession of a weapon on company property or on a job site.
Destructive or sabotaging actions against company or personal property.
Stalking.
Violation of a restraining order.
High levels of conflict or tension with a work unit.
Threats of suicide.

A major educational complex, San Diego State University in California, also provides campus denizens with illustrations of what is meant by threatening behavior. The SDSU list includes actions such as:

Making menacing gestures.
Displaying an intense or obsessive romantic interest that exceeds the normal bounds of interpersonal interest.

Behavior indicating that the individual is significantly out of touch with reality and that he or she may pose a danger either to himself or herself or
to others.
Volatile or violent personal situations such as found in some custody
battles.

A municipality in the same state—the city of El Centro—provides its
workers with specific examples of "threats or acts of violence," both of
which are prohibited. The examples include:

- Intimidating or attempting to coerce an employee to do wrongful acts
  that would affect the business interests of the City.
- Harassing surveillance, also known as "stalking," the willful, malicious
  and repeated following of another person and making a credible
  threat with intent to place the other person in reasonable fear of his
  or her safety.
- Making a suggestion or otherwise intimating that an act to injure
  persons or property is "appropriate," without regard to the location
  where such suggestion or intimation occurs.

Another municipality, the city of Fort Lauderdale, Florida, bans "paranoid behavior" and "moral righteousness."
In order to preclude foolhardy heroics and reinforce the need for a
nonviolent approach, a policy might also define the expected role of the
employee in responding to a dangerous situation. The Oregon Department of Human Resources, for example, recommends this formulation:

In responding to a threatening or violent behavior, no employee, management or represented, shall take any action that will risk his or her own safety
or the safety of other individuals in the area. No attempt should ever be made
by any employee or volunteer to restrain or forcibly evict an armed person or
dangerous person from the premises.

Employee shall use non-physical skills when attempting to de-escalate aggressive behaviors. This is not meant to prohibit a person from using physical
force for self-defense, or to defend a third person, if determined by the employee to be necessary. If an employee is not able to reduce aggressive behavior using non-physical skills the employee shall attempt to remove him or
herself from the situation, if doing so would not increase risk, and obtain assistance from law enforcement by following the steps in the Emergency Action Handbook.

Each approach to policy making has advantages and disadvantages. Keeping the policy general in nature obviates the need to specify in advance every form of behavior that may be considered objectionable. As the examples above illustrate, catalogs of specific offenses tend to be idiosyncratic. The general approach also encourages reporting of threats, because employees need not worry whether conduct meets some arbitrary definition before contacting the crisis response team. But if discipline results, an employee could argue that the policy is unfairly vague and fails to give adequate notice of what is prohibited.

The specific approach allows the policy to be targeted against those dangers detected in the violence risk profile of each organization. But no list can anticipate every possible form of undesirable conduct. Promulgating a catalog of specific offenses makes it more difficult to discipline an employee for a type of behavior that has not been specified, even though it might fall under the general heading of aggression or harassment.

Moreover, specificity could raise troublesome questions of fairness. For example, would it be reasonable to hold an individual employee responsible for "high levels of conflict or tension within a work unit"? Or would that charge more plausibly lie at the door of management, a union, or both? Tension is normally thought of as a group phenomenon, the product of the relationship among a number of employees and their managers, rather than the handiwork of an individual.

Hostage taking, it has been argued, must be specifically prohibited.[7] But affirming the general and self-evident principle that crimes are not allowed in the workplace should suffice. There is no need to clutter the rulebook by reiterating every section of the criminal code. Also, in their attempt to be specific, policy drafters may lapse into unhelpful tautology, as when "threatening" behavior is defined as making a "threat."

Zero Tolerance

Some organizations use the phrase "zero tolerance" in their policies, but the term has acquired unfortunate connotations. It is often taken to suggest a harsh and inflexible attitude toward employee conduct. Implying that even minor transgressions deserve draconian penalties may discourage reporting, since an employee may fear that telling the employer about a co-worker's strange behavior will result in that person's automatic discharge. The reporter may wish to have offensive or threatening conduct stopped without causing job loss.

In addition, "zero tolerance" implies rough justice. The phrase may be construed by an arbitrator or court as an indication that the penalty was imposed reflexively, without carefully weighing all the facts and circumstances of the incident at issue and without attempting to ensure that the penalty fits the offense. In the Case of the Fearful Foreman, for example, the arbitrator considered as a mitigating factor the lack of evidence that the employee intended to threaten or frighten the supervisor. Under some forms of "zero tolerance," in contrast, a remark or action that causes panic may violate the rule even if the speaker did not intend to be taken seriously.

Similarly, when employers enforce "zero tolerance" policies against fighting, they often discharge both participants in a brawl without considering the relative culpability of each. Yet arbitrators tend to apply the traditional "just cause" standard to such cases. As a result, a business school study has found, "employers are likely to have a difficult time justifying equal discipline in cases in which participants appear to have different levels of involvement in the fight."[8] Judgments about behavior that fail to take into account mitigating and aggravating factors are at odds with the principle of just cause.

Union officials contend that "zero tolerance" encourages managers to ignore requirements for progressive discipline enshrined in collective bargaining agreements and sometimes offers a pretext for harassing employees.[9] In the case of drug policy, moreover, invoking the term "zero tolerance" has sometimes been a form of posturing for public consumption—a cynical substitute for genuine efforts to reduce substance abuse. It should be possible for employers to fashion a firm and consistent policy of prohibiting violence and threats without resorting to shopworn and possibly counterproductive slogans.

Banning Guns

Prohibitions against weapons could raise special issues in "right-to-carry" states—those where carrying a concealed handgun is permitted by law and indeed encouraged as a personal safety measure. But Dean J. Schaner, a lawyer who has studied the gun policies of several states, concludes that right-to-carry laws "do not prevent an employer from implementing and establishing a 'no weapons' policy . . . on its property. . . . The constitutional right to bear arms has never been extended to include bringing a weapons to another person's property against that owner's desires."[10] Nevertheless, employees with a license may wish at least to keep guns in their cars in company parking areas as protection during lunch hour and during the trip home at the end of the workday. Some female employees have asked their employers for permission to carry guns for defense because they are the targets of stalkers who might follow them to the office. As Schaner aptly questions, might not a jury find the employer liable "if an employee [gun] permit-holder is raped and was unable to defend herself because of the employer's no-weapons policy?"

Granting such exemptions to a general workplace ban might result in a Wild West atmosphere in which guns proliferated. Overall, Schaner concludes, "a gun-free workplace is far safer than a workplace filled with guns" and thus less likely to expose an employer to liability. Yet it cannot be denied that in right-to-carry states bearing firearms is considered a civic virtue, on the ground that an armed citizenry enhances public safety. In such a climate, some employees are bound to believe that taking a gun to work is an entitlement.

Training

All sectors of the workforce should report dangerous situations to the crisis response team as soon as possible. The proper purpose of training is not, as has sometimes been assumed, to enable employees to predict behavior, but to help them carry out their reporting responsibility. Timely reporting is essential to the concept of *coordinated early response*: ordinary employees form an early-warning network that detects signals of incipient danger and passes them along to the team, which coordinates the response. Shop-floor employees, first-line managers and shop stewards are typically the best detectors. Many serious cases of workplace violence stem from the failure to transmit warning signals to the responsible levels of the organization early enough to intervene. Often the failure resulted from the "judgment call" of a shop floor-level person who should have reported to the crisis response team without evaluating the significance of the signal. Only the team is equipped to conduct fact-finding, gather expert advice, perform an assessment, and choose the correct response. Freelance judgment calls should not be allowed to short-circuit that process.

Corporate culture often discourages reporting. Managers have been schooled to take initiative and act independently wherever possible and to avoid bothering superiors with problems. In addition, some workplaces informally tolerate or sanction hostile and threatening behavior in the mistaken belief that only actual physical violence need be addressed. In a postal service training session, which included managers as well as union members, a letter carrier described the frustration of attempting to report that one employee had threatened another. The supervisor to whom he reported replied, "Well, let me know if anything happens." Perhaps the supervisor thought it acceptable for employees to threaten one another, or perhaps she disliked or disbelieved the person who reported the event. By the time the training session was over, however, every manager in the room had come to understand that failing to act on such a report is malfeasance.

At another training session, in a large mail-sorting facility, a young clerk sat pensively as it was explained that a team composed of union and management members would respond to behavioral issues. Raising his hand, the young man identified himself as a union steward and expressed his relief. He said that he had been dealing with a union member who had been acutely suicidal for months. The steward felt he had nowhere to go with the problem because, in his words, "it might have hurt the guy's job security." A good violence prevention policy creates options for diligent union leaders like that steward.

Access to Expertise for Assessment

It is essential that threat assessment not be treated like a standard investigation of a work injury or health claim, because threat assessment has radically different goals. Whereas the purpose of a standard investigation is to determine if someone is fit to do his or her job, the goal of threat assessment is to determine if someone is dangerous, and, if not, to decide why he or she *seemed* to be dangerous. (The difference between appearance and reality could signal other kinds of organizational dysfunction.)

A correct threat assessment is the key to a correct response. If a professional assessor has been carefully selected and informed consent obtained, two critical elements are assured:

- The employee will feel comfortable and open about entering into the assessment process—as Scott was in the Case of the Menacing Mortgage Broker, because he stood to gain from having his learning disabilities thoroughly assessed.
- The crisis response team will have immediate *and legal* access to information about the level of danger, based on first-hand contact with the employee whose conduct is at issue. In the Case of the Muttering Mechanic, the management team that was directing the response alienated the employee by forcing him to undergo a psychiatric examination and thereby sacrificed his cooperation.

Separation Anxiety

Threats of violence are commonly reported in advance of the discharge of an individual for cause or a mass layoff for economic reasons.

Managers often sense a heightened risk of violence when such separations are in the wind, and there is indeed a theoretical basis for linking the two phenomena. Job loss raises fears of humiliation, isolation, and deprivation; the fears produce severe anxiety, which is expressed in acts of violence. It is important to be prepared for such untoward reactions. Let us consider the violence potential of the two most common causes of job loss:

Termination for Cause

The return of the fired employee, bent on murderous revenge—as in the case of the Santa Ana, California, highway crewman (Chapter 4)—has become the specter that stalks the land, despite the low probability of its occurrence in one's own work setting. Job loss need not create a risk of violence, however. No one ever took revenge simply for being fired. Employees who become threatening always talk about *the way they were made to feel* in the process of losing their jobs. The experience of being terminated—if it is degrading or humiliating or leaves a gnawing sense of injustice—certainly helps raise the risk of violence.

Some employers have been verbally brutal in the course of discharging an employee. Writing in a management journal, an employment lawyer recalls an instance in which "a trucker went on a violent rampage when his supervisor told him, during a conversation in which he was being fired, 'guys like you are a dime a dozen.'"[11]

In other instances, the reason for the discharge may not have been adequately or convincingly explained. A feeling that one has been fired without good cause can lead to a burning desire for revenge, as happened in the Santa Ana incident, where the discharged employee evidently believed that his supervisor had treacherously betrayed him. For that reason, it is important to ensure that due process is afforded and that the employee understands—and, one may even hope, accepts—the grounds for the discharge. The security-minded may believe that a brief discharge meeting is the safest, but giving an employee short shrift is likely to induce, rather than reduce, anger. An effort should be made to explain the basis for the termination as clearly as possible, so that the employee does not believe that he has been victimized because of personal animus unrelated to his performance. Some lawyers have advocated according every discharged employee—not just those covered by collective agreements—the right to file a written grievance and to receive an answer in writing.[12]

Another factor that increases the risk of violence or threat is the elapsed time between the onset of extreme behavior and imposition of discharge. That period is often measured in years, as it was in the Royal Oak postal incident and in the Concordia University faculty shooting. A long history of bad behavior and poor performance typically precedes every report of a threat or perception of danger. Often, extreme behavior goes on for years without provoking a response, creating unnecessary risk, because acting in a menacing manner becomes a means of controlling and intimidating others. The strategy usually works. Unless the company has a firm policy of responding to threats, hostility is often ignored. The offender is merely given a wide berth and regarded as "difficult." When aggressiveness finally goes too far, the justification for responding may seem weak, because similarly odious behavior has been tolerated for so long. That is not good for the organization and in the long run not good for the offender either. The decision to terminate should not be unduly prolonged merely because it is disagreeable to confront a hostile employee.

Policies must be clear and consistently applied and documented—even when an employee is menacing or touchy. The employee's file should record meticulously any previous hostile behavior, violation of discipline, or breach of rules pertaining to conduct, safety, or health. If an investigation uncovers a history of violence, problems with alcohol, or excessive involvement with weapons, those details should properly become part of the assessment. Ignoring an employee's behavior out of fear or out of compassion is misguided.

Layoff

In companies large and small, organizational change increases the need for a focused approach to violence prevention. That is true for two reasons. First, psychological uncertainty and economic insecurity create stress that in some employees results in threatening or violent behavior. Second, organizational change can strain management systems so that rapid and smooth decision making, especially in crisis situations (which proliferate in a changing environment), may not be easy. The situation calls for a two-pronged approach:

Enhanced Two-Way Communication. Because of the uncertainty associated with a changing environment, the need for information is unending. Leaders must be prepared to communicate more often with employees and to speak candidly—which means listening and responding to concerns, not just delivering scripted messages. Stress increases if leaders indulge the natural tendency to become more withdrawn in response to the constant need for assurance exhibited by a workforce that is facing the prospect of widespread job loss.

Emotional Health Monitoring. The crisis response team should be tasked with monitoring the emotional health of the organization throughout the transition period. This team, with its finger to the wind and nose to the ground, will be able to respond to needs and crises emerging from the organization daily.

An alert and prepared crisis response team, together with conscientious two-way communication, provides a safety net for an organization undergoing stressful change. Managers should notify the team when layoffs are about to be announced. Inevitably, some individuals will show the effects of stress and manifest signs of breakdown. If there is a mechanism for listening and responding, it will detect the growth of a climate conducive to violence. Frequent information sessions and support meetings can provide a receptive forum for such concerns. Other functions related to organizational change, such as outplacement counselors, should also become part of the stress-detection network that keeps the crisis response team apprised.

CHAPTER 20

Dispute Resolution
as Violence Prevention

Strategies to prevent violence in the workplace must be shaped by an understanding of the root causes of the hazard. Many threats or instances of revenge violence stem from conflict among employees or between employees and nonemployees. Therefore, no prevention plan is truly comprehensive unless it includes an effective conflict resolution component. Conflict resolution methods, such as mediation, facilitated negotiation, and mutual problem solving, should be used to relieve the myriad tensions among workers that arise from the demands of the workplace, as described in Chapter 2. Moreover, conflict resolution can be useful in building consensus among workplace stakeholders in order to ease the transition from a crisis-prone to a crisis-prepared workplace and to ensure that all efforts are directed toward making the prevention plan work.

The organization's violence risk profile, arrived at through a variety of audit techniques, will reveal the extent to which interpersonal conflict is an issue and dispute resolution systems are lacking. Nominal grievance mechanisms are common in the workplace, but many function poorly. Rather than resolving disputes at an early stage and in an informal manner, the grievance procedure often becomes mired in confrontation and fails to identify the sources or risks of hostile behavior. Indeed, it may exacerbate the dangers by inhibiting early recognition and timely, appropriate responses. Royal Oak (Chapter 3) is a classic example.

When unhappiness is rife because of poor management or structural change, there may be few effective channels for worker distress. Those that do exist may be overwhelmed or inappropriately used. At a federal agency, a disaffected professional employee who believed that he was unfairly passed over for advancement repeatedly filed complaints with the agency's Equal Employment Opportunity (EEO) officer. The employee happened to be African American; nevertheless, a thorough investigation determined that his career obstacles stemmed not from racial discrimination, but from interpersonal and organizational issues. He had been reflexively shunted to the wrong forum, and the cumbersome, bureaucratic process of adjudicating EEO claims had dragged on so long that he had begun threatening violence. The EEO officer estimated that fully three-quarters of the complaints she received did not qualify under the antidiscrimination law. Thus, even though it was destined to provide them with no relief and leave them frustrated, the EEO process attracted employees of all kinds who were dissatisfied.

Arbitration is another case in point. Originally an informal, practical, hands-on mode of problem solving in the workplace, this capstone of the grievance process has become increasingly remote, formalized, and given over to lawyerly argument. The emphasis has shifted from "adjustment"— a term quaintly preserved in the names of many industry boards—to adjudication. The norms of litigation have replaced those of collaboration, as a problem-solving ethos has given way to an adversarial, legalistic exercise. As in a judicial forum, the parties strive to win at all costs; it is a zero-sum game. Immersed in a stridently adversarial culture, the parties are encouraged to exaggerate their differences rather than search for common ground. Adopting a scorched-earth mentality in their dealings with one another, the parties often leave the hearing room more hostile than when they entered. The process has been compared to combat by a veteran participant:

The war has sapped our productivity, diverted legal talent to minuscule disputes, generated divisiveness and suspicion, created and fostered lack of mutual respect and loss of pride in work. . . . [A]rbitration continues to take us down a road of acrimonious debilitating disputes; whereas other forms of ADR [Alternative Dispute Resolution] are far better designed to bring an end to the warfare In the workplace. . . . [Employers] should be building real, not illusory, internal dispute resolution systems.[1]

As in litigation, anointing one party the winner or formally assigning blame rarely resolves the underlying conflict, which continues to fester. Although arbitration may dispose of the surface issues, the underlying causes of an outburst or act of insubordination typically are not addressed. Grievants may be left with little sense of "validation," the feeling that their complaints have been taken seriously. Since the absence of effective channels for expressing anger or distress is a hallmark of the crisis-prone organization, the shortcomings of the arbitration system, can have serious implications for safety in the long run.

A Healing, Not a Hearing

The standard union-versus-management configuration, coupled with an adversarial approach, often fails to adequately address the dynamics of interemployee disputes, which are likely to become more prevalent in the future.[2] A true resolution may require a healing rather than a hearing.[3] To achieve lasting results, it is important to allow the expression of emotions. A sincere apology may be more important than a judgment or assignment of blame.

For individual employees who are in conflict with each other or with nonemployees, fortunately, there is a model ready at hand. Such disputes closely resemble those that traditionally have been labeled "community" disputes. Community mediation programs are repositories of relevant problem-solving experience and skills, and they can be a key resource for the workplace. This brand of mediation displays characteristics that are well suited to workplace disputes involving interpersonal and intergroup tension:

- The disputants are typically not organized parties, and the dispute often lacks a neat bilateral configuration.
- The disputants interact face to face, rather than through representatives.
- There is an effort at developing new information, achieving mutual understanding, and fostering beneficial emotional expression and engagement.
- The disputants come from diverse backgrounds; experienced mediators are comfortable with people of all ages, ethnicities, lifestyles, and idiosyncrasies.
- Each disputant tells his story in his own way and in his own words, rather than being subjected to an artificial, question-and-answer style examination.

- The range of issues is broad and may include such highly charged matters as racism, sexism and homophobia.
- The process seeks to restore the harmony of a relationship—such as sharing a workbench—that must continue after the dispute.

Mediation as a Job Skill

The ability to recognize and resolve disputes at work ought to be considered a valuable job skill. Mediation capabilities should be dispersed throughout an organization to maximize the possibility of an early response to incipient crisis. The U.S. Centers for Disease Control, for example, encourages its staff to take courses in dispute resolution, and the Polaroid Corporation's Grievance Assistance Office has trained dozens of employees to serve as in-house mediators of a wide range of disputes.

Since the early 1990s, a growing number of postal service districts have sponsored mediation training for their supervisors and union stewards. By the year 2000 all postal employees nationwide will be offered mediation of EEO complaints through REDRESS (Resolve Employment Disputes Reach Equitable Solutions Swiftly), which began in pilot sites in 1994 as part of a class action lawsuit settlement. Mediators from outside the postal service facilitate face-to-face discussion with supervisors within weeks of the filing of a complaint to address underlying problems before they worsen. The mediators have been trained in a "transformative" mediation process that aims to improve the working relationship between the parties and the way they perceive and understand each other. (The more traditional, "directive" approach tends to focus on obtaining settlement of the specific dispute.) The success of each mediation is measured in an exit survey[4] in which the participants rate their satisfaction in 51 areas, such as:

- The amount the other party listened to your views.
- What the other party learned about your point of view.
- What you learned about the other party's point of view.
- How much the other party acknowledged your perspective, views or interests.
- How much you acknowledged the other party's perspective, views or interests.
- The amount of respect the mediator gave you.
- The control you had over the mediation process.
- The positive impact mediation will have on the long-term relationship of the parties.

Much like firefighters and emergency medical technicians, crisis response teams and mediators need to keep their skills updated through recurrent training. Yet the American Management Association survey of human resource managers suggests that less than one-third of employers provide training related to violence prevention.[5]

The goal of recurrent training should be fine-tuning a collaborative effort to reduce hostility, violence, harassment, and threatening behavior on a continuing basis and to prevent potentially dysfunctional persons from exploiting disharmony between management and union. Only by sustained collaborative effort will it be possible to marshal the resources of the workplace to ensure its own safety.

The Model of Transition

In Chapter 1 we discussed the need for a workplace to transform itself from crisis-prone to crisis-prepared. An organization moves from a crisis-prone to a crisis-prepared condition through stages, and dispute resolution can assist at each stage. The main stages are as follows:

1. Identifying stakeholders and breaking through denial. The methods used:

   - Data collection (interviews with leaders and workers, surveys, focus groups).
   - Naming and cataloging the problems.

2. Establishing mutual trust. The methods used:

   - Creating a coalition of stakeholders who acknowledge the problem and accept the need for collaborative problem solving.
   - By using facilitation skills, helping the coalition arrive at an understanding that there is a mutuality of interest, rather than a zero-sum relationship between seemingly opposed parties.
   - Forming a basis for trust, grounded in permission to collaborate.
   - Creating a policy that defines the danger signals and identifies internal and external resources for coping with them. Included should be a catalog of situations worthy of response and conflict resolving mechanisms.

3. Promoting awareness of the policy by training others in the organization. Key goals of training:

   - Demonstrate that the paradigm has shifted and display the collaboration between union and management. For example, union and management might "co-lead" the training sessions.

- Legitimate and establish the safety of asking for help for yourself or others. (The request should not cause job jeopardy.)
- Show that there is somewhere to go with problems, that they should not be ignored, and that employees are individually accountable for using the system.
- Explain to managers, supervisors, and union leaders the causes of stress (e.g., organizational change, family issues) and the relationship of stress to illness and violence. Increase sensitivity to the early warning signs of stress-related problems.
- Measure the degree of organizational change by means of periodic surveys.

Consensus Policy Making

In many workplaces, the relationship between management and the employees can best be described as adversarial. Executives assert management's right to promulgate rules unilaterally. Employees then resist the rules, which they see as an unduly punitive, or formally challenge them through arbitration, litigation, and administrative proceedings. Such labor-management friction can exacerbate the very tensions that a violence prevention policy should alleviate. For that reason, it is sensible to construct such a policy by consensus.

One of the most positive trends in industrial relations has been the formation of Labor-Management Committees (LMCs), composed of employer and employee representatives, to undertake consensus policy making. In this constructive alternative to the adversarial model, health and safety are typically placed high on the agenda. And among the chief threats to worker health and safety, as well as productivity, are violence and uncontrolled hostility. For that reason, the LMC represents a potentially effective vehicle for helping the workforce cope with insecurity. By developing a comprehensive, bilateral violence prevention policy, the LMC could become the nucleus for the formation in each workplace of a coalition of stakeholders committed to bringing about the transition to preparedness.

At the moment, that potential remains largely unrealized because LMCs, particularly those in smaller workplaces, have an insufficient information resource base for developing sound policies. Joint violence prevention initiatives would be more common if the committees received direct technical assistance in the formulation of policy and assessment of individual cases.

The LMC should draw upon the knowledge of outside experts, such as psychologists and dispute resolution specialists. Their expertise would help in identifying the sources of workplace stress and trauma and creating effective mechanisms to deal with tensions before they erupt. LMC members would collaboratively seek guidance from medical and mental health professionals and, if necessary, expert assessment of potentially dangerous situations. This mutual approach would replace the wasteful, usually counterproductive, and often hazardous practice of pitting medical or psychological experts against each other in an adversarial proceeding. In association with the LMC, professional expertise could be utilized in a preventive fashion.

Dispute resolution skills should also be enhanced. LMC members typically have basic labor-management negotiating skills, but these could be buttressed by learning skills akin to those of the community mediator in order to meet the newer and more nuanced challenges of interemployee conflict. The LMC members also should become familiar with safeguards for individual privacy.[6] Neutral facilitators could assist the LMCs in reaching consensus agreements. Experts could be drawn from academic and professional bodies, as well as from organizations in which policies on workplace violence and related subjects have been negotiated and incorporated in joint protocols or in collective bargaining agreements.

There have been remarkably successful examples of consensus policy making in the field of workplace substance abuse.[7] These models could be adapted to workplace violence prevention by uniting two major premises, derived from industrial relations and the study of workplace trauma:

- Policy derived from labor-management collaboration is superior to that which emerges from extreme adversarial confrontation.
- Programs with high employee participation are more likely to be effective in preventing violence and hostility than programs that are imposed unilaterally.

High participation is an advantage because employees need to be enlisted in the effort to identify situations with the potential for violence; peer pressure should be harnessed for constructive ends. High-participation programs no doubt will be more comprehensive and multifaceted, encompassing not just sanctions and searches for "bad apples" but positive remedial strategies for dealing with the roots of conflict.

If technical assistance is furnished directly to the parties in a bilateral setting, they are more likely to forge policies that reflect their mutual interest. Once such a policy has been created, management and labor will feel equally invested in it and will devote their best efforts to making it work. Indeed, the very existence of a technical assistance program, combined with the urgency and pervasiveness of the violence issue, could promote the formation of LMCs where none now exist. Violence prevention thus could become an attractive model for joint policy development on other issues.

Constructing an Action Plan

Once an entry point for technical assistance—such as a labor-management committee—is identified, a blueprint for reengineering and reinvigorating the dispute resolution process can be prepared by the LMC or other joint body.

The primary goals are to:

1. *Synthesize* the insights, skills, and techniques of three approaches:

   - interest-based negotiation.
   - community dispute resolution.
   - organizational crisis management.

2. *Implement* that synthesis by empowering the workplace stakeholders to change the posture of the organization.

The steps by which change occurs are as follows:

- Creating transition teams consisting of experienced neutral facilitators/dispute resolvers and organizational crisis management specialists.
- Designating the Labor-Management Committee as an entry point at selected pilot sites, and facilitating the adoption of a bilateral violence prevention policy that breaks though institutional denial.
- Enlarging the coalition upward and downward by enlisting the cooperation of top leaders from management and the union, as well as leaders of significant constituent groups.
- Facilitating the introduction of effective problem solving in the workplace and enhancing the parties' relationship by giving them an opportunity to focus on violence prevention as an area of demonstrable mutual interest.
- Imparting strategies and skills drawn from community mediation to reduce conflict arising from:
  - Stress factors inherent in the organization of work.
  - Intergroup strains in multiethnic, multilingual, and multicultural settings.

- Sexual harassment and interpersonal tension.
- Intrusion of domestic violence and abuse.

Unlike traditional systems, which are relatively rigid, the "softer" strategies are designed to provide the maximum opportunity for communication, participating, and recognition of individual perspectives. Furthermore, they are more likely to allow for the flexibility needed to handle the complex, delicate multiparty issues that arise in cases of threat and violence.

Demonstration Projects

Workplace Solutions, a nonprofit consortium of professionals in dispute resolution and crisis management, has been demonstrating the value of combining dispute resolution and crisis management techniques. (The authors are associated with that organization, which is supported by a grant from the William and Flora Hewlett Foundation.) A model program was created at an urban nursing home facility in 1997. Management and the union at the facility agreed that morale and staff behavior justified an evaluation. There were manifestations of tension and conflict among line staff, as well as poor communication and mistrust between supervisors and nursing assistants. Discipline was inconsistent or ineffective. There had been several incidents of outright violence, and in some units the "climate" was not conducive to good performance.

A Workplace Solutions team met with seven focus groups of nursing home staff during a two-day period. Each group was composed of a single category of employee: nursing assistants, nursing supervisors, dietary and environmental workers, or administrators. Staff members were questioned about job stress and satisfactions. The team also reviewed the records of grievances for the previous three years.

Goals Identified

After analyzing the data, Workplace Solutions identified the following goals for the facility:

- Better communication within work units and between the administration and all levels of the workforce, eliminating the "us and them" problem.
- Early response to warning signs of stress and conflict.
- Constructive, nonconfrontational resolution of grievances.
- Improved support for managers through skills training and enhanced opportunities for collaborative quality improvement.

Specific Changes

The following specific changes were recommended:

1. *A standing committee* or team to address:

   - Workplace climate problems.
   - Interpersonal and job-related disputes.
   - Reward structure and other morale-building programs.
   - Staff training and skills enhancement.

2. *A well-defined dispute resolution and grievance process* for all employees. The process should make use of mediation and other dispute resolution techniques, and be open to issues, such as interpersonal tensions, that may be ill suited to a conventional union-management grievance procedure.

3. *An upgraded, broad-brush Employee Assistance Program*, dealing with such matters as domestic and family problems. The existing program was underutilized and limited to substance abuse.

4. *A series of facilitated meetings* in each unit to:

   - Identify issues of morale, work organization, and communication.
   - Develop plans for better communication, including agreements for regular meetings or training.

5. *Training for managers*, the specific form and content to be determined by the sense of the meetings.

6. A community or "town" meeting, attended by representatives of the administration and each work unit, to agree upon a consensus statement of core values for the facility.

Workplace Solutions proceeded to help the facility implement the plan, beginning with a Conflict Management Survey designed to measure how much confidence workers had in the existing resolution modes. Among the perceptions that the survey measured were:

- Fairness of dispute resolution system.
- Efficacy of dispute resolution system.
- Supervisor fairness.
- Supervisor support.
- Co-worker fairness.
- Co-worker support.
- Organizational support and reward system.

In another effort to introduce dispute resolution as an adjunct to violence prevention, Workplace Solutions participated in designing demonstration programs for the U.S. Department of Health and Human Services. In 1997, the secretary of HHS released departmental guidelines on workplace violence as part of an overall strategy to improve the quality of work life for employees. The guidelines encourage HHS offices to establish crisis response teams to help prevent and respond to potential or actual violent incidents. The HHS Workplace Violence Task Force, which represents all the stakeholders in that department, asked Workplace Solutions to help form and train the crisis response teams. After evaluation, the results are to be revised and disseminated throughout the department in order to demonstrate the effectiveness of the model in a variety of contexts.

Even when effective dispute resolution programs are in place, some cases of severe distress will not be resolved. If the stress becomes serious enough, there may be threats, which should be examined according to the threat assessment procedures described earlier in the book.

CHAPTER 21

Preventing Violence in the Schools

In Springfield, Oregon, a 15-year-old armed with a semiautomatic rifle begins firing in a crowded high school cafeteria, leaving two students dead and 22 others wounded.[1] In Buffalo, New York, a deputy sheriff pursues his estranged wife into their children's elementary school, fatally shoots her, and wounds a school aide as teachers and pupils cower nearby.[2] In Costa Mesa, California, the distraught father of a disabled student takes hostage the administrator of the county special education program and is shot to death by a police SWAT team.[3]

School life once resembled gentle scenes from *Goodbye, Mr. Chips*, but in recent years bloody scenarios like these have been acted out in secondary and middle schools throughout the country. These high-profile incidents of fatal violence underscore the fact that fights, displays of weapons, and serious injury are daily occurrences in the schoolyard, lunchroom, and even classroom. Schools have become an arena for violent conflict, not only in urban areas associated with street crime but also in tranquil rural regions and well-to-do suburbs.

Shootings, assaults, harassment, and bullying at school can be viewed as a manifestation of the worldwide eruption in workplace violence. This unprecedented mayhem demonstrates an urgent need for school districts to emulate other private and public sector workplaces by adopting a comprehensive violence reduction strategy, marrying the insights of conflict resolution and crisis management. The strategy should embrace both prevention and intervention. Prevention focuses on relieving the stress, hostility, and tension that can precede violence, and on ensuring detection of danger signals. Intervention entails responding promptly and effectively to threats and danger risks.

The strategy should rely heavily on dispute resolution skills. Mediation, facilitation, and conciliation can ensure collaborative problem solving by a violence prevention and response team and mobilize the necessary school and community resources. Dispute resolvers, moreover, are needed to help design and operate a variety of mechanisms for reducing tension and conflict on a day-to-day basis.

Schools, like other workplaces, may be divided into the crisis-prone and the crisis-prepared.[4] The crisis-prone school denies the possibility of outbreaks of violence and does nothing to prevent or prepare for them, thereby increasing the chance of severe disruption and harm. It reacts to events, rather than reading the warning signs that might allow tragedy to be averted or mitigated. Such a school is typically mired in adversarial standoff, thwarting genuine internal communication and problem solving.

The crisis-prepared school, in contrast, systematically collects and analyzes early signs of distress, and it cultivates stakeholders' sense of mutual interest in responding effectively to incipient strains. Far from denying the possibility of crises, the school determines in advance how to deal with them. Rather than hunting for a few supposed "bad apples" in the barrel, it checks the barrel itself for defects.

As in other workplaces, violence in school is a human response to stress. Even "normal" persons can react violently when stress becomes unbearable. Symptoms and signals of individual and organizational breakdown typically precede every threat or act of violence. The potential for serious harm increases when a school does not read the signals or interrupt the downward spiral. A good school prevention program seeks to identify and relieve the sources of stress and put in place mechanisms to deal with threats to safety.

School violence is an especially complex phenomenon, fueled by a rich mixture of "stakeholders." They include employees (teachers, administrators, and nonteaching staff) and the consumers of educational services (students and parents). Each category of stakeholder is subject to its own variety of stress. The inner turmoil of adolescence and the demand for academic performance put pressure on students. Job demands and labor-management tension affect teachers, particularly when they are locked into hyperadversarial relationships with school authorities and scapegoated in public discourse for student underachievement. The Case of the Ambiguous Alert (Chapter 15) is an example of how extreme these tensions can become. At the same time, parsimonious taxpayers may be denying resources to administrators, who must cope with a plethora of government mandates and demands for services such as bilingual education and special education. Conflict over special education has produced dangerous—even fatal—levels of tension, as demonstrated by the Costa Mesa hostage incident. In an era of rapid technological change, parents may be desperate to ensure that their children are equipped with an education that prepares them for an uncertain future. Exponents of the gang lifestyle, moreover, may be lurking just beyond the schoolyard fence. The "culture wars" of recent decades—struggles over AIDS, illegal drug use, homosexuality, religious freedom, and free speech rights—have to a large extent been fought in the school setting, adding to the climate of tension.

There may be interplay among various types of tension. It would not be surprising if antipathy in labor-management relations affected student attitudes. Conversely, ethnic and racial disputes among students can disrupt the relationship between the district, parent groups, and the unions. Effective violence prevention thus depends on the ability of the school to deal comprehensively with the violence potential of employees, students, and parents.

An act of lethal violence committed by a school child is inherently disturbing. Something clearly needs to be done, as President Clinton has commented, "when high schools in small towns . . . are torn apart by disturbed children with deadly weapons."[5] His observation was germane to a spate of multiple shootings. In Kentucky, a 14-year-old killed three classmates and wounded five others at a prayer meeting in Heath High School in West Paducah (December 1997). In Arkansas, the police charged that a 13-year-old joined with an 11-year-old friend to murder five persons at the Westfield Middle School in Jonesboro (March 1998). That incident was followed by the lethal rampage in Springfield, Oregon, for which Thurston High School freshman Kip Kinkel was arrested (May 1998).

In the next school year occurred an even more horrific incident— a massacre at Columbine High School in Littleton, Colorado, a suburb of Denver (April 1999). Twelve fellow students and a teacher died at the hands of Eric Harris and Dylan Klebold, who deployed three long guns, a semiautomatic pistol, and scores of homemade pipe bombs. The two were members of the "Trench Coat Mafia," a clique of self-styled outcasts, and apparently sought revenge for being taunted by the more popular "jocks."

The episode culminated in the suicide of the perpetrators, whose fascination with the theme of violence had been evident in school activities—an essay and a video production—and on a Web site that they created.

Teachers, parents, and students have been left to wonder how persons of tender age could be responsible for such savage slaughter. The media have been chastised for glorifying gore. According to a study by the Annenberg Public Policy Center of the University of Pennsylvania, "television is putting a premium on attracting children aged 5 to 11, but many of the programs aimed at them contain violence and harsh language."[6] The Internet is blamed for disseminating recipes for bombs—and implying that they should be used. The easy availability of guns has also been cited as an inducement to violence. Nearly a million U.S. students took guns to school during the 1997–98 academic year,[7] apparently undeterred by the expulsion of about 6,000 of their peers for that offense in the previous school year.[8]

Cultural traits that affect child rearing have also come under suspicion. William Pollack, a clinical psychologist at Harvard University, points to a "gender straitjacket" that affects boys, creating anger, despair, and aggression. Pollack believes that almost all boys experience a sense of loneliness and isolation, because they are taught, starting at about age five, to be "little men" who stolidly repress their emotions: "We ask them to take a whole range of feelings and emotions and put those behind a mask. . . . We tell them they have to stand on their own two feet. And we shame them if they show any emotion." Barred from showing empathy, boys become depressed and interested in guns as a socially acceptable means of expressing the only emotion that is allowed them: anger. "What makes them aggressive is how we shape them in our society," Pollack contends. Violence is the result of the "intolerable burden a boy is forced to carry and simply cannot handle."[9]

Garden-variety sibling rivalry has also been proffered as a reason for some incidents. Michael Carneal, who pleaded guilty but mentally ill to charges of murder and attempted murder in the Kentucky shooting, told psychiatrists that he had felt pressured by the accomplishments of his older sister, who was the valedictorian of her graduating class.[10] A similar theory has been advanced about Kip Kinkel, an underachiever whose older sister was already a university student.

In the eyes of Gregory Holtz, a public administration specialist at Pace University who monitors federal education grants, "There is a steady state of violence in our schools." Most of it is verbal harassment and bullying, caused by dysfunctional home life, bad role models, and an apparent epidemic of Attention Deficit Disorder, contained pharmacologically with doses of Ritalin. Low-level violence can, however, escalate and become more serious. It is important to deal with violence in the early stages, Holtz maintains, because trying to deal with extreme cases is like devising "a program that remedies hurricanes."[11]

A variety of legislative and technological fixes have been attempted. The Federal Gun-Free Schools Act, initially passed in 1994, mandates expulsion for a least a year and referral to the juvenile justice system whenever a student brings a firearm or explosive to school. Some jurisdictions are opting for "smart-gun" technology, which allows a weapon to be fired only by its owner, making it "child-proof." And measures such as the television V-chip have been proposed to limit youngsters' viewing of violence.[12]

Restricting access to weapons and monitoring entertainment may contribute in the long term to a reduction in violence, but many of these measures involve highly contentious issues, such as the interpretation of the Bill of Rights. School officials cannot responsibly wait until those issues are resolved. They need to take immediate practical steps on their own initiative to forestall a repetition of Oregon's carnage in the cafeteria. The most immediate practical step would be to formulate a plan for responding to danger signals.

Reading the Signs

Although killings are often described as a surprise, in school as in other workplaces there are usually signs that a person may be at risk for committing violence. All too often the signs are ignored, owing to the absence of coherent systems for ensuring timely detection and effective countermeasures. In the aftermath of the Oregon incident, the U.S. Department of Education published a guide to safe schools which listed 16 early "behavioral and emotional signs" that suggest a child may become violent.[13] The early signs are:

- Social withdrawal, often stemming from feelings of unworthiness and rejection.
- Excessive feelings of isolation and being alone.
- Excessive feelings of rejection.
- Being a victim of violence, either in the school or at home.
- Feelings of being picked on and persecuted, which can include ridicule or teasing.
- Low school interest and poor academic performance, particularly when there is a sudden downturn.
- Expression of violence in writings and drawings, particularly when it is directed at specific persons.
- Uncontrolled anger that is expressed "frequently and intensely."

- Patterns of impulsive and chronic hitting, intimidation, and bullying behaviors.
- History of discipline problems, which may be the result of behavior linked to unmet emotional needs.
- Past history of violent and aggressive behavior, including animal cruelty and arson.
- Intolerance for differences and prejudicial attitudes, based on race, gender, or physical appearance.
- Drug and alcohol use, which can reduce self-control.
- Affiliation with gangs that "support antisocial values."
- Inappropriate access to, possession of, and use of firearms, particularly by children with a history of aggressiveness or impulsiveness.
- Serious threats of violence—considered the most reliable indicator of dangerousness.

The department emphasizes that the early warning signs are not predictors of violence but merely grounds for further examination of the child's emotional condition. They are not listed in order of importance, nor are they all of equal weight. They are meant to be reported to specialists who are trained in evaluating behavioral disorders and, if necessary, attempting an intervention. Besides *early* warning signs, the department listed *imminent* warning signs—indicators of immediate anger. The signs include serious fighting, property destruction, unexplained bouts of rage, threats of suicide, or "detailed threats of lethal violence."

Measured against the federal guidelines, the districts that suffered fatalities in 1998 were sorely wanting. In both the Oregon and Arkansas incidents, the students had articulated an intention to harm and a plan of dangerous action—which amounts to an "imminent warning sign." In Arkansas, the young shooters voiced an intention to commit violence at the middle school in order to avenge a perceived slight; one allegedly said, "I have a lot of killing to do." Young Kinkel apparently had spoken to other students in Thurston High about doing "something stupid" and had been voted by his fellows "Most Likely to Start World War III," a jest that proved to be figuratively prophetic. He idolized the Unabomber, boasted about stuffing "lit firecrackers into the mouths of squirrels and chipmunks,"[14] and bragged about having blown up a cow.[15] In speech class, he chose as his subject building a bomb. "He really knew what he was talking about," a classmate marveled. "His speech was well-delivered. It was very detailed, 'This is how you do it. You connect this wire to this . . .' He even drew a picture."[16]

Clearly, the youth had been signaling to peers. Fellow students felt uncomfortable talking to their elders about it and feared reprisal. Teachers who did hear of Kinkel's extreme statements were not perturbed, apparently because threats of mass destruction had been uttered by other children and because, in the classmate's words, he "didn't seem like a bizarre psychotic kid or anything. He was funny. He made you laugh in class, and what he joked about wasn't death or killing anyone. He just seemed like a perfectly normal, friendly little freshman."[17] Kinkel's pronouncements simply did not register on the district's radar, owing to denial and wishful thinking.[18] As John Lenssen, an official of the Oregon State Department of Education, has observed:

> There were many students at Thurston High School who knew Kip Kinkel and who knew the problems that he had. And there were many people who actually thought that he posed a danger. . . . But a powerful part of school culture for young people is not to share that information, not to tell, to be loyal, to be supportive, to minimize, to hope for the best, to look on the bright side. The students lacked commitment to the safety of their own school. They didn't have the training. They didn't have the background. They didn't know what to do. They didn't know what steps to take. . . . It was missing in their culture. The staff also lacked that background and that perspective, and the training to know how to respond.[19]

There is evidently a yawning gap between what is common knowledge on the school bus and what parents, teachers, counselors, or law enforcement authorities learn or take seriously. A cornerstone of violence prevention is the reporting of even casual threats. Students, like employees, should be encouraged—for their own safety—to report all menacing remarks or behavior, and these should be evaluated carefully by the violence prevention team and its experts.

The Oregon incident, as well as those in Colorado and Arkansas, involved students who displayed or practiced with weapons and bombs, another imminent warning sign. The discovery of a Beretta handgun in Kinkel's school locker the day before the fatal incident led to its confiscation and his suspension. He was placed in police custody, booked, and released, because the authorities found no cause to detain him. But confiscation failed to neutralize the danger, since the youth had ready access to other firearms and a stockpile of self-manufactured explosive devices at home. The suspension also gave him a motive for revenge. Although the legal grounds for detention may have been insufficient, there was still a potential for harm. The authorities neglected to undertake a prompt and thorough assessment of the risk, an essential element in violence prevention programs.

That a student brought a weapon to school signified a need for protective measures. Interviewing classmates and teachers about the behavior that preceded the incident surely would have shown that some form of intervention was needed, particularly since the parents had noticed a sudden decline in academic performance. It was the boy's father—later found murdered, along with the mother, in the family home—who seemed to recognize that necessity; shortly before shots rang out in the school, he made a desperate phone call, seeking to enroll the son in a program for troubled teens.

As in many safety crises, there was apparently no coordinated effort to evaluate the potential danger or shield possible targets when Kip first appeared in school with a gun. The school and the police department each followed its own, ultimately ineffective routine. Just as summarily discharging a disruptive or threatening employee rarely leaves the workplace more secure, suspension of a student without evaluation and remedial action is an inherently hazardous step. In the wake of Springfield, many schools have pledged to monitor students after expulsion or suspension.[20] The measures include alternative schools for those who are expelled and special training for their parents. The U.S. Conference of Mayors has proposed that school officials be authorized to detain students for 72 hours for evaluation purposes if they bring guns to school.[21]

There has been an unseemly rush to place schools in "lock-down" mode by installing metal detectors, security cameras, and mirrors. In some instances, school districts have offered students financial rewards for "ratting" on friends, and innocuous essays or fictional accounts of violent incidents became suspect. But the need to determine whether a student poses a danger should not be an excuse for a witch-hunt. Early warning signs must not be misused as if they were a junior version of the supposed "profile" of the violent adult. Although there have been calls to make reporting of ominous remarks mandatory—following the model of child abuse laws—a mechanistic process for dealing with perceived threats is no substitute for judgment based on knowledge of the individual and the context.

Intervention Strategies

An important lesson to be drawn from Littleton, Springfield, and Jonesboro is that each district should have a standing crisis prevention and response team to identify potential threats, consult experienced risk assessors, and coordinate the school and community resources needed to assure safety. A representative team is essential to ensure "buy-in" by all stakeholders, so that menacing remarks—like those that preceded the

Colorado, Oregon, and Arkansas shootings—are reported promptly. "Too often," the Department of Education guide aptly observes, "caring individuals remain silent because they have no way to express their concerns."[22] The team should also be a place to discuss severely maladapted children. In the aftermath of the Kentucky shooting teachers at the stricken high school, in the words of its principal, "try to be much more aware of students that are not seeming to adjust to high school or . . . kids that are troubled and why they're troubled. That's very much on your mind."[23]

Intervention should be as early as possible and should include, in the words of the guide, "teaching the child alternative, socially appropriate replacement responses—such as problem solving and anger control skills." Children who are at risk for violence "often need to learn interpersonal, problem solving and conflict resolution skills at home and in school." They also may need to be taught to restrain impulsive behavior and to develop a personal sense of empathy.

In various parts of the country efforts have already begun to give school children the wherewithal to behave nonviolently. In Clackamas County, Oregon, near Portland, the Family Court Services agency has launched a "peer mediation" program in six middle and high schools. Students are trained to mediate conflicts among their fellow students. As an exercise, trainees at McLoughlin Middle School are asked: "What problems do you see students struggling with . . . that might show up in mediation sessions?" They are also instructed to explain their role to the disputants:

- We don't take sides.
- We don't make decisions for you.
- We don't decide who's right or wrong.
- We are here to help you negotiate.

The ground rules include "no physical fighting or threats." The trainees learn to distinguish between that which must be reported to authorities and that which is confidential.

Teen mediators also participate with adults in sessions designed to help students whose barely contained aggressiveness is linked to dysfunctional family life. In one case, seven middle school boys were brought together around a table in a counselor's office with two teen mediators and a staff person. "The scars displayed on their faces and arms gave an immediate indication that these youths are not strangers to violence," recalls Amy Swift, the social worker who manages the program. The mediators probed for the reasons why the boys battled with each other. Eventually, out poured stories about the boys' neighborhood, which they called "Felony

Flats." It was a story, according to Swift, about "gangs to protect themselves, the neighbors selling drugs, the parents at the bars."[24] Such sessions, Swift believes, are more effective than having adults try to browbeat students.

The teen mediator program is an example of the "cadre approach," which focuses on a small number of relatively well-trained students. An alternative is the "total student body approach," in which conflict resolution is viewed as a life skill to be diffused throughout the school population. In the latter approach, students take turns serving as mediator in order to internalize what educators David W. Johnson and Roger T. Johnson call the "credo of nonviolence." The Johnsons tested that theory in a variety of schools, concluding that "it is the actual experience of being a mediator that best teaches students" how to settle their own disputes:

> We found that before training, most students had daily conflicts, used destructive strategies that tended to escalate the conflict . . . and did not know how to negotiate. After training, students could apply the negotiation and mediation process to actual conflict situations, as well as transfer them to nonclassroom and nonschool settings, such as the playground, the lunchroom, and at home. Further, they maintained their knowledge and skills throughout the school year.[25]

At the publicly funded Upstate School Safety Center in New Paltz, New York, the presence of conflict resolution skills is treated as a "protective" factor that offsets such violence risk factors as domestic abuse in students' homes. The center encourages the formation of school safety teams capable of defusing situations that might lead to violence. In many schools, according to Joakim Lartey, a program coordinator at the center, "there is poor communication, and the teachers don't know how to de-escalate the kids." His observation is supported by a survey of 348 Oregon schools conducted around the time of the Springfield incident; more than half the schools agreed with the proposition: "Many teachers do not have appropriate conflict resolution skills." And fully 81 percent of the schools believed that the statement was true of students as well.[26] The lack of communication and conflict skills could help foster ethnically based gangs in districts with particularly diverse populations.

The center uses a naturalist's taxonomy to rate the keenness of districts to prepare for the unthinkable. Those who are reluctant to acquire the necessary training—on the grounds that it "can't happen here"—are classified by the center as "ostriches." Those who prepare diligently and arm themselves with the skills needed to avoid dangerous confrontation are regarded more flatteringly as "beavers." The center takes pains to ensure proper teamwork, so that the violence prevention plan does not suffer "death by committee." It advises the safety teams to set measurable numerical goals, such as halving the number of suspensions by a target date.

Another approach to overly aggressive students draws upon the ancient notion of reintegration of an offender into the community. Ulster-Sullivan Mediation, based in Highland, New York, has developed a Suspension Re-Entry Program that resembles victim-offender mediation, a technique often used as an adjunct to law enforcement. The program facilitates the return of students who have been suspended for making serious threats or using physical force against a teacher. A community mediator meets separately with the teacher and the student, and then brings them together for a kind of spiritual healing in which a plan is made to avoid any repetition of the offense. "The suspension is turned into a cooling off period," according to Clare Danielson, executive director of Ulster-Sullivan Mediation:

> Punitive discipline does not solve the problem. It simply puts the emotional aspects of the conflict in the closet—to be taken out (or fall out) whenever the emotional door opens again. . . . There is resentment, anger, fear—all the negative emotions the person being disciplined feels. . . . [The re-entry program] is the opportunity to work out the past difficulties in the relationship and establish a new way of being with each other. . . .[27]

The program was initiated in an upstate New York school district in the spring of 1996, and 12 students were brought back from suspension. All completed the school year.

An imaginative violence prevention program was also developed at an unlikely site: Boston University Medical Center. Among the center's patients are teens who have sustained spinal injuries in gang wars. Many of the wounded, now bound to wheelchairs, have been profoundly transformed by the experience. As one wrote in the program's newsletter, "When you are lying there, gasping for air, bleeding, going into shock, rushing towards death, all that hard core is gone." Teens in the center are inducted into the Spinal Cord Injury Violence Prevention Club, whose members "offer a positive alternative to retaliation" in their home neighborhoods, according to the project coordinator, Joan Vaz Serra Hoffman. They help resolve peacefully disputes that might otherwise further the cycle of violence. Because of their ability to relate to peers, Hoffman urges that young persons be included in the planning of violence prevention efforts.

The Union-Management Climate

Ideally, a violence prevention and response team should include a representative of the unions in the school district, inasmuch as the safety of their members is at stake. All too often, however, the district is beset by union-management strife, which prevents cooperation on violence prevention.

As an example, rancorous union-management relations plagued a rural school district of the northeast that had gone for years without a collective bargaining contract between the board and the teachers.[28] Mutual animosity had reached fever pitch. In a letter to a local newspaper, a school board member condemned the teachers as "underworked, overpaid prima donnas" and an "army of occupation." He complained: "They are mostly non-residents who come into our town to take our tax dollars . . . and cheat our children out of a good education. . . . These people simply want to go on raping our children. . . ."

The inflammatory language of the board member was matched on the other side by lurid displays on bulletin boards in the teachers' lounge. In one cartoon, the board and the administration are shown holding a dagger, dripping with blood, over the head of a figure marked "education." In another, a gory scimitar is portrayed as cleaving the union logo in half. Other drawings threatened "scabs" with flat tires, and some tires actually did lose air mysteriously.

At a tumultuous meeting in the school auditorium, a teacher later claimed, she was publicly "dehumanized" by a board member's comments. She filed a grievance, asserting that the incident amounted to an improper evaluation. During the arbitration hearing, a vaguely worded settlement was arranged through mediation. But it merely papered over the simmering resentment between the parties.

Given the hyperbole that marred the relationship between management and the union, the district would have benefited from an intensive intervention. In all, it took the parties six harrowing years to reach an agreement. The experience is somewhat extreme, but spending many years negotiating is not unusual. As the 1998–99 school year opened, for instance, several districts in New York State were without a contract for a fourth or fifth year.[29]

The persistence of contemptuous, intemperate language and subtle menace is harmful, not least because it represents a poor role model for students. Seeing their elders locked into unrelenting combat no doubt influences the way young people deal with each other. Moreover, the free-floating anger could well turn into something more sinister. The destructive potential of tension between a teacher and a district is well illustrated by the Case of the Ambiguous Alert.

Constructing a Comprehensive Strategy

Sometimes undue aggressiveness in labor relations and in student behavior can be addressed in tandem. In California's Huntington Beach Union High School District, a comprehensive violence prevention strategy aimed at students emerged from the use of dispute resolution techniques to alter a poor labor relations climate.

The district encompasses three Orange County cities—Westminster, Huntington Beach, and Fountain Valley—along with six comprehensive high schools, a continuation school, and an adult education school. In the late 1970s, the district suffered from three teacher union strikes in five years as well as a plague of gang violence. In 1985, Bonnie Prouty Castrey, a federal mediator who resided in the district, was put forward as a candidate for the school board because of her professional expertise in promoting labor-management cooperation. Castrey was told, "Look, we've got to stop fighting. Kids aren't learning, and what's really happening is that we're having a terrible time trying to negotiate contracts." There had not been a contract for 18 months, and children were being forced to decide whether they should cross picket lines in order to attend school.

Castrey was elected, creating a majority that was ready to make labor-management peace. The board, the administration, and the district's three unions embarked upon a conflict resolution process called Relationship By Objective (RBO). RBO is a form of "preventive mediation" pioneered by John Popular at the Federal Mediation and Conciliation Service. FMCS describes RBO as "strong medicine."[30] The process is designed to remedy the "strained labor-management relationship," which is characterized by "mistrust, suspicion and animosity." In RBO, the parties analyze their problems jointly, decide on common objectives, and take steps to reach those goals. Popular became a consultant to the district, helping to build a cooperative relationship and cultivate a sense of trust.

As a result of the newly achieved harmony, the parties were able to confront one of the district's most pressing issues: gang violence. The police had informed the board that there were 35 gangs in the district's three cities. "We knew that if there were 35 gangs in those cities, there were gangs on our campuses," Castrey recalls. "We needed to know how to prevent any gang operations—or we were going to have dead teachers, dead staff members or dead kids. None of us wanted that to happen."

Galvanized by the murder of a 16-year-old in a gang battle, all the stakeholders realized that a preventive strategy was needed. The newspapers were asking whether the campuses were safe. By means of the RBO process, the disciplinary guidelines were revised. In 1988, mediators from the Northern California Community Justice Center began instructing the faculty and students in conflict resolution. Since then, several hundred have graduated from the Student Conflict Mediation Program. According to Superintendent Susan Roper, "This program emphasizes prevention and gives students the skills to build better relationships. Student mediators handle common disputes between students, such as rumors, damaged friendships, misunderstandings, arguments, fights, bullying and disputes over personal property."

The district also initiated a highly participatory form of strategic planning. The safety component of the strategy called for mediation and conflict resolution programs on every campus, underwritten by grants as well as district funds. In addition, the district set about drafting policies on violence prevention and ensuring that all the stakeholders—including the unions and the community—bought in.[31]

Hundreds of residents attended public hearings about a board proposal to bring police sniffing dogs onto campuses. The community was assured that the policy would be noninvasive, that the dogs would search lockers and vehicles only for weapons and for drugs. If either were found, the student would be removed from class and the parents informed. As a result of the policy, students know that school is not a place to smoke, drink, or carry weapons. All of this came about as a result of creating labor-management peace; without it, the constituent groups in the district would have been unable to trust each other sufficiently to work together on safety and security, even though it affected all of them.

Given their core educational mission, schools should be uniquely well suited to preventing violence. As the Johnsons point out, allowing students "to fail, remain apart from classmates and be socially inept and have low self-esteem, increases the probability that students will use destructive conflict strategies."[32] On the other hand, an ability to deploy higher-order reasoning and analytical skills in order to solve problems is closely linked with peaceful outcomes. Thus, the propensity for violence, both in school and in later life, can best be cured in the long run by enlarging understanding and self-confidence. Until that goal is achieved, however, it is prudent for school districts to rely for their safety on well-drilled, consensus-based violence prevention and response teams.

PART V

DOCUMENTARY RESOURCES

APPENDIX A

Sample Policies

This appendix contains an illustrative selection of provisions excerpted from workplace violence prevention policies that have been adopted or proposed as models by private enterprise, unions, federal, state, and local government, universities, and advocacy groups. This array of formulations is intended to serve as a reference and source of ideas for those who are responsible for framing policy in their own workplaces. Inclusion in this selection does not imply endorsement by the authors. Rather, the selections are intended to represent the broad spectrum of approaches that have been tried by workplace decision makers.

General Policies

Example 1. A corporate policy that explains the role of its threat response team and creates an open channel of communication between employees and the team. Source: DuPont Corporation.

. . .[C]onduct creating an intimidating, hostile, offensive, or threatening working environment through unwelcome words, actions, or physical contact will not be tolerated. Those violating this practice may be subject to disciplinary action up to and including discharge.

Sources of Workplace Violence

- Random Criminal Violence by a perpetrator who works at the same company
- Domestic Violence by a perpetrator who is a family member or significant other
- Stalking
- Toxic Work Environment

Threat Management Response Team

Purpose 1: Provide guidance that promises a safe workplace for all persons working for the company, through their business units, by providing a holistic approach guided by multidisciplinary expertise.

Purpose 2: Provide quality consultation and response in a way that promotes early identification, intervention and response in acute and potential situations.

Our goals are to:

- Reduce frequency.
- Reduce seriousness.
- Reduce employee impact.
- Reduce Company impact.
- Provide consultation with business/site management and HR assessing potentially volatile employees and/or situations.
- Emergency assistance to business/site management during acute situations.
- Assistance during investigations (harassment, threats, violence).
- Consultation to ensure path forward that assures safe and fair resolution for all stakeholders.
- 24 hour/day, 7 day/week access to Threat Management Response Team via Sky Page.
- Also provides linkage to EAP services, including Critical Incident Debriefing.

Employee Assistance Program

Provides consultation to Threat Management Response Team regarding harassment, threats, and violence. At times, information of a threatening nature is revealed during the assessment and/or treatment process. If it is determined at any point that a true threat exists, the EAP will share this information with appropriate personnel to forewarn potential victims.

Confidential Employee Hotline

- Originally put in place as part of DuPont's Personal Safety Program.
- Today, it serves as a non-threatening avenue of support for all employees, providing advice and counsel concerning battering, rape crisis, all forms of harassment (sexual, racial, etc.) and other related issues and concerns.
- It is staffed 24 hours a day, 7 days a week.
- When a call is received, an operator will put the caller in touch with a volunteer trained in crisis intervention.
- The volunteer can advise the caller about the local availability of medical, psychological and rape crisis assistance programs and can advise callers about options and available support systems.
- Individuals calling the Hotline may choose to remain anonymous and need not disclose their location or organizational affiliation.
- Hotline volunteers will work with the caller to understand the issue or concern and will help develop strategies for dealing with them.
- Should they so desire, callers may ask for assistance in bringing their concern or situation to the attention of management.

Example 2. A policy designed for a national retailing chain, here called the Acme Corporation. Source: CMG Associates.

Acme Corporation believes that all associates are entitled to a non-threatening workplace where the basic safety of each associate is promoted. *Therefore, any form of violence, whether actual or perceived, will not be tolerated.*

This includes, but is not limited to:

- Disruptive activity in the workplace
- Threatening, hostile or intimidating behavior
- Possession of a dangerous weapon
- Violation of restraining orders
- Fighting
- Verbal abuse
- Stalking
- Sabotaging another associate's work

- Harmful misuse of equipment or other company property.
- Any behavior which is perceived as threatening by the recipient

An associate who believes he or she is or has been subjected to threatening or intimidating behavior related to the workplace by a fellow associate, a customer, a family member or other, should report such conduct to the individual(s) specified in the complaint procedure. Complaints of intimidation or violence will be promptly and discreetly investigated. Any associate who violates this policy will be subject to serious disciplinary action, up to and including discharge. . . .

Management Responsibility

Violence, or the threat of violence, whether committed by supervisory or non-supervisory personnel, is against stated company policy, and may be considered as unlawful as well. In addition, management is responsible for taking action against threats or acts of violence by company personnel or others (customers/outside vendors, family members or others), regardless of the manner in which the company becomes aware of the conduct.

All complaints must be treated as serious violations of company policy and investigated accordingly. It is management's responsibility to show associates that the company is serious about prohibiting and preventing violence in the workplace.

If a supervisor becomes aware of any action, behavior, or perceived threat that may violate this policy, the supervisor is responsible for immediately contacting a member of the Crisis Management Team.

Complaint Procedure

- Complaints of violence or of intimidating behavior should be brought to the attention of the Crisis Management Team. Any one of the following may be contacted: Senior Vice President of Compliance, Vice President of Human Resources, or the Director of Security. In addition, depending on the severity of the situation, the CEO may need to be informed.
- After the Crisis Management Team has been notified of a complaint, or when it receives knowledge that a situation involving a possible threat of violence exists, then the Team will undertake a thorough investigation to gather all pertinent facts.
- Non-Retaliation—This policy prohibits retaliation against any associate who brings complaints of violent or intimidating behavior, or

who helps in investigating complaints; the associate will not be adversely affected in terms and conditions of employment, nor discriminated against or discharged because of the complaint.

- After the investigation has been completed, a determination will be made regarding the resolution of the complaint. If a violation of this policy is found, disciplinary action will be taken, up to and including termination of employment.

Example 3. A template memorandum from a federal agency director to employees, explaining the workplace violence prevention policy. Source: Federal Office of Personnel Management.

It is the [agency's] policy to promote a safe environment for its employees. The Department is committed to working with its employees to maintain a work environment free from violence, threats of violence, harassment, intimidation, and other disruptive behavior. While this kind of conduct is not pervasive at our agency, no agency is immune. Every agency will be affected by disruptive behavior at one time or another.

Violence, threats, harassment, intimidation, and other disruptive behavior in our workplace will not be tolerated; that is, all reports of incidents will be taken seriously and will be dealt with appropriately. Such behavior can include oral or written statements, gestures, or expressions that communicate a direct or indirect threat of physical harm. Individuals who commit such acts may be removed from the premises and may be subject to disciplinary action, criminal penalties, or both.

We need your cooperation to implement this policy effectively and maintain a safe working environment. Do not ignore violent, threatening, harassing, intimidating, or other disruptive behavior. If you observe or experience such behavior by anyone on agency premises, whether he or she is an agency employee or not, report it immediately to a supervisor or manager. Supervisors and managers who receive such reports should seek advice from the Employee Relations Office . . . regarding investigating the incident and initiating appropriate action. [PLEASE NOTE: Threats or assaults that require immediate attention by security or police should be reported first to security . . . or to police at 911.]

I will support all efforts made by supervisors and agency specialists in dealing with violent, threatening, harassing, intimidating or other disruptive behavior in our workplace and will monitor whether this policy is being implemented effectively. . . .

Example 4. A policy, also written for a federal agency, that contains precise definitions of the main concepts. Source: Lewis Research Center, National Aeronautics and Space Administration.

Definitions:

Threat—A communicated intent to inflict physical or other harm on any person or property.

Threatening Behavior—Any behavior that is provoking and unsafe, which by its very nature could cause physical or other harm to any person or property. It may or may not include an actual physical attack.

Physical Attack—Aggression resulting in a physical assault with or without the use of a weapon.

Violence—Unjustified or unwarranted use of physical force so as to injure, damage, or abuse a person or property.

Policy:

The safety of employees and Agency property is of paramount importance to the mission and goals of the NASA Lewis Research Center. In order to ensure the safety and security of Center personnel, violence and threatening behavior including verbal and/or written threats or physical attacks in the workplace are prohibited. The possession of firearms, ammunition, dangerous or deadly weapons (18 U.S.C. Sec. 930) on Agency premises or in Agency controlled/occupied space, except by authorized personnel, is also prohibited. Such conduct will not be tolerated by employees and/or visitors to the NASA Lewis Research Center.

Implementation of the Policy:

Violations of this policy will be treated seriously and may result in disciplinary action, up to and including removal from Federal service.

All employees are required to promptly report violent or threatening behavior by:

- calling 911 if the situation warrants immediate emergency assistance, or
- notifying his/her supervisor or appropriate management official of the situation.

Managers and supervisors are accountable for providing a safe working environment for all employees. They are responsible for:

- Communicating the workplace violence policy to all employees and ensuring its compliance.

- Identifying actual and striving to identify potential violent and/or threatening behavior and arranging for the investigation into such matters.
- Taking appropriate action when actual incidents are reported or when potential violent or threatening behavior situations are identified, in accordance with the Workplace Violence Plan (appendix to Emergency Preparedness Plan). . . . This includes keeping management, up to and including the Center Director, informed of such actions.
- Attending required training provided by the Center, regarding preventing workplace violence.

Awareness programs for all Center employees and required training for managers, regarding violence in the workplace will be established, as outlined in the Emergency Preparedness Plan.

Example 5. A policy, adopted by a medium-sized city in the Pacific northwest, that pays special attention to the meaning of the term "violence." Source: City of Bellevue, Washington.

The word violence in this policy shall mean an act or behavior that:

- is physically assaultive;
- a reasonable person would perceive as obsessively directed, e.g. intensely focused on a grudge, grievance, or romantic interest in another person, and reasonably likely to result in harm or threats of harm to persons or property;
- consists of a communicated or reasonably perceived threat to harm another individual or in any way endanger the safety of an individual;
- would be interpreted by a reasonable person as carrying potential for physical harm to the individual;
- is a behavior, or action, that a reasonable person would perceive as menacing;
- involves carrying or displaying weapons, destroying property, or throwing objects in a manner reasonably perceived to be threatening; or
- consists of a communicated or reasonably perceived threat to destroy property.

Violent actions on City property or facilities, or while on City business, will not be tolerated or ignored. Any unlawful violent actions committed by employees or members of the public while on City property, or while using City facilities, will be prosecuted as appropriate. The City intends to use reasonable legal, managerial, administrative, and disciplinary procedures to secure the workplace from violence and to reasonably protect employees and members of the public.

Policy Goals and Objectives

The objective of this policy is to achieve the following:

- reduce the potential for violence in and around the workplace;
- encourage and foster a work environment that is characterized by respect and healthy conflict resolution; and
- mitigate the negative consequences for employees who experience or encounter violence in their work lives. . . .

All employees are responsible for:

- refraining from acts of violence and for seeking assistance to resolve personal issues that may lead to acts of violence in the workplace; and
- reporting to managers and supervisors any dangerous or threatening situations that occur in the workplace.

Employees are encouraged to report to their managers/supervisors situations that occur outside of the workplace which may affect workplace safety, i.e., instances where protection orders have been issued, etc.

Managers/Supervisors

Managers and supervisors are responsible for assessing situations, making judgments on the appropriate response, and then responding to reports of or knowledge of violence and for initiating the investigation process.

Any report of violence will be evaluated immediately and confidentially, and appropriate action will be taken, where possible, in order to protect the employee from further violence. Appropriate disciplinary action will be taken when it is determined that City of Bellevue employees have committed acts of violence.

Where issues of employee safety are of concern, managers and supervisors should evaluate the workplace and make appropriate recommendations regarding a reasonable response.

The City Manager

In so far as is reasonably possible, the City Manager, or the City Manager's designee, is responsible for developing procedures that are designed to reasonably achieve:

- prompt and appropriate response to any act of violence;
- accountability among employees for acts of violence committed in the workplace;
- establishment of oversight of investigations of violence;
- establishment of a Crisis Management Team to provide immediate response to serious incidents;
- establishment of avenues of support for employees who experience violence; and
- communication of this policy and administrative procedures to employees, managers and supervisors.

Example 6.   A municipal policy, drafted by a small California city, that deals in detail with threats of violence. Source: City of El Centro, California.

Acts or Threats of Violence Defined

"Threats or acts of violence" include conduct against persons or property that is sufficiently severe, offensive, or intimidating to alter the employment conditions at the City of El Centro, or to create a hostile, abusive, or intimidating work environment for one or more City of El Centro employees.

Examples of Workplace Violence

General examples of prohibited workplace violence include, but are not limited to, the following:

- All threats or acts of violence occurring on City of El Centro property, regardless of the relationship between the City and the parties involved in the incident.
- All threats or acts of violence not occurring on City property but involving someone who is acting in the capacity of a representative of the City of El Centro.

- All threats or acts of violence not occurring on City property involving an employee of the City of El Centro if the threats or acts of violence affect the legitimate interests of the City of El Centro.
- Any threats or acts resulting in the conviction of an employee or agent of the City of El Centro, or of an individual performing services on the City's behalf on a contract or temporary basis, under any criminal code provision relating to threats or acts of violence that adversely affect the legitimate interests and goals of the City of El Centro.

Specific Examples of Prohibited Conduct

Specific examples of conduct that may be considered "threats or acts of violence" prohibited under this policy include, but are not limited to, the following:

- Hitting or shoving an individual.
- Threatening to harm an individual or his/her family, friends, associates, or their property.
- The intentional destruction or threat of destruction of property owned, operated, or controlled by the City of El Centro.
- Making harassing or threatening telephone calls, letters or other forms of written or electronic communications.
- Intimidating or attempting to coerce an employee to do wrongful acts that would affect the business interests of the City.
- Harassing surveillance, also known as "stalking," the willful, malicious and repeated following of another person and making a credible threat with intent to place the other person in reasonable fear of his or her safety.
- Making a suggestion or otherwise intimating that an act to injure persons or property is "appropriate," without regard to the location where such suggestion or intimation occurs.
- Unauthorized possession or inappropriate use of firearms, weapons, or any other dangerous devices on City property.

While employees of the City may be required as a condition of their work assignment to possess firearms, weapons or other dangerous devices, or permitted to carry them as authorized by law, it is the City's policy that employees are to use them only in accordance with departmental operating procedures and all applicable State and Federal laws.

Example 7. A municipal policy that lists behaviors which should be taken seriously. Source: City of Fort Lauderdale, Florida.

All employees have a responsibility to act upon any event or occurrence that may indicate a need for help and assistance or another employee who has displayed an indicating "signal" that help is warranted. Any employee or supervisor who becomes aware of a threat made by another employee and has observed one or more of the following behaviors from that employee should contact his/her immediate supervisor who then has the responsibility to contact the Personnel Director and/or the Employee Relations Director.

- Carrying a concealed weapon or flashing a weapon to test reactions.
- Direct or veiled threats of harm.
- Intimidation of others. (This can be physical or verbal intimidation. Harassing phone calls and stalking are obvious examples.)
- Disregard for the safety of co-employees.
- Paranoid behavior. Perceiving that the whole world is against them.
- Moral righteousness and believing the organization is not following its rules and procedures.
- Unable to take criticism of job performance. Holds a grudge, especially against a supervisor. Often verbalizes hope for something to happen to the person against whom the employee has the grudge.
- Obsessive involvement with the job, often with uneven job performance and no apparent outside interests.
- Extreme interest in semi-automatic or automatic weapons and their destructive power to people.
- Fascination with incidents of workplace violence and approval of the use of violence under similar circumstances.
- History of violent behavior.
- Expression of extreme desperation over recent family, financial or personal problems.

No employee acting in good faith, who reports real or implied violent behavior, will be subject to retaliation or harassment based upon their report.

Collective Bargaining Agreement Language

Example 1. A provision on workplace violence that has been added to the sections of a collective bargaining agreement dealing with health and safety. Source: National Federation of Federal Employees (NFFE), Local 997, and the NASA-Ames Research Center.

Article XI—Environment, Health and Safety

Section 1. Safe Working Conditions—It is the Center's responsibility to provide a work environment free of recognized hazards. It is also the Center's goal to comply with applicable federal, state, and local laws and regulations regarding the environment, health and safety of the employees covered by this Agreement. . . .

Section 22. Preventing Workplace Violence—The Union and the Center agree to work together to prevent violence This cooperation may include co-sponsoring training and sharing information. If an employee has a protective order from a court, the employee is encouraged to notify the Protective Services Office of such order. The employee may request security assistance to help ensure personal safety while at the Center. If a violent incident occurs, and it involves members of the bargaining unit, the Center shall brief the Union and discuss ways of preventing a recurrence.

Example 2.   Contract language recommended by a major North American public sector union. It adopts a preventive approach and seeks to ensure that sufficient trained staff are available to deal with foreseeable emergencies. Source: Canadian Union of Public Employees.

Function of Workplace Union-Employer Health and Safety Committee

All incidents involving aggression or violence shall be brought to the attention of the health and safety committee. The employer agrees that the health and safety committee shall concern itself with all matters relating to violence to staff, including but not limited to:

- developing violence policies;
- developing measures and procedures to prevent violence to staff;
- receiving and reviewing reports of violent incidents; and
- developing and implementing violence training programs.

Where no union-employer health and safety committee has been established, the employer agrees to consult with the Union.

Staffing Levels to Deal with Potential Violence

The employer agrees that, where there is a risk of violence, an adequate level of trained employees must be present. The employer recognizes that workloads can lead to fatigue and a diminished ability both to identify and to subsequently deal with potentially violent situations.

The Employer agrees:

- to reach an agreement about the minimum number of staff for nights, weekends and changeover periods between shifts;
- that where there is an established risk of violence, there shall be an agreed minimum number of appropriately trained staff on duty at any one time;
- that employees will not be required to work alone, especially in situations where there is a recognized potential for violence; and
- that where a patient, resident or client is assessed as being actually or potentially violent or aggressive, no employee will be required to approach that patient, resident or client without being accompanied by at least one other person.

Training

The employer agrees to provide training and information on the prevention of violence to . . . all employees who come into contact with potentially aggressive persons. The training program will include adequate opportunities for participation by union instructors.

All employees working in areas where there is a risk of violence shall be trained with a course including but not limited to:

- causes of violence;
- factors that precipitate violence;
- recognition of warning signs;
- prevention of escalation;
- controlling and defusing aggressive situations; and
- details of the employer's policies, measures and procedures to deal with violence and the availability of legal counsel and supportive counseling.

The employer agrees to provide adequate time and resources for this training. The employer shall pay each employee his/her wages as set out in the collective agreement while he/she undergoes such training or any subsequent training.

University Policies

Example 1.   A university policy that incorporates a broad definition of workplace violence and links it with a highly structured response mechanism. Source: Medical College of Georgia.

For purposes of this policy, "workplace violence" shall mean any behavior, act or statement that:

- would be interpreted by a reasonable person to be aggressive, intimidating, harassing, or unsafe; and
- which carries an expressed or implied intent to cause harm to a person or property; and
- is related to [a workplace] activity. . . .

Crisis Management Team (CMT)

There shall be a CMT appointed by the Vice President for Business Operations and Legal Advisor to the President to serve as a resource for issues related to workplace violence. The CMT shall consist of: the Director of Human Resources, one representative from the Legal Office, one representative from Public Safety, one representative from Employee/Faculty Assistance Program, one representative from Institutional Relations, two representatives at-large and one representative from Student Affairs if a student is involved in the incident. The Vice President shall designate one member of the CMT as the chair and it shall meet from time to time as necessary.

The CMT shall serve as a resource for supervisors and other employees in situations involving workplace violence. The CMT will provide advice and guidance on MCG policies and procedures, intervention, counseling and prevention. Supervisors responding to allegations of workplace violence shall report all such allegations and their resolution to the CMT. CMT shall conduct a post-incident review and, where appropriate, make recommendations for preventing or responding to future incidents.

The CMT shall be responsible for designing and implementing workplace violence training and education for MCG faculty, students, and employees. Such training programs will be reviewed by the CMT at least annually, administered and tracked by the Personnel and Training Section and will be offered at least once each year. . . .

Example 2. A policy that offers advice about how to conduct oneself when confronting a potentially violent situation. Source: University of Michigan.

Threats can be direct and immediate or vague and occur either verbally or in writing. Acts of aggression include abusive behavior, stalking, and tampering with property and are intended to intimidate, create fear, inflict harm, or destroy property. Violent behavior is behaving in a way that poses an immediate threat to self or others by acts of physical harm.

Acts of violence cannot be predicted with absolute certainty, although we can minimize the risk to everyone when behaviors that are observed are reported to appropriate authorities. Often threats or acts of aggression escalate to a level of violence when there is poor communication with the person and the person cannot cope under the stress. The reason for violence is often a person being angry with the organization and they are seeking retaliation. In addition when a customer, patient, or guest feels they have been denied a product or service they may become threatening, aggressive or violent.

Paying close attention to behavior and warning signs, to your own response to the events will help prevent a crisis and increase everyone's safety. When interacting with a potentially aggressive or violent person be aware of your reactions, report all behaviors to others, and follow the suggested guidelines:

- Introduce yourself and acknowledge their difficulties.
- Remain calm, speak in a low voice . . . don't argue or agree with the distortions.
- Let them know of consequences . . . "I'll call security if you don't sit down and stop yelling . . . I can't help you if you don't calm down."
- Monitor your nonverbal cues (tone, volume and rate of voice; maintain a stance that is not challenging . . .).
- Avoid invasion of a "personal space"; keep a safe distance of 3–6 feet.
- Use empathetic listening . . . be interested, helpful, and supportive. What is the person really saying?
- Treat people with respect regardless of their behavior.
- Avoid being judgmental or defensive.
- Apologize if appropriate . . . provide helpful verbal responses or short-term options, if possible.
- Do not make promises that you cannot fulfill.

If the person has an appeal to a higher authority then so inform them. Report all behaviors to appropriate authorities or call Public Safety at "911." If the behavior reaches the point of violence then:

- Remain calm . . . dealing with the person calmly and confidently will help reduce further communication problems.
- Call "911" . . . report your name and location, and information on "who, what, where, and when."
- Direct the adversaries to leave the scene of a confrontation.
- Do not try to physically force a person to leave. Do not touch the person.
- If violent behavior is occurring, escape, hide if not already seen, or . . . [take cover] if injury is likely.
- Make every possible effort to get others out of the immediate area.
- Position yourself, if possible, so that an exit route is readily accessible.
- Never attempt to disarm or accept a weapon from the person in question.
- If a weapon is involved, calmly ask the person to put it in a neutral location while you continue to talk with him/her. Don't argue, threaten, or block their exit.

Example 3. A policy that incorporates a set of "action guidelines" keyed to the level of aggressiveness displayed by a threatening person. Source: University of San Francisco.

Behavior Level of Subject

Level I—The subject may:

- Show signs of increasing stress, perhaps involving negative changes in behavior
- Show signs of a deterioration in work performance
- Show signs of increasingly unkempt appearance
- Show signs of alcohol or substance abuse
- Show signs of distress over personal or workplace problems
- Act "strange" or "unusual" by appearing confrontational, argumentative, stressed, anxious, withdrawn or secretive

[If] behavior is such to cause concern for person's own well-being or possibly others:

- Engage subject in conversation to gain insight into behavior
- Carefully offer help
- Report concerns, if continuing, to next higher-level authority and seek specific outcome
- Seek consultation from Provost's Office/Human Resources

Level II—The subject may:

- Make veiled threats to harm
- Intimidate others
- Have a history of violent behavior and lose temper easily
- Be chronically disgruntled, inflexible
- Refuse to take responsibility for problems or actions
- Find fault with and blame others
- Have a deep sense of entitlement
- Have an obsession with weapons and empathy with those who resort to violence

[Response]

- Report concerns to next higher-level authority before any effort to engage person
- Engage person in conversation, if appropriate, to gain insight into potential for violent behavior
- Consult with next higher level of administration as follow-up
- Seek consultation from Provost's Office/Human Resources

Level III The subject may:

- Make blatant threats to harm others and/or destroy property
- Carry a weapon on campus
- Engage in aggressive behavior such as verbal abuse, physical "in your face" posturing

[Response]

- Warn those who may be in immediate danger
- Immediately report behavior to next higher-level authority and press for quick intervention

- If subject is present and seriously acting-out, call 911 and ask for assistance

Level IV—The subject:

- Is violent toward others or property
- Displays overt acts of violence or out-of-control behavior
- May or may not use a weapon or cause death

[Response]

- Call 911 for immediate assistance.
- Attempt to get others out of harm's way.
- Inform next higher-level authority.

Example 4. A policy that emphasizes the early warning signs of imminent violence. Source: San Diego State University.

. . . [A]cts and/or threats of violence against the life, health, well-being, family or property of individuals in the workplace or in connection with an employee's conduct of . . . business . . . will not be tolerated. Any such acts or threats by employees . . . toward others may be grounds for immediate dismissal . . . whether or not the employee making the threat intended to carry it out.

. . . [E]mployees may be better prepared to avoid or prevent violence if they are able to recognize early warning signs in advance and follow appropriate response procedures. Employees will therefore play a crucial role in the administration of this anti-violence policy.

Early Warning Signs

Employees should understand that certain risk factors and behavior patterns may offer early warning signs of violent conduct. Examples of such warning signs include the following:

- A history of emotional or mental disturbance
- A history of threatening or violent behavior
- Paranoia or easily panicked behavior
- A fascination or preoccupation with weapons, particularly weapons or explosives that could be used for mass destruction, such as semi-automatic guns

- Extreme stress from personal problems or a life crisis
- Events affecting workplace conditions and/or generating stress
- Identifying with incidents of workplace violence reported in the media and either condoning or sympathizing with the actions of the individuals committing the violence
- Being a loner with little or no involvement with other employees
- Engaging in frequent disputes with supervisors or co-workers
- Persistent violation of company policy
- Obsessive involvement with one's job, particularly where it occurs with no apparent outside interest
- Volatile or violent home or other personal situation that has the potential to bring violence into the workplace.

If a supervisor or another employee becomes aware of risk factors and behavior patterns of the type described above, the Director of Personnel Services should be contacted. The Director of Personnel Services will evaluate the matter and, where appropriate, provide the supervisor or employee with direction and assistance to deal with the situation. If outside assistance is needed, the Director of Personnel will arrange for that assistance.

Threats of Violence

Every threat of violence is serious and must be treated as such. Threatening behavior can include such actions as:

- Throwing objects
- Making a verbal threat to harm another individual or destroy property
- Making menacing gestures
- Displaying an intense or obsessive romantic interest that exceeds the normal bounds of interpersonal interest
- Attempting to intimidate or harass other individuals
- Behavior indicating that the individual is significantly out of touch with reality and that he or she may pose a danger either to himself or herself or to others
- Volatile or violent personal situations such as found in some custody battles.

Employees who become aware of any threats of workplace violence must report the threats immediately to their supervisor. The supervisor will, in turn, be responsible to notify the Director of Personnel Services who will consult with the appropriate resources in order to complete an assessment of the incident and the surrounding circumstances.

Imminent Risk of Violence

If an employee becomes aware of any actual violence, imminent violence, or threat of imminent violence, obtaining emergency assistance must be a matter of first priority. The employee should immediately contact Public Safety or local law enforcement by dialing 911.

Immediately after contacting the law enforcement authorities for emergency assistance, the employee must report the incident to his or her supervisor if the supervisor is available. The supervisor must then notify the Director of Personnel Services immediately. If the supervisor is not immediately available, the employee should contact the Director of Personnel Services . . . immediately after contacting the law enforcement authorities. Employees may report any incidents of violence or threats of violence without fear of any reprisal of any kind.

Domestic Violence

Example 1. A statewide policy covering public employees who are affected by the overspill of domestic violence into the workplace. Source: Governor's Executive Order 96-05, State of Washington.

[E]ach state agency and institution of higher education [is directed] to:

1) Initiate actions to create a workplace environment that provides an avenue for assistance for domestic violence victims without fear of reproach.
2) Ensure that personnel policies and procedures are responsive to victims of domestic violence.
3) Develop and make available to all employees a policy that:

   • Clearly directs that the state will not tolerate domestic violence. This includes harassment or the display of violent or threatening behavior that may result in physical or emotional injury to any state employee while in state offices. . . .

- Offers a method for providing assistance to domestic violence victims in a confidential setting.
- Provides for immediate assistance to victims. This assistance shall, at a minimum, include: referral to the Department of Personnel's Employee Advisory Service or other available counseling services; information about community resources. . . .
- Following any applicable rules or statutes, assures that every reasonable effort will be made to adjust work schedules and/or grant accrued or unpaid leave to allow employees who are victims of domestic violence to obtain medical treatment, counseling, legal assistance, to leave the area, or to make other arrangements to create a safer situation for themselves.
- Assures that every reasonable effort will be made to assist employees who are victims of domestic violence to find continued state employment when there is a need for the employee to relocate for safety reasons.
- Encourages state employees who are perpetrators of domestic violence to seek assistance.
- Provides for assistance to perpetrators. This assistance shall, at a minimum, include: referral to the Department of Personnel's Employee Advisory Service or other available counseling services; and information about available certified domestic violence perpetrator treatment programs.
- Provides that corrective or disciplinary action may be taken against state employees who: misuse state resources to perpetrate domestic violence; harass, threaten, or commit an act of domestic violence in the workplace or while conducting state business.
- Provides that employees will not be penalized or disciplined solely because they have been victims of domestic violence.

4) Provide training on their respective policies and domestic violence awareness. The training shall include, at a minimum, information as to: what domestic violence is; what resources are available to victim.
5) Have information about domestic violence and available resources posted in the worksite. Also, information needs to be available where employees can obtain it without having to request it or be seen removing. . . .

Example 2. A corporate policy, titled "Recommended Safety Procedures for Protection from Family Violence Situations." It outlines the responsibilities of the employee, the manager, and the human resources administrator when a case of domestic violence impinges upon the workplace. Source: Polaroid Corporation.

Definition

Family violence is any act of physical aggression that causes physical harm, or any statement that could be perceived as an intent to cause physical or emotional harm. Examples would include, but are not limited to, homicide, assault and battery, rape or stalking. Statistics note that most incidents of family violence are attributed to males, but no one should ignore the fact that such abuse can also be attributed to females or occur in same-sex relationships.

How to Respond

Employee

- Notify your supervisor/manager of the situation and the possible *need* to be absent. Supervisors/managers *cannot* assist until an employee self-discloses.
- Discuss options available to you with your supervisor and Human Resources Administrator. Involve your local Employee Assistance Program (EAP) Counselor, if necessary. The EAP Counselor can assist the employee in developing a safety plan.
- Be clear about your plan to return to work.
- Make arrangements for receiving your pay check while you are absent.
- Submit a recent photo of the abuser to Corporate Security so that a possible identification can be made if the abuser appears at the Polaroid work site.
- Maintain communications with the Human Resources Administrator throughout your absence.

Supervisor/Manager

- Be aware of unusual absences and/or behavior of employees as job performance concerns.
- Be aware of signs of bruises to face, arms, etc. Remember, the employee must self-disclose.
- Consult with your local Employee Assistance Program (EAP) Counselor and/or Human Resources Administrator to discuss your concerns and how to approach the employee. The EAP Counselor can formally contact the employee.

- Maintain confidentiality at all times.
- Honor all civil protection orders (i.e., vacate, restraining or no-contact orders or judgments in effect). Contact the EAP Counselor if there are concerns.
- Contact the local Corporate Security office and make sure that the employee has provided a photo of the abuser and other pertinent safety information.
- Be sensitive to the seriousness of the situation.

Human Resources Administrator

- Be a resource to both the employee and supervisor/manager in handling the situation. Follow recommended procedures for absences and use appropriate community resources.
- Contact the local EAP Counselor immediately.
- Discuss a safety plan for the employee with the EAP Counselor.
- Maintain communications with the employee during his or her absence. Work with the supervisor/manager on pay and absence arrangements.

Employee Assistance Program Counselor

- Be a resource to the employee, the supervisor/manager and the Human Resources Administrator.
- Collaborate with the Human Resources Administrator in all situations.
- Be available during the employee's absence, including referrals to community family violence services.
- Develop a safety plan with the Human Resources Administrator, This safety plan should accompany the protection order once it is obtained.
- Maintain a liaison position between the local shelter staff and the corporation for the purpose of counseling needs.

Elements of a Safety Plan

- Review the travel route between the employee's home and work.
- Review safety of child care arrangements.
- Make sure that current civil protection orders have not expired and are in hand at all times.
- Determine if substance abuse is involved.
- Make sure that Security has a picture of the abuser.
- Have an emergency contact person if the employee cannot be reached.

- Consider if health care is a concern (i.e., diabetes, AIDS, cancer). Shelter staff requires this information.
- Make sure that an address/phone number is provided to the company contact person.
- Review the safety of the employee's parking arrangements.
- Review the employee's work schedule with the supervisor/manager (in case stalking is involved).

Example 3. A "Model Policy on Domestic Violence in the Workplace," drafted by an advocacy group. It recommends an elaborate set of protections and care provisions for affected workers, combined with sanctions for those who perpetrate violence. Source: Family Violence Prevention Fund.

A. Early Intervention and Education Prevention Strategies

1) It is the policy of [the employer] to use early prevention strategies in order to avoid or minimize the occurrence and effects of domestic violence in the workplace. [The employer] will provide available support and assistance to employees who are survivors of domestic violence. This support may include: confidential means of coming forward for help, resource and referral information, additional security at the workplace, work schedule adjustments or leave necessary to obtain medical, counseling or legal assistance, and workplace relocation. Written resource and referral information should be available in all the languages spoken by employees. Other appropriate assistance will be provided based on individual need. In all responses to domestic violence, [the employer] will respect the confidentiality and autonomy of the adult survivor to her or his own life, to the fullest extent permitted by law.
2) [The employer] will attempt to maintain, publish, and post in locations of high visibility, such as bulletin boards and break rooms, health/first aid offices, company phone directories, and on information data bases, a list of resources. . . .

B. Leave Options for Employees Who Are Experiencing Threats of Violence

1) At times an employee may need to be absent from work due to family violence, and the length of time should be determined by the individual's situation. This time period shall be determined through

collaboration with the employee's supervisor/manager, Human Resources representative, and union representative, where the employee is represented.

2) Employees, supervisors, and managers are encouraged to first explore whether paid options can be arranged which will help the employee cope with a family violence situation without having to take a formal unpaid leave of absence. Depending on the circumstances, this may include:

- Arranging flexible work hours so that the employee can handle legal matters, appropriate housing and child care.
- Consider sick, annual, shared, leave, compensatory time, or leave without pay, especially if requests are for relatively short periods.

C. Procedures for Employees with Performance Issues Related to Domestic Violence

1) While the employer retains the right to discipline employees for cause, [the employer] recognizes that victims of domestic violence may have performance or conduct problems, such as chronic absenteeism or inability to concentrate, as a result of the violence. When an employee subject to discipline confides that the job performance or conduct problem is caused by domestic violence, a referral for appropriate assistance should be offered to the employee.

2) The manager, in collaboration with the employee, Employee Assistance counselor, Human Resource representative, [and union representative, where employee is represented] should allow a reasonable amount of time for the employee to obtain assistance regarding the domestic violence. Managers should be mindful that the effects of domestic violence can be severe and may take extended periods of time to address fully.

D. Disciplinary Procedures for Employees Who Commit Acts or Threats of Domestic Violence

1) [The employer] is committed to providing a workplace in which the perpetration of domestic violence is neither tolerated nor excused. Any physical assault or threat made by an employee while on [the employer's] premises, during working hours, or at a [employer] sponsored social event is a serious violation of [the employer's] policy. This policy applies not only to acts against other employees, but to acts

against all other persons, including intimate partners. Employees found to have violated this policy will be subject to corrective or disciplinary action, up to and including discharge:

2) Employees who are convicted of a crime as a result of domestic violence may be subject to corrective or disciplinary action, up to and including discharge, when such action affects the work performance of the employee or affects the normal operation of [the employer].

Weapon Control Policy

Example. A model policy on carrying of weapons by employees. Source: State of Washington Department of Labor and Industry.

In order to ensure a safe environment for employees and customers, our establishment prohibits the wearing, transporting, storage, or presence of firearms or other dangerous weapons in our facilities or on our property. Any employee in possession of a firearm or other weapon within our facilities/property or while otherwise fulfilling job responsibilities may face disciplinary action including termination. Possession of a valid concealed weapons permit authorized by the state of Washington is *not* an exemption under this policy. To the extent allowed by law, our company prohibits clients or visitors from carrying weapons in our facilities or on our property. (Note: A company's right to prohibit firearms in public areas of their facilities or property may be limited in some situations. Check with your legal counsel before implementing a weapons policy that covers clients or visitors.)

Definition

Firearms or other dangerous weapons mean:

- any device from which a projectile may be fired by an explosive
- any simulated firearm operated by gas or compressed air
- sling shot
- sand club
- metal knuckles
- any spring blade knife
- any knife which opens or is ejected open by an outward, downward thrust or movement
- any instrument that can be used as a club and poses a reasonable risk of injury.

Exemptions

This policy does not apply to:

- any law enforcement personnel engaged in official duties
- any security personnel engaged in official duties
- any person engaged in military activities sponsored by the federal or state government, while engaged in official duties

A P P E N D I X   B

Equal Employment Opportunity Commission Enforcement Guidance: The Americans with Disabilities Act and Psychiatric Disabilities

Excerpt from EEOC Notice Number 915.002, March 25, 1997, ADA Division, Office of Legal Counsel

Introduction

The workforce includes many individuals with psychiatric disabilities who face employment discrimination because their disabilities are stigmatized or misunderstood. Congress intended Title I of the Americans with Disabilities Act (ADA) [1] to combat such employment discrimination as well as the myths, fears, and stereotypes upon which it is based. [2]

The Equal Employment Opportunity Commission ("EEOC" or "Commission") receives a large number of charges under the ADA alleging employment discrimination based on psychiatric disability. [3] These charges raise a wide array of legal issues including, for example, whether an individual has a psychiatric disability as defined by the ADA and whether an employer may ask about an individual's psychiatric disability. People with psychiatric disabilities and employers also have posed numerous questions to the EEOC about this topic.

This guidance is designed to: facilitate the full enforcement of the ADA with respect to individuals alleging employment discrimination based on psychiatric disability; respond to questions and concerns expressed by individuals with psychiatric disabilities regarding the ADA; and answer questions posed by employers about how principles of ADA analysis apply in the context of psychiatric disabilities. [4]

What is a psychiatric disability under the ADA?

Under the ADA, the term "disability" means: "(a) A physical or mental impairment that substantially limits one or more of the major life activities of [an] individual; (b) a record of such an impairment; or (c) being regarded as having such an impairment."[5] This guidance focuses on the first prong of the ADA's definition of "disability" because of the great number of questions about how it is applied in the context of psychiatric conditions.

Impairment

What is a "mental impairment" under the ADA?

The ADA rule defines "mental impairment" to include "[a]ny mental or psychological disorder, such as . . . emotional or mental illness."[6] Examples of "emotional or mental illness[es]" include major depression, bipolar disorder, anxiety disorders (which include panic disorder, obsessive compulsive disorder, and post-traumatic stress disorder), schizophrenia, and personality disorders. The current edition of the American Psychiatric Association's Diagnostic and Statistical Manual of Mental Disorders (now the fourth edition, DSM-IV) is relevant for identifying these disorders. The DSM-IV has been recognized as an important reference by courts[7] and is widely used by American mental health professionals for diagnostic and insurance reimbursement purposes.

Not all conditions listed in the DSM-IV, however, are disabilities, or even impairments, for purposes of the ADA. For example, the DSM-IV lists several conditions that Congress expressly excluded from the ADA's definition of "disability."[8] While DSM-IV covers conditions involving drug abuse, the ADA provides that the term "individual with a disability" does not include an individual who is currently engaging in the illegal use of drugs, when the covered entity acts on the basis of that use.[9] The DSM-IV also includes conditions that are not mental disorders but for which people may seek treatment (for example, problems with a spouse or child). Because these conditions are not disorders, they are not impairments under the ADA. Even if a condition is an impairment, it is not automatically a "disability." To rise to the level of a "disability," an impairment must "substantially limit" one or more major life activities of the individual.

Are traits or behaviors in themselves mental impairments?

No. Traits or behaviors are not, in themselves, mental impairments. For example, stress, in itself, is not automatically a mental impairment. Stress, however, may be shown to be related to a mental or physical impairment.

Similarly, traits like irritability, chronic lateness, and poor judgment are not, in themselves, mental impairments, although they may be linked to mental impairments.

Conduct

Maintaining satisfactory conduct and performance typically is not a problem for individuals with psychiatric disabilities. Nonetheless, circumstances arise when employers need to discipline individuals with such disabilities for misconduct.

May an employer discipline an individual with a disability for violating a workplace conduct standard if the misconduct resulted from a disability?

Yes, provided that the workplace conduct standard is job-related for the position in question and is consistent with business necessity. For example, nothing in the ADA prevents an employer from maintaining a workplace free of violence or threats of violence, or from disciplining an employee who steals or destroys property. Thus, an employer may discipline an employee with a disability for engaging in such misconduct if it would impose the same discipline on an employee without a disability. Other conduct standards, however, may not be job-related for the position in question and consistent with business necessity. If they are not, imposing discipline under them could violate the ADA.

Example A: An employee steals money from his employer. Even if he asserts that his misconduct was caused by a disability, the employer may discipline him consistent with its uniform disciplinary policies because the individual violated a conduct standard—a prohibition against employee theft—that is job-related for the position in question and consistent with business necessity.

Example B: An employee at a clinic tampers with and incapacitates medical equipment. Even if the employee explains that she did this because of her disability, the employer may discipline her consistent with its uniform disciplinary policies because she violated a conduct standard—a rule prohibiting intentional damage to equipment—that is job-related for the position in question and consistent with business necessity. However, if the employer disciplines her even though it has not disciplined people without disabilities for the same misconduct, the employer would be treating her differently because of disability in violation of the ADA.

Example C: An employee with a psychiatric disability works in a warehouse loading boxes onto pallets for shipment. He has no customer contact and does not come into regular contact with other employees. Over the course of several weeks, he has come to work appearing increasingly disheveled. His clothes are ill-fitting and often have tears in them. He also has become increasingly anti-social. Coworkers have complained that when they try to engage him in casual conversation, he walks away or gives a curt reply. When he has to talk to a coworker, he is abrupt and rude. His work, however, has not suffered. The employer's company handbook states that employees should have a neat appearance at all times. The handbook also states that employees should be courteous to each other. When told that he is being disciplined for his appearance and treatment of coworkers, the employee explains that his appearance and demeanor have deteriorated because of his disability which was exacerbated during this time period.

The dress code and coworker courtesy rules are not job-related for the position in question and consistent with business necessity because this employee has no customer contact and does not come into regular contact with other employees. Therefore, rigid application of these rules to this employee would violate the ADA.

Must an employer make reasonable accommodation for an individual with a disability who violated a conduct rule that is job-related for the position in question and consistent with business necessity?

An employer must make reasonable accommodation to enable an otherwise qualified individual with a disability to meet such a conduct standard in the future, barring undue hardship. Because reasonable accommodation is always prospective, however, an employer is not required to excuse past misconduct.

Example A: A reference librarian frequently loses her temper at work, disrupting the library atmosphere by shouting at patrons and coworkers. After receiving a suspension as the second step in uniform, progressive discipline, she discloses her disability, states that it causes her behavior, and requests a leave of absence for treatment. The employer may discipline her because she violated a conduct standard—a rule prohibiting disruptive behavior towards patrons and coworkers—that is job-related for the position in question and consistent with business necessity. The employer, however, must grant her request for a leave of absence as a reasonable accommodation, barring undue hardship, to enable her to meet this conduct standard in the future.

Example B: An employee with major depression is often late for work because of medication side-effects that make him extremely groggy in the morning. His scheduled hours are 9:00 AM to 5:30 PM, but he arrives at 9:00, 9:30, 10:00 or even 10:30 on any given day. His job responsibilities involve telephone contact with the company's traveling sales representatives, who depend on him to answer urgent marketing questions and expedite special orders. The employer disciplines him for tardiness, stating that continued failure to arrive promptly during the next month will result in termination of his employment. The individual then explains that he was late because of a disability and needs to work on a later schedule. In this situation, the employer may discipline the employee because he violated a conduct standard addressing tardiness that is job-related for the position in question and consistent with business necessity. The employer, however, must consider reasonable accommodation, barring undue hardship, to enable this individual to meet this standard in the future. For example, if this individual can serve the company's sales representatives by regularly working a schedule of 10:00 AM to 6:30 PM, a reasonable accommodation would be to modify his schedule so that he is not required to report for work until 10:00 AM.

Example C: An employee has a hostile altercation with his supervisor and threatens the supervisor with physical harm. The employer immediately terminates the individual's employment, consistent with its policy of immediately terminating the employment of anyone who threatens a supervisor. When he learns that his employment has been terminated, the employee asks the employer to put the termination on hold and to give him a month off for treatment instead. This is the employee's first request for accommodation and also the first time the employer learns about the employee's disability. The employer is not required to rescind the discharge under these circumstances, because the employee violated a conduct standard—a rule prohibiting threats of physical harm against supervisors—that is job-related for the position in question and consistent with business necessity. The employer also is not required to offer reasonable accommodation for the future because this individual is no longer a qualified individual with a disability. His employment was terminated under a uniformly applied conduct standard that is job-related for the position in question and consistent with business necessity.

How should an employer deal with an employee with a disability who is engaging in misconduct because s/he is not taking his/her medication?

The employer should focus on the employee's conduct and explain to the employee the consequences of continued misconduct in terms of uniform disciplinary procedures. It is the employee's responsibility to decide about medication and to consider the consequences of not taking medication.

Direct Threat

Under the ADA, an employer may lawfully exclude an individual from employment for safety reasons only if the employer can show that employment of the individual would pose a "direct threat." Employers must apply the "direct threat" standard uniformly and may not use safety concerns to justify exclusion of persons with disabilities when persons without disabilities would not be excluded in similar circumstances.

The EEOC's ADA regulations explain that "direct threat" means "a significant risk of substantial harm to the health or safety of the individual or others that cannot be eliminated or reduced by reasonable accommodation." A "significant" risk is a high, and not just a slightly increased, risk. The determination that an individual poses a "direct threat" must be based on an individualized assessment of the individual's present ability to safely perform the functions of the job, considering a reasonable medical judgment relying on the most current medical knowledge and/or the best available objective evidence. With respect to the employment of individuals with psychiatric disabilities, the employer must identify the specific behavior that would pose a direct threat. An individual does not pose a "direct threat" simply by virtue of having a history of psychiatric disability or being treated for a psychiatric disability.

When can an employer refuse to hire someone based on his/her history of violence or threats of violence?

An employer may refuse to hire someone based on his/her history of violence or threats of violence if it can show that the individual poses a direct threat. A determination of "direct threat" must be based on an individualized assessment of the individual's present ability to safely perform the functions of the job, considering the most current medical knowledge and/or the best available objective evidence. To find that an individual with a psychiatric disability poses a direct threat, the employer must identify the specific behavior on the part of the individual that would pose the direct threat. This includes an assessment of the likelihood and imminence of future violence.

Example: An individual applies for a position with Employer X. When Employer X checks his employment background, she learns that he was terminated two weeks ago by Employer Y, after he told a coworker that he would get a gun and "get his supervisor if he tries anything again." Employer X also learns that these statements followed three months of escalating incidents in which this individual had had several altercations in the workplace, including one in which he had to be restrained from fighting with a coworker. He then revealed his disability to Employer Y. After being given time off for medical treatment, he continued to have trouble controlling his temper and was seen punching the wall outside his supervisor's office. Finally, he made the threat against the supervisor and was terminated. Employer X learns that, since then, he has not received any further medical treatment. Employer X does not hire him, stating that this history indicates that he poses a direct threat.

This individual poses a direct threat as a result of his disability because his recent overt acts and statements (including an attempted fight with a coworker, punching the wall, and making a threatening statement about the supervisor) support the conclusion that he poses a "significant risk of substantial harm." Furthermore, his prior treatment had no effect on his behavior, he had received no subsequent treatment, and only two weeks had elapsed since his termination, all supporting a finding of direct threat.

Does an individual who has attempted suicide pose a direct threat when s/he seeks to return to work?

No, in most circumstances. As with other questions of direct threat, an employer must base its determination on an individualized assessment of the person's ability to safely perform job functions when s/he returns to work. Attempting suicide does not mean that an individual poses an imminent risk of harm to him/herself when s/he returns to work. In analyzing direct threat (including the likelihood and imminence of any potential harm), the employer must seek reasonable medical judgments relying on the most current medical knowledge and/or the best available factual evidence concerning the employee.

Example: An employee with a known psychiatric disability was hospitalized for two suicide attempts, which occurred within several weeks of each other. When the employee asked to return to work, the employer allowed him to return pending an evaluation of medical reports to determine his ability to safely perform his job. The individual's therapist and psychiatrist both submitted documentation stating that he could safely perform all of his job functions. Moreover, the employee performed his job safely after his return, without reasonable accommodation. The employer, however, terminated the individual's employment after evaluating the doctor's and therapist's reports, without citing any contradictory medical or factual evidence concerning the employee's recovery. Without more evidence, this employer cannot support its determination that this individual poses a direct threat.

U.S. Occupational Safety and Health Administration *Guidelines for Preventing Workplace Violence for Health Care and Social Service Workers*
Excerpt from OSHA 31481996

Introduction

For many years, health care and social service workers have faced a significant risk of job-related violence. Assaults represent a serious safety and health hazard for these industries, and violence against their employees continues to increase.

OSHA's new violence prevention guidelines provide the agency's recommendations for reducing workplace violence developed following a careful review of workplace violence studies, public and private violence prevention programs, and consultations with and input from stakeholders. OSHA encourages employers to establish violence prevention programs and to track their progress in reducing work-related assaults. Although not every incident can be prevented, many can, and the severity of injuries sustained by employees reduced. Adopting practical measures such as those outlined here can significantly reduce this serious threat to worker safety.

OSHA's Commitment

The publication and distribution of these guidelines is OSHA's first step in assisting health care and social service employers and providers in preventing workplace violence. OSHA plans to conduct a coordinated effort consisting of research, information, training, cooperative programs, and appropriate enforcement to accomplish this goal.

The guidelines are not a new standard or regulation. They are advisory in nature, informational in content, and intended for use by employers in providing a safe and healthful workplace through effective violence prevention programs, adapted to the needs and resources of each place of employment.

Risk Factors

Health care and social service workers face an increased risk of work-related assaults stemming from several factors, including:

- The prevalence of handguns and other weapons as high as 25 percent among patients, their families, or friends. The increasing use of hospitals by police and the criminal justice systems for criminal holds and the care of acutely disturbed, violent individuals.
- The increasing number of acute and chronically mentally ill patients now being released from hospitals without follow-up care, who now have the right to refuse medicine and who can no longer be hospitalized involuntarily unless they pose an immediate threat to themselves or others.
- The availability of drugs or money at hospitals, clinics, and pharmacies, making them likely robbery targets.
- Situational and circumstantial factors such as unrestricted movement of the public in clinics and hospitals; the increasing presence of gang members, drug or alcohol abusers, trauma patients, or distraught family members; long waits in emergency or clinic areas, leading to client frustration over an inability to obtain needed services promptly.
- Low staffing levels during times of specific increased activity such as meal times, visiting times, and when staff are transporting patients.
- Isolated work with clients during examinations or treatment.
- Solo work, often in remote locations, particularly in high-crime settings, with no backup or means of obtaining assistance such as communication devices or alarm systems.
- Lack of training of staff in recognizing and managing escalating hostile and assaultive behavior.
- Poorly lighted parking areas.

Written Program

A written program for job safety and security, incorporated into the organization's overall safety and health program, offers an effective approach for larger organizations. In smaller establishments, the program need not be written or heavily documented to be satisfactory. What is needed are clear goals and objectives to prevent workplace violence suitable for the size and complexity of the workplace operation and adaptable to specific situations in each establishment.

The prevention program and startup date must be communicated to all employees. At a minimum, workplace violence prevention programs should do the following:

- Create and disseminate a clear policy of zero-tolerance for workplace violence, verbal and nonverbal threats, and related actions. Managers, supervisors, co-workers, clients, patients, and visitors must be advised of this policy.
- Ensure that no reprisals are taken against an employee who reports or experiences workplace violence. Encourage employees to promptly report incidents and to suggest ways to reduce or eliminate risks. Require records of incidents to assess risk and to measure progress.
- Outline a comprehensive plan for maintaining security in the workplace, which includes establishing a liaison with law enforcement representatives and others who can help identify ways to prevent and mitigate workplace violence.
- Assign responsibility and authority for the program to individuals or teams with appropriate training and skills. The written plan should ensure that there are adequate resources available for this effort and that the team or responsible individuals develop expertise on workplace violence prevention in health care and social services.
- Affirm management commitment to a worker-supportive environment that places as much importance on employee safety and health as on serving the patient or client.
- Set up a company briefing as part of the initial effort to address such issues as preserving safety, supporting affected employees, and facilitating recovery.

Worksite Analysis

Worksite analysis involves a step-by-step, commonsense look at the workplace to find existing or potential hazards for workplace violence.

This entails reviewing specific procedures or operations that contribute to hazards and specific locales where hazards may develop. A "Threat Assessment Team," "Patient Assault Team," similar task force, or coordinator may assess the vulnerability to workplace violence and determine the appropriate preventive actions to be taken. Implementing the workplace violence prevention program then may be assigned to this group. The team should include representatives from senior management, operations, employee assistance, security, occupational safety and health, legal, and human resources staff.

The team or coordinator can review injury and illness records and workers' compensation claims to identify patterns of assaults that could be prevented by workplace adaptation, procedural changes, or employee training. As the team or coordinator identifies appropriate controls, these should be instituted.

The recommended program for worksite analysis includes, but is not limited to, analyzing and tracking records, monitoring trends and analyzing incidents, screening surveys, and analyzing workplace security.

Workplace Security Analysis

The team or coordinator should periodically inspect the workplace and evaluate employee tasks to identify hazards, conditions, operations, and situations that could lead to violence. To find areas requiring further evaluation, the team or coordinator should do the following:

- Analyze incidents, including the characteristics of assailants and victims, an account of what happened before and during the incident, and the relevant details of the situation and its outcome. When possible, obtain police reports and recommendations.
- Identify jobs or locations with the greatest risk of violence as well as processes and procedures that put employees at risk of assault, including how often and when.
- Note high-risk factors such as types of clients or patients (e.g., psychiatric conditions or patients disoriented by drugs, alcohol, or stress); physical risk factors of the building; isolated locations/job activities; lighting problems; lack of phones and other communication devices, areas of easy, unsecured access; and areas with previous security problems. . . .
- Evaluate the effectiveness of existing security measures, including engineering control measures. Determine if risk factors have been reduced or eliminated, and take appropriate action.

Administrative and Work Practice Controls

Administrative and work practice controls affect the way jobs or tasks are performed. The following examples illustrate how changes in work practices and administrative procedures can help prevent violent incidents.

- State clearly to patients, clients, and employees that violence is not permitted or tolerated.
- Establish liaison with local police and state prosecutors. Report all incidents of violence. Provide police with physical layouts of facilities to expedite investigations.
- Require employees to report all assaults or threats to a supervisor or manager (e.g., can be confidential interview). Keep log books and reports of such incidents to help in determining any necessary actions to prevent further occurrences.
- Advise and assist employees, if needed, of company procedures for requesting police assistance or filing charges when assaulted.
- Provide management support during emergencies. Respond promptly to all complaints.
- Set up a trained response team to respond to emergencies.
- Use properly trained security officers, when necessary, to deal with aggressive behavior. Follow written security procedures.
- Ensure adequate and properly trained staff for restraining patients or clients.
- Provide sensitive and timely information to persons waiting in line or in waiting rooms. Adopt measures to decrease waiting time.
- Ensure adequate and qualified staff coverage at all times. Times of greatest risk occur during patient transfers, emergency responses, meal times, and at night. Locales with the greatest risk include admission units and crisis or acute care units. Other risks include admission of patients with a history of violent behavior or gang activity.
- Institute a sign-in procedure with passes for visitors, especially in a newborn nursery or pediatric department. Enforce visitor hours and procedures.
- Establish a list of "restricted visitors" for patients with a history of violence. Copies should be available at security checkpoints, nurses' stations, and visitor sign-in areas. Review and revise visitor check systems, when necessary. Limit information given to outsiders on hospitalized victims of violence.

- Supervise the movement of psychiatric clients and patients throughout the facility.
- Control access to facilities other than waiting rooms, particularly drug storage or pharmacy areas.
- Prohibit employees from working alone in emergency areas or walk-in clinics, particularly at night or when assistance is unavailable. Employees should never enter seclusion rooms alone.
- Establish policies and procedures for secured areas and emergency evacuations, and for monitoring high-risk patients at night (e.g., open versus locked seclusion).
- Ascertain the behavioral history of new and transferred patients to learn about any past violent or assaultive behaviors. Establish a system such as chart tags, log books, or verbal census reports to identify patients and clients with assaultive behavior problems, keeping in mind patient confidentiality and worker safety issues. Update as needed.
- Treat and/or interview aggressive or agitated clients in relatively open areas that still maintain privacy and confidentiality (e.g., rooms with removable partitions).
- Use case management conferences with co-workers and supervisors to discuss ways to effectively treat potentially violent patients.
- Prepare contingency plans to treat clients who are "acting out" or making verbal or physical attacks or threats. Consider using certified employee assistance professionals (CEAPs) or in-house social service or occupational health service staff to help diffuse patient or client anger.
- Transfer assaultive clients to "acute care units," "criminal units," or other more restrictive settings.
- Make sure that nurses and/or physicians are not alone when performing intimate physical examinations of patients.
- Discourage employees from wearing jewelry to help prevent possible strangulation in confrontational situations. Community workers should carry only required identification and money.
- Periodically survey the facility to remove tools or possessions left by visitors or maintenance staff which could be used inappropriately by patients.
- Provide staff with identification badges, preferably without last names, to readily verify employment.
- Discourage employees from carrying keys, pens, or other items that could be used as weapons.
- Provide staff members with security escorts to parking areas in evening or late hours. Parking areas should be highly visible, well lighted, and safely accessible to the building.

- Use the "buddy system," especially when personal safety may be threatened. Encourage home health care providers, social service workers, and others to avoid threatening situations. Staff should exercise extra care in elevators, stairwells and unfamiliar residences; immediately leave premises if there is a hazardous situation; or request police escort if needed.
- Develop policies and procedures covering home health care providers, such as contracts on how visits will be conducted, the presence of others in the home during the visits, and the refusal to provide services in a clearly hazardous situation.
- Establish a daily work plan for field staff to keep a designated contact person informed about workers' whereabouts throughout the workday. If an employee does not report in, the contact person should follow up.
- Conduct a comprehensive post-incident evaluation, including psychological as well as medical treatment, for employees who have been subjected to abusive behavior.

Post-Incident Response

Post-incident response and evaluation are essential to an effective violence prevention program. All workplace violence programs should provide comprehensive treatment for victimized employees and employees who may be traumatized by witnessing a workplace violence incident. Injured staff should receive prompt treatment and psychological evaluation whenever an assault takes place, regardless of severity. . . . Transportation of the injured to medical care should be provided if care is not available on-site. Victims of workplace violence suffer a variety of consequences in addition to their actual physical injuries. These include short and long-term psychological trauma, fear of returning to work, changes in relationships with co-workers and family, feelings of incompetence, guilt, powerlessness, and fear of criticism by supervisors or managers. Consequently, a strong follow-up program for these employees will not only help them to deal with these problems but also to help prepare them to confront or prevent future incidents of violence. . . .

There are several types of assistance that can be incorporated into the post-incident response. For example, trauma-crisis counseling, critical incident stress debriefing, or employee assistance programs may be provided to assist victims. Certified employee assistance professionals, psychologists, psychiatrists, clinical nurse specialists, or social workers could provide this counseling, or the employer can refer staff victims to an outside specialist.

In addition, an employee counseling service, peer counseling, or support groups may be established.

In any case, counselors must be well trained and have a good understanding of the issues and consequences of assaults and other aggressive, violent behavior. Appropriate and promptly rendered post-incident debriefings and counseling reduce acute psychological trauma and general stress levels among victims and witnesses. In addition, such counseling educates staff about workplace violence and positively influences workplace and organizational cultural norms to reduce trauma associated with future incidents.

Training and Education

Training and education ensure that all staff are aware of potential security hazards and how to protect themselves and their co-workers through established policies and procedures.

The training should cover topics such as the following:

- The workplace violence prevention policy.
- Risk factors that cause or contribute to assaults.
- Early recognition of escalating behavior or recognition of warning signs or situations that may lead to assaults.
- Ways of preventing or diffusing volatile situations or aggressive behavior, managing anger, and appropriately using medications as chemical restraints.
- Information on multicultural diversity to develop sensitivity to racial and ethnic issues and differences.
- A standard response action plan for violent situations, including availability of assistance, response to alarm systems, and communication procedures.
- How to deal with hostile persons other than patients and clients, such as relatives and visitors.
- Progressive behavior control methods and safe methods of restraint application or escape.
- The location and operation of safety devices such as alarm systems, along with the required maintenance schedules and procedures.
- Ways to protect oneself and co-workers, including use of the "buddy system."
- Policies and procedures for reporting and record-keeping.

- Policies and procedures for obtaining medical care, counseling, workers' compensation, or legal assistance after a violent episode or injury.

Evaluation

As part of their overall program, employers should evaluate their safety and security measures. Top management should review the program regularly, and with each incident, to evaluate program success. Responsible parties (managers, supervisors, and employees) should collectively reevaluate policies and procedures on a regular basis. Deficiencies should be identified and corrective action taken.

An evaluation program should involve the following:

- Establishing a uniform violence reporting system and regular review of reports.
- Reviewing reports and minutes from staff meetings on safety and security issues.
- Analyzing trends and rates in illness/injury or fatalities caused by violence relative to initial or "baseline" rates.
- Measuring improvement based on lowering the frequency and severity of workplace violence.
- Keeping up-to-date records of administrative and work practice changes to prevent workplace violence, to evaluate their effectiveness.
- Surveying employees before and after making job or worksite changes or installing security measures or new systems, to determine their effectiveness.
- Keeping abreast of new strategies available to deal with violence in the health care and social service fields as these develop.
- Surveying employees who experience hostile situations about the medical treatment they received initially and, again, several weeks afterward, and then several months later.
- Complying with OSHA and state requirements for recording and reporting deaths, injuries, and illnesses.
- Requesting periodic law enforcement or outside consultant review of the worksite for recommendations on improving employee safety. Management should share workplace violence prevention program evaluation reports with all employees. Any changes in the program should be discussed at regular meetings of the safety committee, union representatives, or other employee groups. . . .

Notes

Chapter 1. Introduction: An Everyday Event

1. "Fear and Violence in the Workplace: A Survey Documenting the Experiences of American Workers," Northwestern National Life Insurance Company, Minneapolis, 1993.

2. "Workplace Violence: Policies, Procedures & Incidents," American Management Association, 65th Annual Human Resources Conference & Exposition Onsite Survey, April 9–13, 1994.

3. S. L. Smith, "Violence in the Workplace: A Cry for Help," *Occupational Hazards*, October 1993, p. 29.

4. U.S. Centers for Disease Control, Atlanta, "Fatal Occupational Injuries—United States, 1980–1994," April 24, 1998.

5. "Violence in the Workplace Survey Results," Society for Human Resource Management, December 1993. "Survivors of murdered employees have won sizable sums in civil suits against employers or others with [security] responsibilities in workplaces," according to M. Purdy, "Workplace Murders Provoke Lawsuits and Better Security," *New York Times*, February 14, 1994.

6. *Workplace Violence*, Society for Human Resource Management, Alexandria, Va., June 1996. See also, "Workplace Violence Threats Common, SHRM Finds," *Individual Employment Rights*, July 2, 1996.

7. *1997 Annual Employment Survey*, Thomas Staffing, Irvine, Calif., pp. 41–55.

8. O. M. Kurland, "Workplace Violence," *Risk Management*, June 1993, p. 76.

9. "Sources of Information on the Incidence of Domestic Violence at Work and Its Effects," Briefing Memo, Women's Bureau, U.S. Department of Labor, 1994.

10. "Violence in the Workplace—Oregon, 1991–1995," Research and Analysis Section, Oregon Department of Consumer and Business Services, December 1996.

11. Scott Richardson, "Workplace Homicides in Texas, 1990–91," *Fatal Workplace Injuries in 1991: A Collection of Data and Analysis*, U.S. Department of Labor, Bureau of Labor Statis-

tics Report 845, April 1993, p. 2. Richardson is a manager at the Texas Worker Compensation Commission.

12. Susan E. Davis, "Working Scared," *California Lawyer*, April 1998, pp. 41–43, 91, at 42, quoting Karen D. Kadushin, dean of Monterrey College of Law.

13. Michael Atkinson, Mr. Showbiz Review, ABC News Online, December 1997.

14. Duncan Chappell and Vittorio Di Martino, *Violence at Work*, International Labor Organization, Geneva, 1998.

15. "Violence on the Job—a Global Problem," International Labor Organization statement, July 20, 1998.

16. "9 Fatally Shot in California in 2 Incidents in 2 Days," *New York Times*, July 20, 1995; "Armed and Angry," *Los Angeles Times*, June 6, 1997. Woods survived and was sentenced to life in prison.

17. "Ford Plant Gunman Gets Life," *Detroit News*, May 1, 1998.

18. "Milwaukee Postal Worker Kills Co-Worker, Self," CNN, December 19, 1997.

19. "Killer Linked His Caltrans Supervisor to Pilfering," *San Diego Union Tribune*, December 20, 1997.

20. "Connecticut Lottery Accountant Kills Four of His Bosses," *New York Times*, March 7, 1998.

21. "Rampage Brings Death to Industrial Plant," *Las Vegas Sun*, November 11, 1998.

22. "Atkins Guilty in Wixom Plant Death," *Detroit News*, April 21, 1998.

23. "Desperadoes Seeking a Baffling Endgame: Suicide by Cop," *New York Times*, June 21, 1998.

24. Vittorio Di Martino of the ILO, quoted in "When Working Becomes Hazardous," *World of Work*, no. 26, September-October 1998.

25. R. A. Baron and J. H. Neuman, "Workplace Violence and Workplace Aggression: Evidence on Their Relative Frequency and Potential Causes," *Aggressive Behavior* 22 (1996): 161–173.

26. "Violence on the Job—a Global Problem," ILO statement, July 20, 1998.

27. Definition of the Manufacturing, Science and Finance Union (MSF), United Kingdom.

28. Loraleigh Keashly, "Emotional Abuse in the Workplace: Conceptual and Empirical Issues," *Journal of Emotional Abuse*, 1, no. 1 (1998): 85–99. For a discussion of the psychological consequences of verbal assault, see James C. Scott, *Domination and the Arts of Resistance: Hidden Transcripts* (New Haven: Yale University Press, 1990).

29. K. D. Grimsley, "Leaner—and Definitely Meaner: The Growing Problem of Incivility on the Job Is Hurting Profits as Well as Feelings," *Washington Post* (Weekly Edition), July 20–27, 1998.

30. "Cal/OSHA Guidelines for Workplace Security," Division of Occupational Safety and Health, California, Department of Industrial Relations, August 15, 1994.

31. Judith L. Catlett [King]and David G. Alexander, "Violence in the Workplace: The Union Perspective," Center for Labor Education and Research, University of Alabama at Birmingham, 1995.

32. Greg Warchol, *Workplace Violence, 1992–96*, Washington, D.C., U.S. Department of Justice, Bureau of Justice Statistics, 1998.

33. L. Bensley et al., "Injuries Due to Assaults on Psychiatric Hospital Employees in Washington State," *American Journal of Industrial Medicine* 31 (1997): 92-99.

34. "Woman Charged in Slaying of Nurse," *Buffalo News*, November 26, 1998.

35. *New York Times*, September 22, 1991. The 17-hour siege, in a Utah hospital, resulted in a fatality.

36. J. A. Lipscomb and C. C. Love, "Violence toward Health Care Workers: An Emerging Occupational Hazard," *American Association of Occupational Health Nurses Journal*, May 1992, p. 222.

37. Jordan Barab, "Workplace Violence: How Labor Sees It," *New Solutions* (AFSCME), Spring 1995.

38. *A Matter of Life and Death: Worksite Security and Reducing Risks in the Danger Zone*, Civil Service Employees Association, October 1993.

39. "Armed and Angry," *Los Angeles Times*, June 6, 1997.

40. "Atkins Guilty in Wixom Plant Death," *Detroit News*, April 21, 1998. The state of Washington uses a fourfold classification system in which "Violence by Personal Relations" is Type IV.

41. "Sources of Information on the Incidence of Domestic Violence at Work and Its Effects," Briefing Memo, Women's Bureau, U.S. Department of Labor, 1994.

42. "Domestic Violence against Women," Resolution no. 135, AFL-CIO Convention 1995, Committee Reports on Resolutions, p. 42.

43. "Armed and Angry," *Los Angeles Times*, June 6, 1997.

44. Ibid.

45. "Ex-Postal Worker's Life 'Disintegrated'," *Las Vegas Review-Journal*, December 3, 1997.

46. "Two Die as Hearing Turns Violent," *Denver Post*, December 9, 1998.

47. "Routine Turns to Tragedy," *Los Angeles Times*, April 24, 1998.

48. "Hilbun Given 9 Life Terms for Rampage," *Los Angeles Times*, January 15, 1997.

49. Benjamin Weiser, "Electronic Version of Putting Krazy Glue in Locks," *New York Times*, November 25, 1997.

50. David W. Chen, "Man Charged with Sabotage of Computers," *New York* Times, February 18, 1998.

51. "Annual Cost of Computer Crime Rises Alarmingly," Computer Security Institute, San Francisco, February 24, 1998. Peter H. Lewis, "Threat to Corporate Computers Is Often Enemy Within," *New York Times*, March 2, 1998.

52. Timothy Egan, "Sabotage Suspected in San Francisco Blackout," *New York Times*, October 25, 1997.

53. "Thirteen Ways to a Better Termination," Cambridge Human Resources Group, Cambridge, Mass., 1995. Reported in the "Checkoffs" column, *Wall Street Journal*, May 23, 1995.

Chapter 2. Origins of Workplace Violence

1. P. Shrivastava, "Crisis Theory/Practice: Towards a Sustainable Future," *Industrial and Environmental Crisis Quarterly* 7, no.1 (1993): 23–42.

2. T. C. Pauchant and I. I. Mitroff, *Transforming the Crisis Prone Organization* (San Francisco: Jossey-Bass, 1993).

3. See J. A. Klein, "The Human Costs of Manufacturing Reform," *Harvard Business Review*, March-April 1989.

4. Basil Hargrove, "Workplace Change and Stormy Weather—The Canadian Experience," *Arbitration 1996 at the Crossroads: Proceedings of the 49th Annual Meeting of the National Academy of Arbitrators* (Washington, D.C.: BNA Books, 1997), p. 311. Hargrove is president of the Canadian Automobile Workers Union.

5. Edward N. Luttwak, "America's Insecurity Blanket," *Washington Post* (Weekly Edition), December 5–11, 1994.

6. Robert Kanigel, *The One Best Way: Frederick Winslow Taylor and the Enigma of Efficiency* (New York: Viking, 1997), p. 534.

7. Charles Heckscher, *White-Collar Blues* (New York: Basic Books, 1995), p. 16.

8. Reuters dispatch by Robert Woodward, datelined London, October 14, 1996 [in *Financial Times*]. Reuters report broadcast on BBC World Service, October 14, 1996.

9. David Shenk, *Data Smog: Surviving the Information Glut* (San Francisco: Harper Edge, 1997).

10. "Meetings May Result in Lost Productivity," *USA Today*, December 8, 1997.

11. "Telecommuting: Dream Come True?" Newshour, Public Broadcasting System, November 14, 1997, citing Dr. Michelle Weil, co-author of *TechnoStress: Coping with Technology @Home, @Work, @Play*.

12. Tia Schneider Denenberg and R. V. Denenberg, *Alcohol and Other Drugs: Issues in Arbitration* (Washington, D.C.: BNA Books, 1991); T. S. Denenberg and R. V. Denenberg, eds.,

Attorney's Guide to Drugs in the Workplace (Chicago: American Bar Association Section of Labor and Employment Law, 1996).

13. "Work: No Place for Privacy," *USA Today,* January 21, 1998.

14. "Electronic Monitoring and Surveillance," American Management Association, New York, 1997.

15. "New Study on Workplace Surveillance Highlights Lack of Protections, ACLU Says," May 23, 1997 [ACLU Press Release].

16. Steven Greenhouse, "Pro-Union Plastics Worker Is Reinstated," *New York Times,* May 28, 1998.

17. Kathleen Ohlson, "Recreational Web Surfing at Work Is on the Rise," IDG [International Data Group], August 13, 1998; "Employee Net Abuse Draws Scrutiny," Knight-Ridder News Service, November 30, 1998.

18. "Big Brother as Workplace Robot," *New York Times,* July 24, 1997.

19. Jonathan Rauch, "Offices and Gentlemen," *New Republic,* June 23, 1997, pp. 22–28.

20. Ibid.

21. "'Performance Testing' Is Helping Employers Gauge Worker Acuity," *Wall Street Journal,* April 22, 1992.

22. Denenberg and Denenberg, *Attorney's Guide to Drugs in the Workplace,* p 25.

23. Bruce S. McEwen, "Protective and Damaging Effects of Stress Mediators," *New England Journal of Medicine,* January 15, 1998.

24. Gina Kolata, "Study of Stress in Mice Offers Possible Explanation for Gulf War Syndrome," *New York Times,* May 28, 1998.

25. R. Karasek and T. Theorell, *Healthy Work: Stress, Productivity, and the Reconstruction of Working Life* (New York: Basic Books, 1990).

26. P. L. Schnall et al., "Relation between Job Strain, Alcohol and Ambulatory Blood Press," *Hypertension,* May, 1992, pp. 488–94.

27. P. L. Schnall et al., "The Relationship between 'Job Strain,' Workplace Diastolic Blood Pressure, and Left Ventricular Mass Index: Results of a Case-Control Study," *Journal of the American Medical Association,* April 11, 1990.

28. Rhonda Rowland, "Stressed? Depressed? Health Experts Commiserate?" CNN, June 12, 1997.

29. Al Hinman, "If You're Stressed, Go Ahead—Spit!" CNN, April 21, 1997.

30. Gwen Robinson, "Stress: Death by Overwork Suits on the Rise in Japan," *Financial Times,* November 27, 1996.

31. "Researcher Says Some Pilots Nap in Cockpit," *New York Times,* December 26, 1986; "The Sleep Factor: Pilots on Transoceanic Flights Keep Hours That Could Be Dangerous," *Frequent Flyer* 40 (June 1987).

32. "The Peach Bottom Syndrome," *New York Times,* March 27, 1988.

33. National Transportation Safety Board, *Safety Study: Fatigue, Alcohol, Other Drugs, and Medical Factors in Fatal-to-the-Driver Heavy Truck Crashes* (Volume I), Report No. NTSB/55–90/01, Washington, D.C., 1990.

34. D. Dinges et al., "Attending to Inattention," Letter, *Science,* July 28, 1989, p. 342.

35. "Increased Daytime Sleepiness Enhances Ethanol's Sedative Effects," *Neuropsychopharmacology* 1 (1988): 284–285.

36. Heffring Research Group of Canada, *Substance Abuse in Transportation: Airports, Aviation, Surface, (Bus/Trucking), and Marine,* Integrated Report 32, January 1990.

37. "On-the-Job Naps Could Be Pause That Refreshes, " CNN, March 26, 1998.

38. The Census Bureau predicted that Hispanics will make up 24.5 percent of the nation's population by 2050, compared to 10.2 percent today, and that Asians will make up 8.2 percent, compared to the current 3.3 percent. The black share of the population was expected to remain relatively stable, rising only to 13.6 percent from the current 12 percent. *New York Times,* March 14, 1996.

39. "Panel Balks at Multiracial Category," *New York Times,* July 9, 1997. The task force recommended that each person be allowed to identify themselves as a member of more than one race.

40. *Taking America's Pulse: The National Conference Survey On Intergroup Relations*, National Conference of Christians and Jews, 1994. See also "Survey Finds Minorities Resent One Another Almost as Much as They Do Whites," *New York Times*, March 3, 1994, and L. E. Stallworth and M. H. Malin, "Conflict Arising out of Workforce Diversity," *Proceedings of the Forty-Sixth Annual Meeting*, National Academy of Arbitrators, 1993, p. 104.

41. *Garcia v. Spun Steak Company*, 114 Sup. Ct. Reporter 2726 (June 20, 1994); case below 998 F.2d 1480; 13 F.3d 296. See also *Daily Labor Report* (BNA), June 21, 1994; Christopher Cameron, "How the Garcia Cousins Lost Their Accents: Understanding the Language of Title VII Decisions Approving English-only Rules as the Product of Racial Dualism, Latino Invisibility, and Legal Indeterminacy," *California Law Review* 85 (1997): 1347 [*La Raza L.J* 10. (1998): 26]; and R. M. Rodriguez, "Misplaced Application of English-Only Rules in the Workplace," *Chicano-Latino Law Review*, Winter 1994.

42. "Gunman Felt Mocked, Police Say," *Los Angeles Times*, June 7, 1997.

Chapter 3. Royal Oak, Michigan: A Post Office Massacre

1. *U.S. Postal Service v. National Association of Letter Carriers* (C7N-4B-D 29760).

2. U.S. Air Force "Guidelines for Separation and Service Characterization" (August 12, 1994), quoted in Dennis W. Gibson, "Assessing Military Service: Honorable or Under Honorable Conditions? A Small Difference in Words, a Big Difference in Meaning," paper delivered to a meeting of the Alabama Chapter of the Industrial Relations Research Association, September 15, 1997, p. 3.

3. Ibid.

4. *U.S. Postal Service v. National Association of Letter Carriers.*

5. Michael Grunwald, "Wisconsin Shooting Sign of Hidden Epidemic; Job Violence Not Just 'Postal'," *Boston Globe*, December 20, 1997.

6. "Chief Operating Officer New Postmaster General," Associated Press dispatch, May 13, 1998.

7. Grunwald, "Wisconsin Shooting."

8. Aaron Nathans, "Workplace Tension, Monotony May Have Set Off Gunman, Postal Workers," Associated Press dispatch, December 20, 1997.

9. Ibid.

10. "Milwaukee Postal Worker Kills Co-Worker, Self," CNN, December 19, 1997.

11. "Fired Postal Worker Kills Supervisor," Associated Press dispatch, December 20, 1996.

12. "Ex-Postal Worker's Life 'Disintegrated,'" *Las Vegas Review-Journal*, December 3, 1997.

13. "Seizing of Workers 'Rageful,' Experts Say," *Denver Post*, December 25, 1997.

14. Vern Baxter, *Labor and Politics in the U.S. Postal Service* (New York: Plenum, 1995) p. 193.

15. Mark Braverman, Ph.D., Testimony before Subcommittee on Postal Personnel and Modernization and Subcommittee on Postal Operations and Services, United States House of Representatives, September 15, 1992.

Chapter 4. Santa Ana, California: A Highway Worker's Revenge

1. Larry Gerber, "Killer Linked His Caltrans Supervisor to Pilfering," *San Diego Union Tribune*, December 20, 1997.

2. *In the Matter of Appeals by Arturo R. Torres and James H. Torres*, California State Personnel Board, Sacramento, Calif., Case Nos. 97–2586 and 97–2587, October 1997.

3. Ibid.

4. Bruce Crawford, "The Caltrans Tragedy Had a Familiar Ring to It," *Orange County Register*, December 28, 1997.

5. Ibid.

6. Esther Schrader, "A Rifle's Journey, from Import to Orange County," *Los Angeles Times*, January 25, 1998.

Chapter 5. Hartford, Connecticut: An Unlucky Day at the Lottery

1. The incident was well covered in local and regional newspapers. See Jonathan Rabinovitz, "Connecticut Lottery Accountant Kills Four of His Bosses," *New York Times*, March 7, 1998; Frank Bruni, "Friends and Colleagues Remember Slain Lottery Officials," *New York Times*, March 7, 1998; Jim Yardley, "In the Province of Winners, One Who Lost Out Takes Revenge," *New York Times*, March 8, 1998; Andrew Julien, Lyn Bixby, and Colin Poitras, "Friends Saw Anger Growing in Beck," *Hartford Courant*, March 7, 1998; Lyn Bixby, "Matt Beck Took His Grudge to the Newspaper," *Hartford Courant*, March 7, 1998; Liz Halloran, "Could Others Share Blame in Beck's Attack?" *Hartford Courant*, March 13, 1998. This account is also based on interviews with Robert Kinker, executive director, Connecticut State Employees Association and Michael Sartori of the Administrative and Residual Employees Union (AFT).

2. *Diagnostic and Statistical Manual of Mental Disorders*, 4th ed. (DSM IV), American Psychiatric Association, 1994, p. 732.

3. R. M. Hirschfeld et al., National Depressive and Manic-Depressive Association, "Consensus Statement on the Undertreatment of Depression," *JAMA*, January 1997, pp. 333–340.

4. Jonathan A. Segal, "When Charles Manson Comes to the Workplace," *HRMagazine*, June 1994, p. 38.

5. J. Mintz et al., "Treatments of Depression and the Functional Capacity to Work," *Archives of General Psychiatry* 49 (1992): 761–768.

6. *Managing the Impact of Depression in the Workplace: An Integrated Approach*, Washington Business Group on Health, 1996; D. J. Conti and W. N. Burden, "The Economic Impact of Depression in a Workplace," *Journal of Occupational Medicine* 36 (September 1994): 983–988.

7. W. B. Mendelson; C. Thompson; T. Franko (Sleep Research Laboratory, University of Chicago), "Adverse Reactions to Sedative/Hypnotics: Three Years' Experience," *Sleep* 19 (November 1996): 702–706.

8. *Department of Energy Retaliation Complaint Study*, National Academy of Public Administration, Washington, D.C., 1995.

Chapter 6. Watkins Glen, New York: A Social Service Office under Siege

1. *Preventing Workplace Violence: A Union Representative's Guidebook*, American Federation of State, County and Municipal Employees, Washington, D.C., 1998, p. 8.

2. Ibid., p. 6.

3. Ibid.

4. Lekan Oguntoyinbo and Jack Kresnak, "Social Worker Beaten to Death," *Detroit Free Press*, May 23, 1998.

5. "State Acts to Protect Employees," *Detroit News*, June 18, 1998.

Chapter 7. Iowa City, Iowa: The "Darkest Hour" of a Campus

1. Jennifer Cassell, "Remembering the UI's Darkest Hour," *Daily Iowan*, November 1, 1996.

2. M. Sagen and B. Schwartz, "Campus Violence: The University of Iowa Response," paper presented to the Nineteenth Annual Conference of the California Caucus of College and University Ombudsmen, November 1993.

3. Ibid.

4. Ibid.

5. "University Policy on Violence," University of Iowa, January 1992.

6. Kenneth P. Swan, "Workplace Violence—The Proper Role for Arbitration," *Proceedings of the 49th Annual Meeting, National Academy of Arbitrators* (Washington, D.C.: BNA Books, 1996), p. 85.

7. Harry W. Arthurs, Roger A. Blais, and Jon Thompson, *Integrity in Scholarship: A Report to Concordia University*, April 1994, pp. 2–3.

8. Swan, "Workplace Violence," p. 87.

9. John Scott Cowan, *Lessons from the Fabrikant File: A Report to the Board of Governors of Concordia University*, May 1994, p. 1.

Chapter 16. Understanding Violent Behavior

1. For this simple and powerful formulation, as well as the definition of violence as the outcome of unbearable stress, the authors are grateful to Drs. John Daignault and Robert Fein, who in turn credit Dr. Shervert Frazier.

2. For discussions of the difficulties in predicting violent behavior, see the following: L. DiLorenzo and D. Carroll, "Screening Applicants for a Safer Workplace," *HRMagazine*, March, 1995, pp. 55–58; C. W. Lidz et al., "The Accuracy of Predictions of Violence to Others," *JAMA* 269, no. 8 (1993): 1007–1011; J. Monahan, "Mental Disorder and Violent Behavior: Perceptions and Evidence," *American Psychologist* 47, no. 4 (1992): 511–521; J. Monahan and H. Steadman, *Violence and Mental Disorder: Developments in Risk Assessment* (Chicago: University of Chicago Press, 1994); John Monahan, *Predicting Violent Behavior: An Assessment of Clinical Techniques* (Beverly Hills, Calif.: Sage, 1989); Robert Menzies et al., "The Dimensions of Dangerousness Revisited: Assessing Forensic Predictions about Violence," *Law and Human Behavior* 18 (1994): 1; P. E. Dietz et al., "Threatening and Otherwise Inappropriate Letters to Members of the United States Congress," *Journal of Forensic Sciences* 36 (September 5, 1991): 1445–1468; Barbara D. Underwood, "Law and the Crystal Ball: Predicting Behavior with Statistical Inference and Individualized Judgment," *Yale Law Journal* 88 (1979): 1408; E. A. Wenk and J. O. Robison, "Can Violence Be Predicted?" *Crime and Delinquency* 18 (1972):393; C. L. Becton, "Drug Courier Profile," *North Carolina Law Review* 65 (1987): 417.

3. M. David Vaughn, "Comment on Violence in the Workplace: Prevention Strategies," *Arbitration 1994: Controversy and Continuity*, Proceedings of the National Academy of Arbitrators, 1995.

4. *Barefoot v. Estelle*, 463 U.S. 880, 920 (1983) (Blackmun, J., dissenting).

5. John Monahan, *The Clinical Prediction of Violent Behavior* (Rockville, Md.: U.S. Public Health Service, 1981), pp. 47–49.

6. G. B. Palermo et al., "On the Predictability of Violent Behavior: Considerations and Guidelines," *Journal of Forensic Sciences* 36 (September 5, 1991): 1442. See also Menzies et al., "The Dimensions of Dangerousness Revisited";: 1; John Monahan, "Limiting Therapist Exposure to Tarasoff Liability: Guidelines for Risk Containment," *American Psychologist* 242 (March 1993): 244; Joseph J. Cocozza and Henry J. Steadman, "The Failure of Psychiatric Predictions of Dangerousness: Clear and Convincing Evidence," *Rutgers Law Review* 29 (1976): 1084; John Monahan, "Mental Disorder and Violent Behavior: Perceptions and Evidence," *American Psychologist* 511 (April 1992); and Deirdre Klassen and William A. O'Connor, "A Prospective Study of Predictors of Violence in Adult Male Mental Health Admissions," *Law and Human Behavior* 12 (1988): 143. The authors are indebted to Craig Cornish, J.D., for these references.

7. *Employee Relations Law Journal* 22. no. 1 (Summer 1996).

8. Alessandra Stanley, "Disturbed Guard Killed Couple, Then Self, Vatican Says," *New York Times*, May 5, 1998.

9. Martin Blinder, "Profile of a Workplace Killer," *Wall Street Journal,* February 10, 1997.

10. *EEOC Enforcement Guidance on the Americans with Disabilities Act and Psychiatric Disabilities,* March 25, 1997, Paragraph 1.

11. Ibid., Paragraph 16.

12. Linda Micco, "Employers Find Fault with Guidance for Psychiatric Disabilities," SHRM Online, April 1, 1997.

13. *Hindman v. GTE Data Services, Inc.,* 1994 WL 371396 (M.D. Fla.); 3 AD Cases 641 (M.D. Fla. 1994).

14. Letter from Claire Gonzales, director of Communications and Legislative Affairs, U.S. EEOC, to Sen. John Breaux of Louisiana, January 4, 1995, quoted in *ADA Information Brief,* Washington Business Group on Health, 1, no. 4 (199.

15. Dr. E. Fuller Torrey, president of the Treatment Advocacy Center, Arlington, Va., quoted in Fox Butterfield, "Treatment Can Be Illusion for Violent Mentally Ill," *New York Times,* July 28, 1998.

16. "Violence and Mental Disorder: Public Perceptions vs. Research Findings," National Stigma Clearinghouse and MacArthur Foundation Research Network on Mental Health and the Law, New York, 1994.

17. Sandra G. Boodman, "Are Former Mental Patients More Violent? If They Don't Abuse Drugs or Alcohol, the Answer Is Generally No, Study Finds," *Washington Post,* May 19, 1998.

18. Sheila Akabas, "Supervisors: The Linchpin in Effective Employment for People with Disabilities," *The Journal,* WBGH, 1995.

19. Bruce G. Flynn, "Violence, Mental Illness and Reasonable Accommodation in the Workplace," *The Journal,* WBGH, 1995.

Chapter 17. Assessing the Risk of Violence

1. Michael J. Gan, "Responding to Workplace Violence: The EAP Alternative," *BNA's Collective Bargaining Bulletin,* March 27, 1997, p. 50.

2. R. A. Fein, B. Vossekul, and G. A. Holden, "Threat Assessment: An Approach to Prevent Targeted Violence," *Research in Action,* National Institute of Justice, September 1995.

3. The authors are indebted to Steven White, Ph.D., for this analogy.

Chapter 18. Ethical and Legal Dimensions of Violence Prevention

1. Jonathan A. Segal, "When Charles Manson Comes to the Workplace," *HRMagazine,* June 1994.

Chapter 19. Designing a Violence Prevention Program

1. T. C. Pauchant and I. I. Mitroff, *Transforming the Crisis-Prone Organization* (San Francisco: Jossey-Bass, 1993).

2. "Workplace Violence: Policies, Procedures & Incidents," American Management Association, 65th Annual Human Resources Conference and Exposition Onsite Survey, April 9–13, 1994.

3. See Mark Braverman and Susan Braverman, "Seeking Solutions to Violence on the Job," *USA Today Magazine,* May 1994.

4. Judith L. Catlett [King] and David G. Alexander, "Violence in the Workplace: The Union Perspective," Center for Labor Education and Research, University of Alabama at Birmingham, 1995.

5. *Dealing with Workplace Violence,* U.S. Office of Personnel Management, Office of Workplace Relations, Washington, D.C., 1998, p. 16.

6. "Preventing Violence and Threatening Behavior in the Federal Workplace," CDC Policy Guide, U.S. Department of Health and Human Services, August 16, 1994.

7. Jonathan A. Segal, "When Charles Manson Comes to the Workplace," *HRMagazine*, June 1994.

8. Margaret A. Lucero and Robert E. Allen, "Fighting on the Job: Analysis of Recent Arbitration Decisions," *Dispute Resolution Journal*, August 1998, pp. 50–57.

9. *Preventing Workplace Violence: A Union Representative's Guidebook*, American Federation of State, County and Municipal Employees, Washington, D.C., 1998.

10. Dean J. Schaner, "Have Gun, Will Carry: Concealed Handgun Laws, Workplace Violence and Employer Liability," *Employee Relations Law Journal* 22, no. 1 (Summer 1996): 86–87.

11. Daniel Weisberg, "Preparing for the Unthinkable," *Management Review*, March 1994, p. 60.

12. Ibid.

Chapter 20. Dispute Resolution as Violence Prevention

1. R. V. Fitzpatrick, "The War in the Workplace Must End, but Arbitration Is Not the Answer," *Society for Human Resource Management News*, Spring 1994, p. 5.

2. Although a well-known substitute for arbitration, grievance mediation has tended to focus on classical union-management disputes rather than interpersonal conflict.

3. See Tia Schneider Denenberg and R. V. Denenberg, "The Future of the Workplace Dispute Resolver," *Dispute Resolution Journal*, June 1994.

4. Exit Survey for REDRESS Mediation Participants. The completed surveys are reviewed by Professor Lisa Bingham, Indiana University, who monitors the process for fairness. See L. B. Bingham, "Mediating Employment Disputes: Perceptions of Redress at the United States Postal Service," *Review of Public Personnel Administration*, Spring 1997.

5. "Workplace Violence: Policies, Procedures and Incidents," American Management Association, 65th Annual Human Resources Conference and Exposition Onsite Survey, April 9–13, 1994.

6. See C. M. Cornish, "Employer Responses to Workplace Violence: How Will This Affect Individual Privacy?" paper presented at the American Bar Association Committee on Individual Rights and Responsibilities Mid-Winter Meeting, March 9–12, 1994, Scottsdale, Ariz.

7. For an analysis of consensus agreements on drug abuse, see T. S. Denenberg and R. V. Denenberg, *Alcohol and Other Drugs: Issues in Arbitration* (Washington, D.C.: BNA Books, 1991.

Chapter 21. Preventing Violence in the Schools

1. "Deadly Fantasy of a Teen-Ager Became a Reality," *New York Times*, May 24, 1998.

2. "Deputy Arrested in Killing of Wife at a Buffalo School," *New York Times*, May 2, 1998.

3. "Police Kill Hostage-Taker," *Los Angeles Times*, November 24, 1998.

4. T. C. Pauchant and I. I. Mitroff, *Transforming the Crisis-Prone Organization* (San Francisco: Jossey-Bass, 1993).

5. Speech in Worcester, Mass., August 1998.

6. "Study: U.S. TV Exposes Young Children to Violence," Reuters, June 22, 1998.

7. "Survey: 1 Million Students Took Guns to School in '97," Reuters, June 19, 1998.

8. "Schools Faced with Conflicting Pressures in Dealing with Troubled Students," *New York Times*, May 23, 1998.

9. "Double Bind of Boys Concerns Psychologist," *Portland Oregonian*, October 17, 1998.

10. "Pain, Isolation Still Mark Days for Some Paducah Parents," Associated Press, November 28, 1998.

11. Gregory Holtz, interview with authors, September 23, 1998.

12. "Trenton Debates Requiring Guns That Sense Owners," *New York Times*, September 24, 1998; "'Smart Guns' Set Off Debate: Just How 'Smart' Are They?" *New York Times*, October 22, 1998.

13. K. Dwyer, D. Osher, and C. Warger, *Early Warning, Timely Response: A Guide to Safe Schools*, U.S. Department of Education, Washington, D.C., August 1998.

14. "Deadly Fantasy of a Teen-Ager Became a Reality," *New York Times*, May 24, 1998.

15. "Suspect Called Short-Tempered, Fascinated with Explosives," CNN, May 22, 1998.

16. Betsy Hammond, "Did Kinkel Signal Staff at Thurston That He Might Explode into Violence?" *Portland Oregonian*, June 3, 1998.

17. Ibid.

18. Randall Sullivan, "A Boy's Life: Kip Kinkel and the Springfield, Oregon Shooting," *Rolling Stone*, September 1998.

19. John Lenssen, remarks to Twenty-Sixth Annual Conference, Society of Professionals in Dispute Resolution, October 17, 1998, Portland, Ore.

20. "Thurston Shootings Prompt New Emphasis on Security," *Portland Oregonian*, September 6, 1998.

21. "Mayor Vera Katz Endorses Plan to Reduce School Violence," Press Release, City of Portland, Oregon, October 15, 1998.

22. *Early Warning, Timely Response*, p. 24.

23. "Pain, Isolation Still Mark Days for Some Paducah Parents," Associated Press, November 28, 1998.

24. Amy Swift, interview with authors, October 15, 1998, and materials prepared by Family Court Services of Clackamas County, Oregon.

25. D. W. Johnson and R. Johnson, "Why Violence Prevention Programs Don't Work and What Does," *Educational Leadership*, February 1995, p. 67.

26. "Compilation of Conflict Management K-12 Survey Results," Oregon Department of Education, Oregon Dispute Resolution Commission and Resolutions Northwest, Portland, 1998.

27. Memorandum to authors from Clare Danielson, September 28, 1998.

28. This account is based on notes and exhibits in the arbitrator's files.

29. *PERB News*, New York State Public Employment Relations Board, 31, no. 8 (August-September 1998).

30. "Preventive Mediation," *Annual Report for Fiscal Year 1997*, Federal Mediation and Conciliation Service, Washington, D.C.

31. "Safety First Priority in High School District," *The Independent* [Orange County, Calif.], August 27, 1998.

32. Johnson and Johnson, "Why Violence Prevention Programs Don't Work," p. 65.

Appendix B. Equal Employment Opportunity Commission Enforcement Guidance: The Americans With Disabilities Act and Psychiatric Disabilities

1. 42 U.S.C. §§ 12101–12117, 12201–12213 (1994) (codified as amended).

2. H.R. Rep. No. 101–485, pt. 3, at 31–32 (1990) [hereinafter House Judiciary Report].

3. Between July 26, 1992, and September 30, 1996, approximately 12.7% of ADA charges filed with EEOC were based on emotional or psychiatric impairment. These included charges based on anxiety disorders, depression, bipolar disorder (manic depression), schizophrenia, and other psychiatric impairments.

4. The analysis in this guidance applies to federal sector complaints of non-affirmative action employment discrimination arising under section 501 of the Rehabilitation Act of 1973. 29 U.S.C. § 791(g) (1994). It also applies to complaints of non-affirmative action em-

ployment discrimination arising under section 503 and employment discrimination under section 504 of the Rehabilitation Act. 29 U.S.C. §§ 793(d), 794(d) (1994).

5. 42 U.S.C. § 12102(2) (1994); 29 C.F.R. § 1630.2(g) (1996). See generally EEOC Compliance Manual § 902, Definition of the Term "Disability," 8 FEP Manual (BNA) 405: 7251 (1995).

6. 29 C.F.R. § 1630.2(h)(2) (1996). This ADA regulatory definition also refers to mental retardation, organic brain syndrome, and specific learning disabilities. These additional mental conditions, as well as other neurological disorders such as Alzheimer's disease, are not the primary focus of this guidance.

7. See, e.g., Boldini v. Postmaster Gen., 928 F. Supp. 125, 130, 5 AD Cas. (BNA) 11, 14 (D.N.H. 1995) (stating, under section 501 of the Rehabilitation Act, that "in circumstances of mental impairment, a court may give weight to a diagnosis of mental impairment which is described in the Diagnostic and Statistical Manual of Mental Disorders of the American Psychiatric Association . . .").

8. These include various sexual behavior disorders, compulsive gambling, kleptomania, pyromania, and psychoactive substance use disorders resulting from current illegal use of drugs. 42 U.S.C. § 12211(b) (1994); 29 C.F.R. § 1630.3(d) (1996).

9. 42 U.S.C. § 12210(a) (1994). However, individuals who are not currently engaging in the illegal use of drugs and who are participating in, or have successfully completed, a supervised drug rehabilitation program (or who have otherwise been successfully rehabilitated) may be covered by the ADA. Individuals who are erroneously regarded as engaging in the current illegal use of drugs, but who are not engaging in such use, also may be covered. Id. at § 12210(b).

Index